The Promise

1967-Connie age 14

It was difficult at times to get the adult in me out of the way so that the restless fourteen-year-old inside could tell our story. I wouldn't be who I am today without the brave sacrifices, faith, and choices of this inner child. Through the healing process of writing our story, we are no longer shattered and separate. She rests within me peacefully now knowing that she is an intricate part of who we've become today.

The Promise

A Memoir

Connie Rife

To Janice & Keith

Peace, Blessings & Love

Connie Rife

Notes:

It was difficult after so many years to find the actual people who participated in this time of my life. Since I was unable to get their permission to use their names, I changed them. I did the same thing with some of the places I referred to, as well.

To my husband, Tom,
You not only saw the value
in what my story had to teach others,
but used it
to show me my sense of purpose, too.
And to my children
Ginny, Tommy, Shannon, and Teri.
I wrote my story for you
With the hope that in knowing me better,
You might come
to understand yourself as well.

Acknowledgments

It is with great thanks and praise that I offer my acknowledgment to God first. It was through the quirky relationship we shared that this story came to be. If not for His constant presence in my life, I don't think I'd be here today to tell it.

It was my dad who first encouraged me to write my story even though he knew it wouldn't paint a very kind picture of the part he played in creating it. He knew what my story had to offer was bigger than him, even bigger than me.

I spent many hours with my siblings Kathy, John, and Mary, going over the memories of our past.

There have been many friends throughout my life who have encouraged me to write my story. I'm afraid if I mention one, I'll forget another. There is one friend I must mention, Mary Faith Arment, who was always there when I needed her.

I thank Susan Reed, a college librarian and English major who read my first rough draft. It was a test of true friendship and an eye-opener for me that I had a lot of work ahead of me. Virginia Ingram, a retired English school teacher read the second draft, and encouraged me to continue practicing my craft because she thought I had a great story to tell. My sister-in-law Elaine Rife, another school teacher, read my third draft and helped me to refine it with her great input. I thank them all for believing in me.

I can't forget the people who taught me how to be a better writer — my coach from the *Institute of Children's Literature* Brenda Seabrooke and Sarah Clayton from The *Long Ridge Writers Group* now called *The Institute for Writers*. Melissa Green from *Write from the Heart*, who taught me how to use my senses in writing. Marlee LeDai from *Writers.com*, who taught me how to show not tell. Anya Achtenberg from *Writers.com* who told me my story was a golden nugget. *Highlights Foundation* for providing me with a beautiful place to write and share with the other writers I meet, especially Paige Britt, who encouraged me to follow my heart and do it my way.

I can't forget my son-in-law Darrell Roberts who challenged me in so many words that it was time to let my story go and publish it.

Dream lofty dreams,

and as you dream,
so, shall you become.
Your vision is
"The Promise"
of what
you shall one day be;
your ideal is the prophecy
of what you shall at last unveil."

"Dreams are the seedlings of realities."

–James Allen
"As A Man Thinketh"

Prologue

California-Spring of 1964

I often wondered how many people have experienced an encounter with God. I was eleven years old when it happened to me. There was nothing physical or material to prove what happened that day. All I had were God's words, a promise, planted like seedlings in my mind

I can still feel the cold of the cement steps beneath my buttocks, chilling me to my bones, and yet the bright California sun warmed my face. I leaned my head on my arms, looking down at the step below me. I didn't want anyone from the streets to see me crying. My eyes filled like overflowing pools of water. As I blinked, tears dripped onto the step below, almost hitting a roly-poly bug that was scurrying across it. I laid my hand down, feeling the tickle of its tiny bug feet as it walked from one hand to another until it rolled into a protective ball.

"I wish I could curl up in a ball like that and hide from the world," I said to the bug as I let it roll off my hand and into the dirt.

My butt began to feel numb from the cold step, so I stood to find a warmer place to sit. I walked over to the old black Dodge sitting in the driveway and touching the sloping trunk to test its hotness. I sat on the fender and slowly leaned against the heat. Ahh, ...it felt like a soothing hot water bottle against my skin. Between the car and the bright sunlight, I felt wrapped in a blanket of warmth.

I don't understand what I did wrong. Why did Mom beat me across the back with the broom the moment I walked in the house? She whacked me from the backdoor on out to the front, as if I was a dirty rat that snuck in house. "You're just like your father," she said.

I never know what she means by that, but I'd rather be like him than her any day.

God, what's wrong with me? I feel unfinished as if I slipped from the Heavens before You made me lovable. Maybe that's why my mom hates me. It hurts so bad, God. I don't know how much more I can take. Is this the way the rest of my life is going to be?

Even with my eyes closed, I couldn't hold the tears back. I wiped them away as quickly as they leaked from the corners of my eyes. But something was soothing and comforting about being in the light of the sun. Soon I began to feel sleepy, dreamy, and light as a helium balloon floating up toward the heavens. I rested upon a white puffy cloud, gliding gently across the skies like a genie on a carpet ride. I saw families playing in the park, eating dinner, and laughing together. Mothers were snuggling with their babies, hugging their kids, and wiping away their tears. All I wanted was the same kind of loving care. The white puffy cloud became gray, damp, and cold as darkness set in. It was there that I saw what was ahead for me; that my life was going to get worse than it already was. I could not hold back the dam of tears I had built up any longer. As they came flooding out from my eyes, they fell from my cloud down onto the ugliness of my future, washing away the memory of what would happen but leaving behind the feelings it created in me. All that remained was the dreaded question: how will I ever live through anything worse than I already am?

"I will always be with you," I heard a voice from within.

"But you're God, why can't you wave your wand or something and make it better now?" I asked.

"All I can do is promise you that someday your life will be the way you want," God said.

"It's not fair, I'm only a kid and a stupid one at that," I said.

"I believe in you, and I'll always be with you," He said. "Someday, your life will be your own to make any way you want it to be. All you have to do is never give up on your hopes and dreams and hold onto my promise."

Little did I know that God's Promise would become the golden thread woven in and out of the tapestry of my life. How it would turn out, in the end, would be an intertwining of my own creation.

Part 1 -

Stenton Child Care Center

The Promise

Chapter 1 - November 1967
Pennsylvania

S hivering. I hate that feeling as if I'm standing out in the cold. I know what that feels like now that I'm living in Pennsylvania. I love the changing seasons, but I could do without the bitter cold. I miss the way the California sun used to warm my face. But the thing is I'm not outside right now. I'm sitting in the hallway of the Philadelphia Department of Child Welfare, and I don't know why, besides I'm not a child anymore I'm fourteen now, so I don't know what it has to do with me. Maybe mom's just trying to get a little more money to help us out. I hope that's all it is, but something doesn't feel right, and even though my coat is buttoned up and my arms wrapped across me I still can't stop shivering all over

It reminds me of a dog I once found shaking as if scared to death. I picked him up and took it home. No one ever claimed him. So, I kept him and named him Happy because the markings around his mouth that made him look as if he had a permanent smile. Happy eventually ran away. He was always trying to escape as if he was longing to find his way back home. I've run away a few times myself. I never knew where I was going either; just this need to find something better. I wonder if that's the way Dad felt when he left us two years ago in California. Johnny, my brother, left too when he was 16, and Kathy, my sister, left only a few months ago soon after she graduated. Everybody leaves.

Maybe I'm not cold at all, but shivering out of pure fear like Happy was the day I found him. I can't help feeling as if something terrible is about to happen.

The ding of the elevator makes me jump every time the door opens.

"Are they done talking yet?" my sister Mary asks. She reminds me of a jack-in-the-box that keeps popping her head out between the doors. She's been riding the elevator up and down ever since Miss Dolly, the caseworker, asked us to wait in the hallway.

"Come on, Mary, get over here before you get in trouble," I say, with irritation.

She sticks her tongue out at me as the doors slowly closed. Even if I wanted to stop Mary, she wouldn't listen to me. She's a bullheaded ten-year-old, use to doing whatever she wants. I've watched Mary for the past few years while Mom worked at the sewing factory. She fights me every step of the way, so I finally gave up trying. She goes her way, and I go mine.

Sneaking across the hallway, I stand against the wall near the closed door. The voices sound mumbled. I hear my uncle though, loud and clear when he says, "She can't even take care of herself right now, let alone those two girls out there."

I sit back down on the hard bench, biting my nails. I stare at the letters "Child Social Services," printed on the frosted window of the door.

The ding of the elevator makes me jump again, this time a man in a black suit has Mary by the hand. He brings her over to sit beside me and tells us to stay put until he comes back. He goes into the same office where mom is and closes the door behind him. I run across, trying again to hear what they're saying. Mary follows.

"I can't hear anything," she shouts. "What are they saying, Con?"

"Shush!" I say, pulling her back to the bench with me.

The man in the black suit opens the door and motions for us to come inside. Both mom and her brother stare downward when we walk in. My aunt, the stronger of the two, pulls us toward her. Looking at us both in the eyes, she says, "You know your Mother has not been well lately."

Mary looks at mom and says, "What's wrong with you, Mommy?"

Aunt Tee turns Mary's face back toward her and continues to talk. "Your Mother needs some time to rest, so she can get better and take care of you the way she wants to," she goes on.

"So, what does that mean? What's going to happen to Mary and me? Are we going to live with you again like we did when we first came to Philadelphia?"

"No!" my uncle snaps.

"Mr. Nelson here is going to take you to a nice place called Stenton Child Care Center," Miss Dolly, our caseworker says.

"Why can't we stay where we've been living? I like it there," Mary says.

"Because your mother can't afford the rent now that Johnny and Kathy left home," Aunt Tee says.

"Why can't Connie get a job and help out as they did?" Mary asks.

"She's only fourteen, and you have to be sixteen-years-old to get a job. Besides, if she worked, who'd take care of you?"

"I can take care of myself," Mary says as she sits on Mom's lap. I don't think I can ever remember a time that she couldn't twist Mom around her little finger. Tears well up in Mom's eyes as she wraps her arms around Mary, rocking her back and forth, telling her how much she loves her.

Bending down on my knees in front of Mom to get her attention, I plead with her, "Please don't leave us too, Mom. I can help! I'll find a babysitting job or something where I can help with the money. Please don't leave us. Please!"

Her eyes get big, and her skin pulls back like an animal ready to attack. It's that look that makes me freeze in place. "You're no help! All you do is run away. You're just like your father," she spits the words out.

"Oh my God, Ginny! What a thing to say," Aunt Tee says as she helps me up.

Then she pulls Mary gently away from Mom. We're both standing in the doorway looking at her, but she only looks at Mary when she says how sorry she is again. "It will only be for a few weeks. I promise," she says to her.

As we turn to leave, Mom calls out my name, "Connie! Take care of your sister for me."

I feel as if I'm in a bad dream where you're trying to speak, but you can't get the words to come out of your mouth. They're trapped inside along with all the other painful words I've never been allowed to express. Then I realize it doesn't matter anymore. What could Mom do to me that could be any worse than this? All the pent-up hurt, anger, frustration, and abuse came barreling out.

"I hate you! I hate you! I hate you!" I screamed as the elevator doors slowly closed, and everything becomes quiet.

Standing in front of the closed doors, I see a slightly blurry reflection of myself. As the elevator descends, it feels as if I'm falling down a hole like Alice in Wonderland. The ding of the bell as we pass each floor breaks through the silence, making me jump each time it rings. I feel Mary slip her hand in mine as she stands quietly next to me. When the doors finally open, it feels like a scene from the Twilight Zone, as we step across the threshold from our old life into the unknown.

"I'm hungry," Mary says the moment we're off the elevator.

"How about a candy bar to hold you over?" the man in the black suit offers.

As we head out of the building, there is a newspaper stand on the sidewalk with lots of candy. Mary's face lights up as she stands before it, trying to decide which one she wants. The man in the black suit asks me a few times what I want, but I don't answer. He gets impatient with Mary's indecision, so he picks two candy bars out himself and hands one to Mary and me, but I don't react. I feel numb, like a walking corpse. My mouth feels as dry as cotton balls, but I can't get the words out to ask for a drink.

"I'll take it if she doesn't want it," Mary says, but he puts it in his pocket, ignoring her.

The Promise

∞ ∞ ∞

Gliding up and down as if we're riding the waves of the road, the long black Ford station wagon drives smooth and quiet. I'd probably fall asleep if I weren't so upset. I wonder if this is what it feels like to be in the backseat of a police car? Maybe it's more like being a dead body in a hearse. I'm cold enough to be a corpse, that's for sure. I still can't stop shivering all over, even with the heat blasting in the car.

Leaning my head against the window, everything outside the car looks like a blur of life passing by. It reminds me of when Dad left us two years ago. I was sitting on a Greyhound bus looking out the window, feeling the same uncertainty. What would life be like in Pennsylvania? It seemed so far away from California and everything I'd ever known. We were going to Philadelphia to live with Mom's brother and his family, whom I'd never met. At least we were all together, though, going to someplace we could make a new start. Mary and I are all alone now, with no idea where we're going or what the future holds.

The man in the black suit strikes a match at a red light and touches it to his cigarette. I love the smell it creates the moment the two meets. The first drag is always the best. I could sure use a cigarette myself right now. I remember smoking my first cigarette with my cousin when we moved to Philadelphia. I always wanted to smoke cigarettes. Watching the smoke rise and swirl around the man driving reminds me of Dad.

How did I get from that innocent little girl sitting behind Dad in our car, to where I am now?

"What are you singing back there, Connie?" I can still hear Dad asking me.

"Oh, nothing, just something I made up," I tell him.

"Well, it sure sounds pretty," he'd say.

I miss him so much. If he knew what was happening to us, he'd come and get us right away. I know it. I'll never stop looking for him, but the truth is, it's been so long I can hardly remember what he looks like anymore.

I hate Mom for ruining all our lives. I know she drove Dad to drink, and when he couldn't stand her any longer, he left. She pushed Johnny too far until he took off at sixteen, and Kathy couldn't wait to get away as soon as she graduated from high school.

"Hates a strong word," I hear the voice inside me.

"I don't care. I do hate Mom, and I hate you too for at all the bad things you let happen to me."

"I know you don't mean that. You're just feeling hurt right now."

"Go away; I don't want to talk to you. All the good ideas you put in my head get gobbled up by all the bad things that keep happening. I don't believe in you anymore, God. It's all a lie. I wish I'd never been born."

The silence brings the view outside the window into focus. Houses where I imagine happy families live, and I wonder if people love their children the way I wish I could be loved. I don't hear anything after a while and begin to worry that maybe I went too far with my angry words toward God.

"I honestly don't think I could go on if I lost you too, God."

"I'm still here. I'll never leave you no matter how hard you try to get rid of me."

"It doesn't change what's happening though, God. I'm still sitting in this car, heading for where I don't know. I'm glad you're with me, but don't think that gets you off the hook. I'm still mad at you."

"Fifteen minutes, and we'll be there," says the man in black. His voice breaking the silence in the car brings my thoughts back into the present moment.

I notice his eyes in the rear-view mirror as they look up at me. They're sad and puppy-dog-like. "The place you're going is one of the nicer facilities for kids. It won't be so bad. You'll see." His voice is thick like a smoker, but he speaks in a low tone. His mannerisms don't jibe with his military haircut and strait-laced FBI appearance. I wonder if he does this kind of thing all the time.

I take a piece of my long hair and begin to rub it back and forth across my lips as I look over at Mary. She's still holding the licked clean candy wrapper. She seems fine. She always seems fine, no matter what happens.

"You know Mary; Mom's not going to be around to get you out of trouble. If you don't behave where we're going, who knows what will happen." I say to her.

"Well, she told you to take care of me, so I guess you'll have to do it now," she says.

"If you think I'm going to let you get away with the things Mom did, you have another think coming. If you want me to help you out, then you better behave."

"I can take care of myself," she says to me as she looks out the window.

"Well, don't come running to me when you get into trouble," I say.

I don't have any fight left in me right now to argue with her about it. Leaning my head against the window again, I can't help wondering what lies behind the doors of the shelter. I remember the movie with Shirley Temple called, "The Little Princess." It was the one where she had to go to a home for girls while her father went to war.

What I remember most about it was how badly they treated her. The words to one of the catchy songs she sang begin to play in my head, "Animal Crackers in My Soup." Once it starts, I can't make it stop. It spins round in my head like a nervous habit keeping me from focusing.

"Here it is," the man in the black suit says.

As we turn into the horseshoe driveway, I see the silver words "Stenton Child Care Center" pressed deep into the red brick building. Windows line the front of the facility, giving the appearance of a one-level school building. A yellow mural strip runs across the upper edge right below the rain spout with green childlike figures running with birds and animals. It looks like one of those decorative ribbons you sew on a dress. As the shelter spreads out to the right, it grows into a two-story building. All the while, my heart is beating fast. My palms are sweating, and my mouth feels as dry as the desert. When the man opens my door, the crisp November air hits every sweaty part of my body. The dead leaves of Autumn mixed with the moist earthy smell stronger than usual.

As I step closer to the entrance, I hear the faint sound of keys jingling. They get louder and louder as a shadowy figure comes into view. As he hunts for the right key, I notice his blotchy pitted complexion and his thick white hair. He reminds me of a big grizzly bear. The keys bang hard against the metal of the door as he slips the right one into the lock. Pushing down on the long handle, he opens the door, and his face lights up into a Santa Clause smile.

"Welcome to Stenton Child Care Center," the grizzly bear says as he steps out, holding the door open. He takes the files from the man in the black suit and nods to him as he leaves. The grizzly bear shuffles us through the door, and as it shuts, he turns the key, locking us inside.

"My name is Mr. Max, and I'm the superintendent of this facility," he says as he pulls another door open. A whiff of cafeteria food is the first thing I notice. It smells like tomato soup, grilled cheese sandwiches, hamburgers, and French fries. Maybe I'm so hungry I imagine what I want it to be. My mouth is too dry to water, but my stomach growls as loud as a lion. Right around the entrance door to the left, I see a black woman wiping down a serving station.

"That's where the staff eats," Mr. Max says.

"This is my office," he says, pointing across from us.

We proceed down the hallway to the right. All I seem to notice now is the magnified sound of his keys dangling from his belt buckle. A quiver runs down my back; he reminds me of a jailer.

"This is Mr. Filler, the caseworker for the boys," Mr. Max says as we come to the first office. Mr. Filler's a white, chubby, balding man with wire-rimmed glasses.

"Welcome," he says with a cheerful smile. "I work with the boys here, but if there's anything I can do for you, don't hesitate to come and see me."

As we continue down the hallway, we come to the next office where a black woman stands in the doorway. She has a warm, pleasant smile on her face, but she folds her arms across her body as if holding them back from reaching out for us.

"This is Mrs. Becker. She's the caseworker for all the girls. She'll be taking you from here. Do you have any questions before I leave you in her good hands?" he asks.

"Yes. I have a question," I say as I look at the dangling keys. "Are we locked in here all the time?"

"Oh, yes!" he says. "We lock the doors for your safety."

"Are we ever allowed to go out on our own?" I ask.

"All in due time," he says. "Mrs. Becker is going to go over all the rules with you now, but I'm always here as well anytime you want to talk." Mrs. Becker motions for us to sit in the two plastic chairs in front of her big gray desk. She sits in a wooden swivel chair that moves with her every turn. She slides on its wheels over to her filing cabinet as she pulls a few papers out. On her desk are a few neat piles of paper, a pencil cup, a framed picture facing her way, and her nameplate facing us.

Mrs. Becker skims through our files. Then she leans back with her elbows resting on the arms of her chair, her woven fingers supporting her chin. As the late afternoon sunlight streams through the windows, it gives her dark brown skin a bronzy glow. Her smiling cheeks look like the toe of a shoe buffed to a spit shine. Even her black hair shines, but not in a natural way. I don't know what it is, but it looks as if she's combed Vaseline through her hair to make it look straight. A tight curl turns under her chin line.

"As Mr. Max mentioned, I am the girl's caseworker here at Stenton," she says.

"Why do we need a caseworker when we already have one at the welfare office?" I ask.

"Well, I work as the link between the Child Social Service and your mother. My job is to make sure you get the best care we have to offer. I'm also a counselor, like the ones you have in school. That's my favorite part of the job, helping and guiding you in any way I can," she says as she smiles.

"Do you understand why you're here?" she asks.

"They said because our mom was having a nervous breakdown," Mary says. "What is a nervous breakdown anyway?" she asks.

"I don't think there's an easy answer, Mary. Sometimes people get a helpless feeling inside that won't go away no matter how hard they try to do the right thing. It's kind of like being Humpty Dumpty sitting on the wall. You're holding on for dear life, fearing the fall that will crack you open. That's the point where you realize you're not going to get off the wall by yourself. You need to ask for help. Your mother was on the verge of falling off her wall, but she asked for help before things got that bad. That's a good thing. Now she needs to take care of herself to get better. Then she'll be able to take care of the two of you," she says.

"I like that story," Mary says. "That means Mom's not going to fall off the wall and get all cracked-up. Soon she'll be better, and we can go home, Con," she says, looking at me.

"I sure hope so, Mary," I say.

"Can you tell me a little bit about what was going on at home?" Mrs. Becker asks us.

"It's simple. First, our Dad left, then our brother Johnny, and finally, our sister Kathy left in June right after she graduated from high school. Without the extra income they were bringing in, Mom can't afford the rent. We looked into special housing that the Department of Welfare offers to low-income families, but they were dirty, run-down, and the people living there scared us," I say.

"It seems like everyone leaves," she says. "Even you've tried to leave a few times, Connie."

Like the tongue of fire igniting a piece of paper, I feel the flame of embarrassment crawl up my neck and across my face. Mrs. Becker's eyes study me as she waits for a response. I bite my nails, trying to ignore her. I don't like being like this, and I wish I could tell someone what it's like to live with Mom. How unpredictable she is, like Jekyll and Hyde. Loving and laughing with us one minute, then yelling at us to wipe that smile off our faces the next. How I never know what to expect the moment I walk through the door. Will she toss a heavy ashtray at me again or greet me with a smile and a plate of cookies? Will I find her talking and laughing to her invisible friend? It's creepy, and she scares me. I know how dangerous she can be. She stabbed Dad in the arm with a pair of scissors, and she would've gotten him right in the heart if he hadn't put his arm up. But I'd still rather be with her than in here. I ran away at times, it's true, but I always came back. Running away makes me feel like I'm doing something. It's better than sitting, taking the abuse all the time. I can try harder to be more helpful and cooperative. I'd do anything to get out of here.

Mrs. Becker breaks the silence saying, "It's okay. You've both been through enough today. We can talk more on Monday. I'm here to help you in any way I can, so if you want to talk, I'll be here Monday through Friday," she says.

"I want my mommy," Mary says.

"I know you miss her, Mary. I promise it will only be for a little while. In the meantime, do you think you could try to have some fun with the other kids? She asks.

"I guess so," Mary says. "But I'm starving. When do we get to eat?"

"Very soon," Mrs. Becker says. "First, we have to get you checked out by Nurse Jones. By the time she finishes with you, it will be time for dinner."

"We're only going to be here for a few weeks, right?" I ask.

"Let's not worry about that right now," she says, "We'll take one day at a time, okay?"

"Is there a phone I can use?" I ask.

"No phone calls, but you can write letters. Give us the address, and we will mail it for you," Mrs. Becker says.

"Can't I have a few envelopes and address them myself?" I ask.

"No, we prefer you to bring the letter in, and we take care of it for you," she says.

"I was also wondering if we're allowed to go outside?"

"Sure. We have a great playground with a baseball field, and basketball, foursquare court. There are all kinds of things to do out there," Mrs. Becker tells me.

"No, I mean, like go for a walk or hang out with friends?"

"Right now, it's best if you stay within the grounds here. You will walk to school, or take the city bus, and maybe in due time, we can figure out some specials things for you to do. Now let me call Nurse Jones so we can finish getting you processed."

As we come outside her office, Mary asks what's through the doors across from her office.

"This is another place where you will spend lots of time doing fun things," she tells us.

"Like what?" Mary asks with interest.

She takes us closer where we can look through the narrow windows in the doors. It's a gym with a stage like they have in most schools.

"We have sports, movies, crafts, and parties," she says. "There's going to be a dance tomorrow night."

"Can I go too?" Mary asks.

"Of course, you can. It will be a great way for you to meet some of the other kids your age."

Mary smiles as if she can't wait, but all I want to do is turn and run out the front door.

Mrs. Becker takes us to the end of the hallway, where a large woman stands waiting in the doorway.

∞ ∞ ∞

"Girls, this is Nurse Jones. She's going to take you from here. Not to worry now, we're going to take good care of you. I'll check in with you on Monday morning."

I thought at first that it might be the yellow glow of light behind Nurse Jones that makes her look so large. She is wide, tall, and robust, reminding me of a blow-up doll about to burst open. It's as if she's guarding the gateway that takes you deeper into the body of the shelter. No one can enter without going through her first.

She wears a white uniform, a nursing cap, stockings, and shoes to match. There is nothing saintly about the glow around her. She shows no warmth at all.

She stands aside so we can enter the infirmary. Then she shuts and locks the door behind us. It looks just like a doctor's examination room with a table, a white glass door cabinet, and a sink, but we don't stop there. The big blow-up doll shepherds us into an adjoining room where a large bathtub sits right in the middle of the room. It has a long shiny metal shower hose hanging over a hook above the spigot. To the right is a long bench with lockers behind it.

"Okay, ladies," comes a deep husky voice from Nurse Jones. "Strip down!" she demands.

I feel as if I've been punched in the stomach and can't catch my breath at first. My heart is beating fast, and then comes the heat of courage creeping up my neck and face as I gain the strength to stand my ground.

"I'm not taking my clothes off in front of you. No way! I won't do it, and you can't make me."

"You will take your clothes off, or I'll take them off for you," she says. I look up at Nurse Jones, towering over me like a bully with her fists pushed deeply into the folds of her midriff.

She turns the water on adjusting the temperature, then calls Mary over.

"Come here, missy," she says. Mary stands without expression in all her nakedness and does what she's told.

Exasperated, the blow-up doll looks at me and says, "Every kid that comes through those doors has to go through the same procedure. We have to protect each one of you from lice, bed bugs, worms, and any other diseases brought in here," she says.

I watch as she scrubs every inch of my sister from head to toe. Mary sits and stands, and moves her arms like a puppet under the control of its puppeteer. Nurse Jones wraps her in a towel and tells her to sit on the bench.

I watch as the blow-up-doll cleans the tub as if preparing her stage for the next performance. She throws a towel in my direction and waves her index finger at me.

"Don't make me come over there, girl," she says.

I begin to strip down as my eyes pool up with tears. I feel as vulnerable as a turtle without its shell.

"Let's go," she motions with her hand.

I step in from the opposite side, still holding the towel around me when she yanks it hard from my hands. I quickly sit down with my arms across my breasts. She begins with the same routine, Scrubbing my long hair first with an awful smelling disinfectant shampoo. She lathers the washcloth working her way down my back than pries my arms away from my breasts, rubbing hard.

"Stand up," she demands as she scrubs up and down my legs, across my crotch, and between my butt cheeks. She rinses me all over with the metal shower hose, taking her good old time. She turns the water off, hands me the towel, looks me in the eyes with a smirk on her face, and says, "All done!"

I feel like the Tinman, locked in place. I have to make myself move, wrapping the towel slowly around me, clutching it so tightly with both hands that my knuckles turn white. With lowered head and dripping hair, I work my way over to the bench and sit beside Mary. Nurse Jones pulls the plug, and the mouth of the tub begins to drink deeply with long, loud gulps. I feel as if the person I was has been stripped and washed away. The gulping gets slower as the few remnants of who I was trickle down the drain. I wonder if there's anything left of me. I've lost my parents, my home, my friends, my freedom, and even my dignity.

"Put these on," her loud voice makes me jump. She hands us each a hospital gown.

"Why do we have to put these on?" Mary asks.

"Because I need to give you a physical exam next," Nurse Jones says.

As we put on the gowns, she disappears, coming back with a pair of navy-blue sweatshirts and matching pants, underwear, socks, and some toiletries.

"Come with me, missy," Nurse Jones says to Mary. She sits on the examining table in the other room with the door open while I remain perched on the bench. I feel as if this big dark hole is opening, and if I don't do something, I'll get swallowed up by it. Willing myself to move, I put the hospital gown on. I take the comb from the pile of stuff given us and begin working it through my hair. Not only is it tangled, but it feels like wet straw. As I pull and tug through a small section at a time, the sting of each plucked hair awaking's my senses. They become magnified as I smell the disinfectant used on my hair and body. The sound of the blood pressure cuff used on Mary sounds as if she is right next to me. My skin looks red and irritated from the rough scrubbing. I rub my arms up and down to soothe away the burn. I realize I can still feel, hear, see, and think. They can take all they want from me, but they'll never take away who I am. I won't let them.

The big blow-up doll calls me into the examining room. I sit on the crinkled paper as she stuffs the thermometer in my mouth. I can see the things inside the glass cabinet: tongue depressors, cotton balls, alcohol, peroxide, and medications. On the wall is an eye chart, a phone, a calendar, and a medication schedule tacked up beside the cabinet. Nurse Jones comes back to take the thermometer out of my mouth. A shiver goes down my back at the thought of her touching me again. I amuse myself with the idea of popping her with a pin and running out the door.

"Lay back," she tells me as she proceeds to press around my abdomen.

"When was your last period?" she asks me.

"I don't know. I guess about a few weeks ago," I say.

"Are you sexually active?" she asks next.

"No!" I say, insulted at her question.

"I have to ask," she says without compassion.

As Nurse Jones finishes filling out our charts, she tells us to get dressed. I watch her collect our clothes, the last remaining pieces of our old life. She wraps them in a brown paper bag, staples it shut, and writes our name on each one. The only thing she returns to us is our shoes.

"Tomorrow, you will go to the wardrobe room where you can pick something more suitable to wear," she says.

"But what are you doing with our clothes?" I ask. "I made that skirt, and that's my favorite sweater."

"Oh, stop your fussing," she says. "You'll get your things back when you leave this facility." She puts the packages on her desk and instructs us to follow her.

"Where are we going now?" Mary asks.

"I'm taking you to the children's unit," she says. "It's the section where you have to stay until something opens up for you in the girls' section," she tells us.

We walk through yet another doorway at the other end of the nurse's area. The hallway turns to the left, and three small rooms lie within this small area. Two of them have a hospital bed. Nurse Jones explains that they are set aside for those who get sick. The last room, she points out, looks like a prison cell. It has white walls, a cot, and a big window with a black metal screen bolted shut with a long black lock. The door is thick and has a small square window at eye level.

"This is where we put the bad kids...especially when they don't do the things asked of them," she says, looking at me.

She opens the door that leads into the next section, and it feels as if we've entered the belly of the whale that is Stenton Child Care Center.

∞ ∞ ∞

On the other side of the door, it opens into a large room where toddlers stop what they are doing to see who has entered their space. I only see a few white kids, and two babies sit in a playpen; another sits in the arms of a pudgy older woman. Straight ahead is a kitchen with a half wall that divides it from this room. To our right is a wall lined with colorful munchkin chairs. Nurse Jones instructs us to sit down while she gets the supervisor in charge. There is a big window beside us that looks out into a small courtyard that looks like a playground.

Nurse Jones introduces us to Ms. Gore. She is a dark, big-boned woman who stands stoic and unemotional. Her black hair is in a tight French twist. She wears gold, hoop earrings. Her eyes are light brown and have a slight Asian slant. I'd say this is her best feature.

She nods her head when introduced, barely acknowledging us. I've never been around black people before. The only thing I know about them is what I've seen on TV or heard from other people. There's been a lot of unrest and riots lately with the Civil Rights movement in full swing. I've never paid a lot of attention to it. Besides, I've had enough troubles to deal with in my own life. There's not enough room inside me to pay attention to all the craziness going on in the world around me.

"Where are we supposed to put them?" Ms. Gore asks Nurse Jones. "We don't have any room for them here."

"Put Mary in one of the sick rooms, and Connie can sleep in the cell till something else opens up," Nurse Jones suggests.

"Why can't I sleep in the other sick room?" I ask.

"Because we need to keep one of the rooms open in case someone gets sick," Nurse Jones says, standing over me with her fist pushed deep her into waist again.

"It's not like I'm going to lock you in there," Ms. Gore says, looking at me with irritation.

"Yes, it seems we have a bit of a troublemaker here," Nurse Jones says. "But she's all yours now. With that, Nurse Jones returns to her domain, like a big bird in a cuckoo clock she disappears behind the door from which she popped out. I can't say that I'm sorry to see her go, but it feels as if Ms. Gore is about to slip right into her place.

The pudgy older woman comes waddling over, with the baby bouncing on her hip. Her blue and white floral muumuu hangs to her mid-calf. A wavy black wig covers her head, and her big broad smile shows off her bright white teeth.

"This is Mrs. Brown. She's one of the foster grandparents who come in to help with the little ones," Ms. Gore tells us. "She'll help you girls get settled in while I finish my paperwork."

"Now, yawls can call me Grandma Brown like all the little ones do," she says.

She pulls a nearby rocking chair over so she can sit closer to us. She settles the baby on her lap and leans forward, touching both Mary and me tenderly on the knee.

"I know yawls are feeling mighty confused and scared 'bout now. We gonna take good care of yawls, and that's a promise," Grandma Brown says.

I want to crawl up on her big soft lap and cry like a baby, but I'm too old for that. Anyway, I'm afraid if I did, I'd fall apart, and I can't let that happen. It's a relief to be around someone nice.

Grandma Brown points out the window to the building across the courtyard.

"That be the big girl's section where yawls are going."

While Grandma Brown is talking, the baby on her lap stares at me. Her eyes look big, sunken, and shadowy. But when I make eye contact with her, a sudden smile appears; then as quickly as it came, it's gone again.

"How long will we have to wait?" Mary asks.

"Could be a week or more," she tells us.

"Where do the boys stay?" Mary asks.

"They is on the other side of the girl's building, "she says.

"This here shelter breaks up into separate sections. It all connects through a hallway and stretches like long arms, from one building to another. This here place is only 'bouts five-years-old. Yawls lucky to be in such a nice new clean place," Grandmas Brown says.

As Grandma Brown goes on, I'm still distracted by the baby as she continues to stare at me. She reminds me of myself at her age. I never thought much about it until now. I was only three months old when Dad had Mom committed to a mental hospital. Kathy was four. She stayed with Dad's mother and sister, Honey. Johnny was three, and he and I went to live with Dad's brother's family in Pittsburgh. We stayed there for six months before Mom was well enough to come home.

"There ain't much to do in this here children's section, but we need all the help we can gets. This little one here is Sarah. She's been with us for a few days. The little ones, they don't be staying long. They goes on to foster homes much quicker than yawl older ones do," Grandma Brown says.

Ms. Gore comes back to take over, and Grandma Brown gets up to change little Sarah's diaper. As she walks away, Sarah's head bobs up and down over Grandma's shoulder. Her eyes remain fixed on mine with that half-lit smile. As if my pain of abandonment isn't enough, my heart hurts worse for her.

Ms. Gore pulls the rocking chair back to its original place. Before she has a chance to say anything, one of the toddlers comes up to her and pulls at her skirt. "I gots to go pee-pee, Ms. Gore."

"Well, then I guess we best get you to the potty, little man," she says with a smile.

I can't believe the change in her facial expression as she tends to the little boy. It's as if someone flicked a light on in her. She is pretty when her face softens.

Grandma Brown brings Sarah back.

"How'd ya likes to hold this sweet little one so as I can get to work setting ups for dinner?"

"I've never held a real baby before," I say as she sits her on my lap.

"You be just fine," she assures me as she pats me on the shoulder.

My nose moves to the soft fuzz at the top of her head. She doesn't' smell like my Thumbelina doll. She smells pure, clean, and brand new, like baby powder. She turns her head to look up at me. Her eyes are sad, but she gives me that quick smile again. Then she leans her head against my chest. My heart aches inside for her because deep down inside, I know what she's feeling. Holding her is like holding myself when I was her age. It's the same abandoned feeling I get in the recurring dream I have about a baby crying in a crib, and no one ever comes to get her.

"It's time to eat," Ms. Gore announces as she claps her hands to get the children's attention.

"Finally," Mary says as she rushes over to get a seat.

Six colorful munchkin chairs sit around two short tables. I sit next to Mary at a regular size table. Grandma Brown scoots a highchair in next to me and buckles Sarah in. She moves another highchair next to Mary and puts the other baby in that one. A skinny little woman burst through the dining room door, pulling a heavy food cart. She wears a stretched out black net covering over her kinky hair and a white uniform. She looks old, worn, and tired, but she moves fast as she goes into action filling each plate. The skinny woman hands them to Ms. Gore to distribute. As Ms. Gore puts one in front of each child, she gives them her stern look and tells them not to touch until she serves everyone. The children squirm in their seats. When everyone has a plate, we bow our heads to give thanks.

"God is great, God is good, let us thank Him for our food, A...men," they drag the last part out.

Ms. Gore sits across from me, where she is close enough to tend to the kids when needed and tries to eat as well. Grandma Brown also double tasks as she feeds the baby.

I look at my plate of fish sticks, macaroni and cheese, and a pile of peas. I have milk to drink, and red Jell-O for dessert. I can't eat. It feels like the doorway to my throat closes every time I try to swallow. Mary has already gobbled her fish sticks and macaroni down and asks if she can have more.

"No...you may not," Ms. Gore says. "We don't waste anything around here, so if you want more, you best finish up those peas first. You ever know what it's like to be hungry, girl?" she asks, looking at her sternly.

Mary boldly stares back at her until Ms. Gore wins the contest.

As I watch Mary continue to fiddle with her peas, an uncontrollable snort comes bursting out. The harder I try to hold it in, the more hysterical my laughter comes barreling out. It's like trying to hold back a big loud burp, but the force behind it is too overpowering, and it comes ripping out. Mary looks at me, as I point to her peas. She knows right away, why I am laughing. We both start to crack up, but I guess Ms. Gore thinks we are laughing at her.

"I'm sorry, Ms. Gore," I say, "I just remembered something funny I did to Mary one time."

"Well," she says, "why don't you let us all in on it then."

"It was nothing," I say, trying to get around it.

"No, please enlighten us," she keeps insisting.

I don't think she believes me, so I tell her what it's all about.

"Well, Mary was sitting at the table playing with her peas like she is now. I couldn't go out until she finished, and I was getting irritated, so I decided to play a trick on her."

"Oh...lordy, what'd you go and do to that poor girl," Grandma Brown snickers at me?

"I tricked her into looking away, and each time she did, I dropped a few peas in her milk. I was laughing my head off, and she was laughing right along with me, but she didn't have any idea what I was doing. Before long, there was a nice layer of peas at the bottom of her glass. So, I told her if she drank all her milk, she could go play."

"Oh...you is a stinker," Grandma Brown giggles. "What'd happen next?"

"She picked her glass up to take a drink, and as she tilted it back to chug it down. I saw the green glob of peas staring back at me. I burst out laughing hysterically as they slowly started to roll straight into her mouth. As quick as they went in, they came flying back out."

The corner of Ms. Gore's mouth goes up in a slight smile, but she takes it back as quickly as it comes.

"So, what did you do, Mary?" she asks as she puts a forkful of peas in her mouth.

"I was mad at first and started punching her in the arm, but then I started cracking up, too," Mary says.

"Well, don't get any ideas of trying to get around me, missy," she says, looking at Mary. "You eat those peas, or you'll sit there until breakfast," she goes on.

Mary begins shoving the peas into her mouth, chewing them as fast as she can. She tries to swallow but instead gags. Ms. Gore says, "Don't you throw up, girl, or I'll make you eat that, too."

Mary slows down and takes a few swallows of milk to help them slide down. She finishes in time to help clear up the dishes.

Ms. Gore hands me a cloth and tells me to wipe the tables, watching my every move. "Did you drop anything on the floor?" she asks me.

"I don't think so," I say.

"Well, you better look a little closer," she says.

There is a lot of food under the table. I'm thinking to myself. That's what little kids do; they drop things. So, why is she getting on me about the food on the floor? She hands me a broom to sweep everything up, and once again watches every move I make.

"Did you find every pea that fell on the floor," she looks around.

"I think so," I say.

"Well, I still see one," she points out.

I must get down on the ground to find it, and finally, there it is. I picked it up and put it in the dustpan with the rest of the fallen food.

"Do you know what it's like to scrub a smashed dried up pea from the floor?" she asks with that big-eyed stare of hers.

"No," I say.

"I didn't think so," she says with sarcasm in her voice. "It's like trying to scrub glue off the floor," she says as she gazes off into space.

"Ms. Gore," I say, handing the broom back to her. "I've never had to scrub a pea off the floor, but I was beaten across the back with a broom. Have you?" I ask. "I didn't know what I did wrong then...either."

I turn and walk away with nowhere else to go except the cell. It doesn't even matter at this point. I want to be alone. Flicking the light on, I quickly turn it off. Between the white walls and ceiling, the brightness is blinding. It's as empty and cold in here as I feel inside. Pulling the blankets back, I slip under the covers. I'm still wearing the sweatshirt and pants Nurse Jones gave me. Thoughts of the day make me toss and turn as I see one door after another, spinning around in my head. I wonder how many new doors I walked through today? I picture Alice in Wonderland standing in front of all the doors, wondering which one will take her back home.

I dream and wake, off and on, not knowing after a while what's real. One minute I see Nurse Jones standing in the doorway, then I see Ms. Gore looking at me with wicked eyes. She laughs as she shuts the door, locking me in. I try to open it and see her through the small window in the door. She and Nurse Jones stand on the other side, laughing. Mr. Max holds his keys up for me to see. I hear a baby crying in the distance, getting louder and louder. Why doesn't someone pick her up? I go to the crib, startled awake by what I see, the baby crying, it's me. I was dreaming, but I still hear the cry of a baby coming from the other room. I realize the nightmare I was hoping to awake from is real. I'm still here.

The sun shines through the big caged window of the cell, bouncing off the white walls. I turn away from it, pulling the covers over my head. I feel drained after yesterday and my restless night. Now my body doesn't want to wake up. I used to like hiding out in my dreams. Now, I can't trust them any more than my waking hours, never knowing what's going to come next. I hear the children getting louder with the squeaks and squeals of playfulness. I hold my hands over my ears to drown out the noise, but it doesn't help. The food cart bangs through the dining-room door. I wish I could curl up and disappear into myself like a roly-poly bug.

"Come on, missy," a new voice calls out to me, "times ta eat breakfast," she says. Her voice is deep and raspy like a smoker. She introduces herself as Grandma Cobb. She is thinner than Grandma Brown, but about the same age. Her skin is dark, and she wears a black wig styled in a chin-length bob.

I smell bacon and eggs. I don't feel hungry, but my stomach growls back at me. Mary is already sitting at the table, as are the little ones. I sit next to her, and she leans over to tell me about the mush on her plate that looks like cream of wheat.

Grandma Cobb puts a plate of food in front of me and sees Mary poking at the mush. "Ain't you girls never ate grits before?" she asks.

We both shake our head no.

"Um, um! Yawl been missing out on some good food," she says. "Let me fix it up for yawl," she says to Mary. We watch as she adds a pat of butter, broken bacon bits, salt, and pepper mix it all together. Go on now, gives it a try," Grandma Cobb says. Mary takes a bite and looks up at me.

"It is good, Con," she says, "try it."

Whatever it is, I think Grandma Cobb is right when she calls it comfort food. I like it, too.

I help clear away the dishes. Ms. Gore is still here, but she doesn't say anything to me this time. When I finish, I sit beside Grandma Cobb on one of the munchkin chairs along the wall. A little girl stands between her legs as Grandma Cobb works a wide-tooth comb through the girl's nappy hair. She parts it into sections and starts braiding it. Then connects one section to the other until there are rows of braids across her head with little tails that dangle at the neck. I watch how she does it with interest.

"You wanna give this here, plaiting a try?" she asks me.

"Sure," I say. It looks easy enough, I think.

As I work the big comb through the little girl's hair, I can't do it without yanking her head back. I'm afraid I'll hurt her, but she doesn't seem fazed by all the tugging it takes to get the comb through it. I begin as Grandma Cobb did with one section at a time. It's tricky at first to figure out how to connect the braids, but once I start, it gets easier.

"You is good at this, girl," Grandma Cobb smiles at me. "I just might gets you to help me all the time," she says with a chuckle.

As I start with another toddler, a different woman strolls through the same door as the food cart.

"This is Mrs. Jackson," Ms. Gore tells us. "She's gonna take you, girls, to the wardrobe room."

Mrs. Jackson is a light-skinned woman, almost bronze. She wears a short dark brown wig styled with pin curls around her face. She has a pretty smile and speaks in a soft tone when she tells us to follow her.

"You'll need to pick two skirts and three tops to mix and match for school this week. You'll need a few sets of casual clothes as well," Mrs. Jackson says.

The wardrobe room smells like mothballs, and it has racks of blouses, tops, sweaters, skirts, and dresses. There are piles of slacks, jeans, underwear, socks, and nightgowns. All the clothes look used but clean. At any other time, it might be fun to dig through everything, but right now, I feel overwhelmed. Everything I hold up to me is too long. I try the shortest bell-bottom pants I can find. They drag a bit on the floor, but I'll only be wearing them around here, so they'll do. I stick with the straight pencil skirts, one beige and one black, knowing I can roll them up. I grab a ribbed forest green sweater, a white oxford blouse, and a brown turtleneck. Mrs. Jackson hands us underwear, knee socks, and a nightgown.

"You're lucky to be the only two going through the clothes at one time. When you get to the girls' section, you'll come here every Saturday with the rest of them. You learn after some practice how to reach for the things you want before someone else gets them first," she tells us.

When we get back to the children's section, I take a shower, washing the disinfectant soap out of my hair. It still feels like straw, but at least it smells better. It's funny how cleaning myself up and putting fresh clothes on makes me feel a little more like myself. I make my bed and sit on top of it with my legs pulled up and my back against the wall. My chin rests on my knees as I wrap my arms around my legs. I turn to look through the caged window when I notice three girls walking through the hallway. One of them stops to look over. They can see me from across the courtyard because of the way the sun is shining through the window, but the caged screen makes it hard for them to get a good look at me. They put their hands against the window like they're looking through binoculars to get a better view. They look like the three bears standing next to each other, short, medium, and tall. The little one waves at me and I wave back. The one in the middle gives me the finger, and the tall one smacks her on the shoulder, laughing at her gesture. They proceed down the hallway and turn to their right. They are walking in my direction, but soon I can't see them as they seem to be heading toward the nurse's station.

∞ ∞ ∞

Grandma Brown peeks around the door. Being back here away from all the commotion makes an unexpected visitor seem to appear out of nowhere. Each time it makes me jump. She tells me it's time to go to the dance.

"What dance," I ask.

"It be a Thanksgiving dance," she says.

"I'm not feeling very thankful these days," I say. "I'd rather not go."

"Watcha means you ain't got nothin to be thankful fur? You alive, ain't ya'?" Grandma Brown asks me.

"What kind of life is this? I didn't ask to be born," I say. "It wasn't fair for God to give all us kids to parents that don't take care of us. It's not our fault. Why should we have to suffer because of them?" I ask.

"Maybe so ya' can learn ta be the soul you meant to be," she says.

"What do you mean?" I ask.

"Sometimes I be thinking, there be so many lessons we gots ta learn. It gotta take more than one lifetime to learn it all. That mean we has ta keep coming back till we gets it right. I don't knows where I learned it 'cept by what God pressed in my heart and soul.

"Hm! So, all us kids here are going through the same thing so we can learn the same lesson?"

"No, we all has our own stuff ta learn even if we in the same boat. There ain't no one else like you in this whole wide world can learn and give watcha comes here ta do," Grandma Brown says.

"How did you get so wise?" I ask her.

"Through lots of my own trials and error, buts most of all, it be in the letting go," she says.

"Letting go of what?" I ask.

"That fight ya' feel inside when one part of ya' wants to go this way, and the other be going that way. It ain't hows God made us ta be living this here life.

"What do you mean?" I asked.

"Watcha think ya' gots a soul fur?" she asks me.

"I'm not sure I have a soul. I think I must have fallen from the heavens before God had a chance to put one inside me. That's why everyone leaves me, because I have no love inside me," I say.

"Whatcha talking 'bout, girly? God don't make no mistakes; He can't, cause He be God. Everybody gots a soul, that be the part of ya' that makes ya' who ya' really is. If ya' ain't got no soul, you'd be like the walking dead going through this here life without no rhyme or reason.

"Wow! That's heavy; It sure would get my parents off the hook if I did choose them. I'd have to do a lot of forgiving before I could see things that way. How do you forgive when it hurts so much inside?" I ask.

"The healing of pains has ta start from the inside out. Ya has ta stop picking away at the scabs or the scar gonna be worse. Just likes a fever has ta takes its course. So does the pains that touch the heart. Once we learns from them, we can lets 'em go."

"But how do you do that?" I ask.

"That be an answer only ya' can find inside ya' self. It be like standing at one of them crossroads and trying to decide which ways ta go. The soul knows the right way, but it be the flesh that has the feet," she says. "Listen ta that voice inside ya'."

"What if I'm not sure if I hear the right voice?"

"If ya' be asking that question, ya' be knowing the answer," she says to me.

"This is all too confusing," I say.

"That cause ya' thinking from the mind of the flesh and nots the soul. The soul always knows what way ta go, and when ya' follow it they ain't nothin ta question cause ya' can feel it all the way down ta the bones that ya' is going the right way."

"Come on, Con," Mary peeks around the corner, "Let's go!"

I still don't want to go to the dance, but I am curious to check out the other kids that are here. I wonder if any of them are my age and if there are any cute boys. What if they're all black kids. They might hate me, like that girl who gave me the finger.

"How's 'bout if ya' gets freshened up? I be back ta gets ya' girls and takes ya' over ta the gym," she says.

I comb my straw hair out. I don't need to look close to notice how pale my face is. It makes my freckles and the redness around my nose and chin from my swollen pimples stand out. I zoom in close to the mirror so I can pop the whiteheads. I rinse with cold water to close the pores and get rid of the redness. I wish I had my cover-up and a little mascara to bring the green out in my eyes. Oh, what does it matter? I don't want to go anyway. I run back to the cell, throwing myself face down on the bed. I wish I could believe the way Grandma Brown does, but all I want to do is curl up and disappear.

Grandma Brown taps on the door again. "Bout time ta go," she says in her sweet voice.

"I don't want to go," I tell her.

"It be good ta go out, and meet sum 'em, other kids," she encourages me. "They all in the same boat as ya' is, and maybe ya' find some comfort in knowing ya' ain't as alone as ya' think ya' is. Get on up now," she says.

As I sit up on the edge of the bed, she takes the comb out of my hand and gently glides it through my hair.

"There now, ya' is pretty as a picture," she says, tucking my hair behind my ear. "Ya' gonna be just fine," she says, patting me on the back.

We walk through a hallway on the other side of the nurses' station. It has a shower room on one side and two rooms across from the doorway. One says storage on it, and the other is open. I look in, and it's a bedroom with Christmas boxes stacked on top of a bed.

"Whose room is this?" I ask.

"It be the supervisors' room to sleep in when she works through the night, but they ain't allowed to sleep when they ain't gots enough help. None of them uses it anymore.

"Oh, so, no one uses it," I say.

"I thinks they just getting stuff out to decorate for Christmas. They puts all the stuff in there they wants out of the way," she says.

I wonder why they couldn't have put all that stuff in the cell, but I guess they need it ready for unruly kids same as they need the sick rooms open.

When we get to the gym doors, I pause, looking at Grandma Brown.

"Do I have to go?" I ask before going in.

"There ain't nothin like singing and dancing to chase away the blues," she says. "Go on now; it be good fur, ya'."

There's lots of chatter, and the song "I Can't Help Myself" by the Four Tops is playing. As we open the doors to go in, I see Mr. Max sitting at a long table on the stage, looking through piles of 45' records. He looks up, seeing Mary and I standing in the entrance and proceeds to take the arm off the record. Pulling the microphone closer to his mouth, he asked for everyone's' attention.

"I'd like you all to welcome our most recent boarders, Connie and Mary," he introduces us, Mary waves, but no one waves back. The silence is chilling, and their eyes are piercing. I'm thankful for how quickly Mr. Max puts the next record on and dims the lights. A glass mirrored ball spins from the ceiling making twinkling lights flash around the room. Chairs line the front of the stage and the wall to our left. I head for the ones closest to us and tug on Mary's arm to come with me. She protests at first because she wants to check out the snack table. I pull her along anyway, but a few girls rush in front of us, grabbing seats first. They look like the same two I saw in the hallway earlier, the one who gave me the finger and the tall one who laughed. Mary and I move down the row of seats, but they sit down on those too. I can feel myself getting angry, that feeling you get when you want to stand your ground, but it feels like I'm in a different world, and I don't know how to play by the rules yet.

"Come on, Con," Mary says, pulling my arm. "Let's check out the snack table."

"Look at all the goodies, Con," Mary says. She grabs a plate, trying to decide what she wants first. There's punch, popcorn, pretzels, chips, cheese, ring baloney, cake, and a big bowl of penny candy.

A girl comes walking toward us. She looks about nine years old, I think. She's as skinny as a stick with long legs and arms, but her torso is short. She reminds me of a spider. Her hair is dark brown and sits right above her shoulders in a smooth flip. The hairdo doesn't quite fit her age or the shape of her head.

"Hi, my name be Wanda," she says in a deep hollow voice that surprises me as much as her looks do. Everything about her seems off-kilter. "I see ya' this morning from the hallway," she says, looking at me. "When ya' all get here?" she asks.

"Yesterday," I said, still staring at her hair.

"Whatcha looking at?" she snaps at me.

"Oh, nothing, I was just admiring how pretty your hair is," I say.

"Oh, yeah," she says, shifting in back in place, "it be nice. They done got it for me 'cause I ain't got no hair."

"What happened to your hair?" I asked her.

"I gots some kind of disease; it don't let my hairs grow. I ain't gots no eyebrows or eyelashes either."

"Hi, my name's Gina," the other girl who's standing in the background says.

"Yeah, she be glad ta see another white girl in this place, ain't ya' Gina?" Wanda bumps her with her hip.

I smile at her asking, how old she is?

"I'm twelve," she says.

"When did you get here?" I ask her.

"My little brother and I got her a few months ago. He's over in the boys' section. I hardly ever get to see him," she says, looking sad.

"We won't be here that long. Our caseworker told us it would only be a few weeks," I say.

"Yeah, that be what they tell all the newbies. You ain't going no wheres 'cept they find you a foster home or another place like this to live in," Wanda says.

"How long have you been here?" I ask.

"I been here's, um let me think, for over a year now," she says.

"Oh, wow! That's awful. There's no way I'd stay here that long. Besides, our mom promised us, too, that it would only be two weeks," I say.

"Girl!" she says, "you best not get your hopes up, 'cause you gone be real disappointed when ya' finds out ya' has to stay longer. It ain't so bad here. At least we gets a place to sleep and food to eat. I been homeless 'fore I gots here, and ain't no way I wants to go back to living like that."

"It's true," Gina says. "They told my little brother and I the same thing. Now they tell me as soon as there's an opening I'll be going to St. Joseph of Gonzaga's home for girls. I don't know where my brother is going, probably a Catholic foster home," she says.

"Don't start with that crybaby face round here, Gina. They ain't no one around here gonna feels bad for ya. We all hurting just like ya' are," Wanda says.

While she's talking, the two girls who took Mary's and my seats keep giving me dirty looks. After looking over at them a few times, the short, stocky one jumps up like she's going to come charging at me. I don't know for sure if she's a girl or a boy.

She's broad-shouldered like a boy. Her hair is short and nappy with a pick comb sticking out of it, and she walks with a funny looking gait. She might have breasts, or maybe she's just thick around the chest.

"Whatcha looking at?" Wanda asks, turning around so she can see, too.

"Those are the two you were with this morning when you waved at me from across the courtyard. The shorter one keeps giving me the finger," I say.

"Oh, that be Billy Joe," Wanda says.

"Ah, I thought she was a boy," I say.

"Oh, lordy! Ya best not let her hear ya says that. She ain't no, boy. She be as much female as you and me," Wanda says. "I should knows...she be my roommate."

"Why are they so mean to me? I ask.

"Don't pay them no mind. That Billy Joe ain't nothin but a bunch of hot air. The other be Sharon and she ain't nothin but Billy Joe's puppet. She do anything Billy Joe wants hers ta do," Wanda says.

"How old is Sharon? She looks too old to be in here," I say.

"Sharon, she be the same age as Gina and me twelve."

"No way," I say, looking at her. She's tall and slender with curves in all the right places. Why is her hair so short?" I ask.

"They shaved it off when she's first come here cause she had lice. Ain't hardly growed back much in the past few months she been here, Wanda says.

"Does Billy Joe scare you, Gina?" I ask.

"All the time," she says.

"Gina, I tell you not to pay her no mind," Wanda says.

"I know, but you're not always around when Billy Joe is. I try to keep my mouth shut, but sometimes she still pushes me around," she says.

A trumpet blast followed by the raspy voice of James Brown singing, "Papa's Got A Brand-New Bag."

"Come out and dances with us, Wanda says.

"No, thanks, go ahead," I say.

"Come here, sister.

Papa's in the swing

He ain't too hip

About that new breed thing

He ain't no drag

Papa's got a brand-new bag

I watch as she grabs Billy Joe and Sharon out of the floor. They make the moves to the direction of James Brown's voice:

> He's doing the Jerk
> He's doing the Fly
> Don't play him cheap
> cause you know he ain't shy
> He's doing the Monkey
> The Mashed Potatoes
> Jump back Jack
> See you later, alligator".

They don't dance like white people. Their moves are smooth and right in line with the beat. I love to dance. Sometimes if I close my eyes and listen to music, I can feel the beat. It's just letting go and letting it flow from your head down to your toes. The thing is, I haven't quite learned how to do it yet with my eyes open.

Mary and I find a seat at the end of the row of chairs, and Gina follows us. We sit watching the kids moving and grooving. You can't help but feel the beat and rhythm with its magical power that pulls you into it.

"That Billy Joe girl scares me, Con," Mary says.

"I don't think you have to worry, Mary," I say. "I think she's more concerned with me than you."

"She doesn't like us because we're white," Gina says. "I know. I've been here long enough, and she picks on me all the time. As long as I do as she says, it's not so bad," she advises.

"Like what kind of things does she make you do?" I ask.

"She makes me go upstairs and get this and that. Sometimes she makes me do her chores if she can get away with it. She blames everything on me," Gina goes on.

"Well, she's not going to do that to me, that's for sure," I say.

"How are you going to stop her?" she asks me.

"I don't know, but right now, I feel so angry inside with everyone that I might punch her in the nose if she starts up with me," I say.

I grab a candy off Mary's plate, and she yells at me.

"Hey, that's mine. Get your own," Mary says.

"Oh, shut up, or I'll punch you in the nose, too," I say.

"I'm going to tell Mom when I see her that you said that," Mary whined.

"Yeah, where's she now, Mary?"

"Shut up, Connie. I hate you," she says, moving a few seats down.

"How can you treat your sister like that?" Gina says. "I'd do anything if I could make things easier on my little brother."

"I'm sure you would, Gina, but you're not me, and Mary's not your brother. You have no idea what it's like to be us, so don't compare our situation to yours," I say. "Mary goes her way, and I go mine. It's the way it's always been between us, so don't go trying to make me feel bad because I'm not like you."

Wanda comes running back over when the song is over.

"When you start school?" Wanda asks me.

"I guess on Tuesday. Tomorrow we see Mrs. Becker, and she's going to go over more stuff with us," I say.

"She real good ta us here. Just watch whatcha puts in ya' letters cause they reads' um 'fore they mail 'am outs," she tells me. What grade you in?" she asks.

"Ninth," I say.

"Then you go ta Leeds Junior High, same as me," she says.

"What grade are you in?" I ask.

"I'm in seventh grade," she says. Gina, her in seventh grade too, but she go to the Catholic school. "I'll looks fur ya' after school on Tuesday. We can walks home together," she says.

"Walk home? You mean, we get to walk outside all by ourselves?" I ask.

"Sure, this ain't no jail," she says.

"Sure, feels like it is with Mr. Max walking around with all those keys jingling from his belt," I say.

"It ain't as bad as you think it is here. I been worse places than this. At least you has a clean bed and hots food. I been homeless and sleeping on the streets. I ain't got nothin ta complains 'bouts. I be happy ta stay here till I turns eighteen years old," Wanda says.

"I'm sorry, Wanda, I'm not usually like this. I just feel like I want to scream with frustration," I say.

Mr. Max puts on the song "Mr. Postman" by the Marvelettes.

"Come on, dance it out, girly," she says as she starts swaying back and forth. "Come on, like this," she says, as she starts tapping her feet back and forth." That's it, now a little bit faster," she says.

After a while, I'm moving with my eyes closed, feeling the music deep down inside, but the words make me sad as I think of my boyfriend Luke, who all of a sudden stopped writing me a few weeks ago. He probably met someone else. He's just another person to add to the list of people who said they loved me but left me too. Tears well up behind my closed eyes lids. I wipe at them before they start to drip down my cheeks.

"Going to the chapel and we're gonna get married," Gina and Mary, sing along with the Dixie Cups.

They grab my hand, and we start dancing in a circle as we sing and move to the music.

"Hey, Con, Grandma Brown was right when she said, There ain't nothin like singing and dancing to chase away the blues."

"Maybe so," I say.

When the song is over, I notice Gina standing stiff as a board with her head down. I turn to look, and there stands Billy Joe looking at Gina.

"You ain't no nigger girl, so stop trying to dance like one," she says.

"She's not trying to dance like anyone. We're just enjoying the music the same as you," I say.

"I ain't talking to you, white cracker," she says. "Sides, ya' still gots no rhythm, ya' all dance like white people."

"Maybe that's because we are white, but I sure like the way your people dance," I say.

"Your people, what that mean?" She says. "You means us, niggers," she says.

"I didn't say that you did. I love watching all of you dance."

"Shut yoo white mouth, ya ain't nothin round here," she says.

"Now, Billy Joe, that be enough out of you. This girl she ain't done nothin to you. Stop acting so stupid. She be given you a compliment," Wanda says.

"I don't need no compliments from no white trash," she says.

"You best shuts ya' mouth fur I shuts it for ya'," little Wanda says to Billy Joe. "Come on, Billy Joe, they all in the same boat heres as we is. Don't matter what color, we all be hurting just the same," she says.

"And you best shuts ya' mouth or ain't gone like you either," Billy Joe says to Wanda.

"You knows you don't scare me, Billy Joe. I knows who you really is, so stops acting like a bully. You don't has to do that in here with all us. No one out ta gets ya like on the outside. We all family inheres."

"She ain't never gone be family to us, Wanda, takes my word for it, girl," she says. "Come on, Sharon, all this white stuff too blinding to my eyes."

"Likes I keep saying, don't pay her no mind," Wanda says.

"I don't know how you expect me to do that," I say.

"Just likes ya' shoo a fly away; after a while, they go's away."

"No, they don't. That fly keeps coming back, bugging the heck out of you until you swat it with the fly swatter," I say.

"Well, I guess if she keeps coming back, the only choice ya' has is to shush her away or swat her one good. And that be all I gots ta say 'bout it."

∞ ∞ ∞

A tap at the door interrupts me just as I was about to doze off.

"You still sleeping?" Mrs. Becker asks me.

"No, I've been up since 7 am. I ate, showered, helped Grandma Cobb plait the kids' hair, and then just wanted to be alone. I'm so tired all I want to do is sleep,"

"It's normal to feel that way when your life's turned upside down. Give it some time, and you'll start to adjust," she says. "I'm sure it doesn't help to be in this room either. I'm sorry they put you in here," Mrs. Becker said.

"Ms. Gore said they didn't have anywhere else to put me, but when we went to the dance Saturday, we went past a private room that no one is using. Grandma Brown said it used to be for the supervisors to sleep in, but they don't use it anymore," I say.

"Let's get Mary and head over to my office. You can show me this room on the way," she says.

"Um-hm, she says as she walks into the spare room, looking inside the boxes. It looks like they're getting ready to decorate for the holidays," she says to me. "I'll see what we can do about getting you out of that cell and into another room."

Mary and I sit once again in the plastic chairs. They remind me of something from the space age "Jetsons" cartoon show." I see these modern halfmoon chairs everywhere now. The only thing is, my feet don't touch the ground, and that gets uncomfortable after a while. As I look around her office again, the one thing I notice this time is that it's as neat and tidy as her appearance is.

"So, how have you been adjusting since I saw you on Friday?" she asks us.

"Ms. Gore made me eat peas the first night we were here, and I hate peas," Mary says.

"I'm sure that was difficult for you with it being your first day. Next time why don't you ask for a smaller helping? That way you won't have to eat as much of the things you don't like," she suggests to Mary.

"The next morning, we tried something new called grits. I didn't want to eat them at first, but Grandma Cobb showed us how to mix them up with butter and bacon. They were yummy.

33

"Well, good for you, trying something new," she says to her.

"How about you, Connie. Did you enjoy the Thanksgiving dance?" she asks me.

"I hate it here, and I just want to go home," I say.

"I know you want to go home. All the kids here want to go home, but did something happen to make things worse?"

I sit looking at her, not knowing who I can and can't trust. My eyes look down at my nails to avoid her penetrating study of me, that thing adults do to try to get inside your head.

"How did you like the dance, Mary?"

"There was a scary girl," she starts to say.

"Stop, Mary," I say.

"I can say what I want. I'm not afraid to tell Mrs. Becker like you are," she says.

"That's because you don't have anything to worry about, Mary. I do," I say.

"What have you got to worry about, Connie?" Mrs. Becker asks me.

"Nothing, I can handle myself," I tell her.

"It's because of that Billy Joe girl," Mary says.

"Come on, Mary, shut-up," I say.

"No, tell me what happened," Mrs. Becker says.

"She was being mean to us and called us names like a white cracker. What's that mean, anyway? It's a funny name to call someone," she asks.

"That wasn't nice of her to call you names," Mrs. Becker says, avoiding Mary's question. "Did she hurt you?" she asks me.

"Nothing happened," I say.

"She scares me, and Gina too," Mary says.

"I'll talk with Billy Joe," Mrs. Becker says.

"See what you did, Mary? Now she's going to come after me for sure," I say.

"So, you are afraid of her?" Mrs. Becker asks me.

"I can handle this my way. Please stay out of it, Mrs. Becker. You'll only make it worse," I say.

She sits there, studying me again.

"I'll let it go for now, but if it gets worse, I want you to promise me you'll tell me," she says.

"I promise," I tell her.

"I still don't know why she calls us a white cracker," Mary asks again.

"It's an old term the slaves used to call the white man when he'd come along, cracking his whip to get them to do what he wanted," she tells us.

"Well, then we should start calling Billy Joe a black cracker, Con," she says to me.

"And why would I do that?" I ask her.

"Because she's treating Gina the same way, trying to make her do whatever she wants, and she's trying to get you to do the same thing," Mary says.

"I told you she's not going to push me around like that, Mary. Calling her names isn't going to make it better," I say.

"Besides this incident, has anything else gone wrong?" Mrs. Becker asks us.

"Everything is fine," I say. There's no way I'm going to tell her how mean Nurse Jones and Ms. Gore are. "Grandma Brown and Grandma Cobb have been great, and we met Wanda. She sure is wise for her age. She said she'd meet me after school, and we could walk back here together."

"Yes, Wanda has been through a lot but always makes the best of things. I'm glad you got a chance to meet her. Speaking of school, I'll be working on getting you registered today, and you'll both start tomorrow morning," she says.

"So, on Friday, we talked a little bit about your family, how your father, brother, and sister eventually left home. We talked about nervous breakdowns and what that means. Has this kind of thing ever happened to your mother before?" she asked.

"I was only about three months old. I don't remember anything. I've heard bits and pieces about it over the years. Mom went crazy or something, and our dad had to commit her to a mental hospital."

"So, you don't know what was wrong with her?" Mrs. Becker asks.

"Everyone blamed Dad because of his drinking, but if anything, it's Mom who drove him to drink. We watched a movie one time about a woman in a mental hospital. She had shock treatments. Mom spazzed out when she saw it, and she started screaming, "That's what they did to me in the hospital.""

"Did she get better after that?" Mrs. Becker asks.

"I don't know. As long as I can remember, Mom's been strange," I say.

"In what way?" Mrs. Becker asks me.

I start to bite my nails again, thinking of the things Mom would accuse me of doing. It was always something nasty having to do with sex.

"Watch out for men, they're only out to get one thing," she'd say.

What thing? I'd wonder.

Then there was the time she was picking on me, and Dad told her to lay off me. "Why so you can lay on her?" she said. That made me sick.

"It must be difficult for you to know who to trust," Mrs. Becker says as if she's reading my mind.

"My mom is the best mom in the world," Mary says. "She's always telling me how much she loves me and takes good care of me."

"That's because you're the only one she treats that way," I say. The heat of anger and jealousy makes my face turn red again, and my eyes fill up with tears. I will not cry, I say to myself as I shift in my chair, trying to shake it off.

Mrs. Becker sits with her chin resting on her folded hands, looking at me for a few minutes.

I've said and shown too much, more than I want any adults to know about what goes on inside our house.

She breaks the silence with another question pushing for more information.

"Has your Mother ever hurt you physically?" She asks me.

"It's not that bad. Sometimes I blow things out of proportion," I say, trying to avoid Mrs. Becker's eyes.

"How bad is it?" she pushes a little harder for answers.

"I don't want to talk about this anymore. Can we go back now?" I ask.

She sits for a long while, looking at me. My hand goes back up to my mouth as I start chewing on the side of my fingernails.

"That's okay, you don't have to talk about it if you don't want to," Mrs. Becker says. "Hopefully, your mother will get the help she needs while you girls are here."

"Yeah, that would be great. Then in a few weeks, when Mom's better, we can go home and help her stay that way," I say.

"And how are you going to do that?" she asks.

"I could help with the expenses by getting a babysitting job and still look after Mary the way I have for the past year," I say.

"You can't go to school, work, and take care of Mary. Who is going to take care of you?" she asks.

"I don't need anyone to take care of me. I can take care of myself and the rest of us. I know how to cook, clean, and do laundry."

"Where is your father?" Mrs. Becker continues to ask questions.

"Oh, he left us two years ago when we lived in California. We had to take the Greyhound bus all the way to Pennsylvania, and it took five days to get here," Mary says.

"You must have seen a lot of places," Mrs. Becker says.

"It was fun, like an adventure, but I got tired of sitting for so long," Mary said.

I roll my eyes; only Mary could make an adventure out of a difficult situation.

"Have you heard from him at all?" Mrs. Becker asks.

"No," I say. "Dad was going to send for us when he got settled wherever he was going, but Mom didn't stick around to wait. He could be looking for us right now and wouldn't know where to find us."

"Doesn't he know how to reach your mother's brother?" she asked.

"I don't know, but even if he did, I don't think our uncle would help him find us. He hates our dad for everything that's happened to mom," I tell her.

"Tell me about Kathy and Johnny."

"Johnny is seventeen; he left a year ago."

"Why did he leave?" she asks.

"Oh, he didn't get along with Mom very well. That's all," I tell her.

"Where did he go?" Mrs. Becker asked.

"He went to live with a friend and his family. He's a senior in high school now. Kathy graduated from high school in June and moved back to California. She's living with our aunt now."

"Well, I think I have a better understanding of your family situation now. Just like your mother needs help to get better, the two of you can get through this easier by talking things out. That's what I'm here for, so any time you want to talk, come and see me."

Standing in front of my new school, I look up at the silver letters spelling out the name Morris E. Leeds Junior High School. As Mrs. Becker and I walk up the steps toward the entrance, I'm not counting how many steps lead to the door. Instead, I'm counting the number of times I've had to change schools in the past ten years; this will be my seventh since I started kindergarten. It never gets any easier. Every school is different, and walking into that first class is always the same.

After getting me signed in, Mrs. Becker leaves, and I follow the office secretary to my new homeroom class. As we walk down the hallway, I straighten the beige pencil skirt I have rolled up around my waist. The green sweater I have on is big enough to hide the bulkiness around my waistline. At least wearing green makes my hazel eyes stand out, but not as well as black eyeliner does. I'm not sure anything could help me anymore. There's something more than eyeliner missing in my eyes. It's like the sparkle has gone out of them. I have never been good at hiding my feelings, although I sure do try hard not to show them. My hair lays over my shoulders still looking fried and dull. I wonder if I'll ever get that healthy shine back.

The teachers always introduce as Constance. It never fails to make a few people laugh. I don't even associate the name with who I am. It's like being introduced as someone else.

"Do you go by Constance or Connie?" the teacher asks me.

"Connie," I say, relieved.

I don't even have to look at the class to see their gawking eyes. I can feel them crawling all over me like creepy bugs. Their whispering snickers sound magnified in my ears. My thumb rubs across the thick bump on my middle finger. It's a callus built up after years of pressing hard against my pencil, trying to perfect my penmanship. It's weird how numb it feels, but even weirder how much I'm beginning to feel the same numbness growing around my body, like a shield protecting me from the arrows of pain.

They're always a few nice kids who offer to show me how to get to my next class. But the older I get, the harder it is to get to know them. Most of them have been together since kindergarten. Letting someone new into their little cliques usually has to be earned in some way. I don't feel like playing their games, and it's just as well, I'd rather be left alone right now.

Lunchtime is always hard on the first day. I never know where to sit. I don't want to pick someone else's regular seat. I look for the most inconspicuous spot and settle for a table in the back of the cafeteria off in a corner.

I sit for a few minutes, watching students still coming in, as they mingle around, or get in line to buy lunch. It smells the same as it did the first day I walked through the doors of Stenton, like cafeteria food. You never know what it is until you get in line and can see what the choices are.

I notice that there seem to be a few more black than white kids. All the schools I've ever attended before only had a handful of black kids if any. I'm beginning to feel like I'm in a whole different world.

Finally, opening the bag lunch, I was handed this morning; the pungent smell of a browning banana jumps out at me. I Dump the contents of my lunch onto the table, and a dime drops out on top of the wrapped sandwich. I guess that's for milk. Hm! If I don't spend the dime, I can make a phone call on the way home from school or save it up and have enough at the end of this week to buy a pack of cigarettes with a nickel to spare. Unwrapping the crinkly waxed paper from my sandwich, I peel the two pieces of bread apart and smell the unfamiliar red looking lunch meet. The sweet smell grosses me out, so I roll the whole thing back up and stuff it in my paper bag. At least I have the banana and some peanut butter cookies.

As the day goes on, I can't help wondering if the students here know about Stenton Child Care Center, if they've ever known anyone who has lived there. If they have, I wonder if they can tell that I'm from there, too.

At the end of the school day, I make my way back to the front entrance of the school. Standing on the top landing, I look down the steps and see Wanda waiting with Billy Joe and Sharon for me.

"Come on, girl, get your ass down here. What the f— took you so long," Billy Joe says.

"Leave her alone, Billy Joe. She can't help it; she a newbie here finding her way around and all," Wanda says.

Billy Joe and Sharon walk up ahead of us, lighting a cigarette. I watch them pass it back and forth as they walk ahead of us, wishing I could have a drag, too.

I smile to myself, thinking how much they look like Mutt & Jeff next to each other. Billy Joe, with her skirt on, looks more like a short, stocky boy trying to dress like a girl. Sharon has long legs and a perfect shape to go with them. The guys walking past Sharon can't help but comment and whistle. She smiles back, but there's something timid about the way she looks back at them. I can't tell if she's shy or scared of them.

We get in line to take the city bus back to Stenton, just as we're about to get on the bus, Billy Joe and Sharon butt in front of us. Wanda starts to protest, but I pull her off to the side.

"Can we walk?" I ask her.

"Sho can," she says, "but it be long walk."

"I don't care. I'm not in any hurry to get back to Stenton. It feels good to be away from that place.

"I don'ts mind it there. You get used to it eventually," she says.

"That's just it, Wanda, I don't want to get used it," I say.

"Ain't much else ya' cans do," she says. "At least for now, anyways."

As we're walking, I notice how many other kids have the same big-toothed comb tucked in their hair as Billy Joe does.

"Why do some of your people go around with those big-toothed combs tucked in their hair all the time?" I ask Wanda.

"That cause they be proud Negroes taking the shame of their wigs off and showing their crown of glory," she says.

"What do you mean, the shame of their wigs?" I ask.

"My granny used to say that no colored woman could goes anywhere without her wig or straightened hair. She says it just ain't acceptable. But now things is changing, and parts of that freedom is accepting who we is. Wearing close cropped hair or growing it into big Afros is a sign of our proud heritage."

"But why the big comb?" I asked again.

"To keeps it all fluffed out, they gots to keep picking at it all day. That ain't no comb; it be called an Afro pick. They wears it in their hair like a proud crown," she says.

"I think their hair looks cool the way it flops and bounces around their head like a big bubble," I say.

"Yeah, I wish I could grow some hair like that," Wanda says.

"Another thing I wonder is, what's with the strut?" I ask.

"You means like this?" She dips, then swings her arm back, drops her head toward her shoulder, then repeats the same movements as the other leg moves forward. From left to right, she struts down the sidewalk.

"You're so funny, Wanda. You make me laugh," I say. "It's almost like you're walking to a dance step," I say.

"That's cause we gots rhythm, " she says, smiling. "We can't help it we finds song and dance in everything we do. That be how my people been getting through all the tough times for centuries," she goes on.

"You mean what the white people like me put your people through?" I ask.

"Ain't gonna lie, cause it be true, but I knows it ain't yur doing. Thing is, there be lots more Negros out there that's says all white people the same and nothin gonna change what they believe," she says.

"You mean like Billy Joe and Sharon?" I say.

"Yeah, but the thing is as long as you in Stenton in a way that make you no better off thans the rest of us in there. It don't matter if you boy, girl, young, old black or white. We all like a bunch of different colored crayons sitting in the same box ta-gather," she says.

"I sure am glad I met you, Wanda. You make a difficult situation a little bit easier to bear. Plus, you make me laugh."

Billy Joe and Sharon are waiting for us a block away from Stenton. "Whatcha ditch us for, Wanda?" Billy Joe asks.

"We just 'cided to takes our time, is all," she says.

"Whatcha looking at?" Billy Joe snaps at me.

"What did I do to you?" I snap back at her. "I don't even know you, and you want to pick a fight with me."

"What's wrong," Billy Joe says, getting in my face, "is you was born white. Ain't nuthin else I gots to say 'bout it, 'cept you best be watching yo mouth."

"Now Billy Joe, you stop all this meanness. She ain't no different than us right now. She be abandon same as us."

"She ain't never gonna be one of us, Wanda," Billy Joe says.

"Don't pay her no mind. She all talk and no action," Wanda says.

Billy Joe comes over and stands close enough to my face; I can feel the heat coming off her, like a bull. Looking me right in the eyes, she says, "You ain't nothin but white trash around these parts. You best be watching yur back, cause if I don't gets ya, one of us will." Her eyes are opened so wide I can see the white surrounding the black bullseye in the center. I stare back at her not giving in yet not knowing what to do next.

"Ooh wee!" She says, turning away first. I gots to close my eyes fur all this whiteness make me go blind," Billy Joe says.

"Yeh, we gonna have to start wearing some sunglasses long as she be around," Sharon says.

"You be right, Sharon. I guess ya' gots more smarts than I thoughts ya' did, girl," Billy Joe says.

Sharon scratches her head as they head back to Stenton, but as soon as Billy Joe nudges her with her elbow, they both start laughing as if nothing was ever said.

"See, I done told you not to pay them no mind," Wanda says to me.

"Are you serious?" I say to her. "How can I ignore that, and what's going to happen if you're not around?"

"I tell you she ain't nothin but a bunch hot air going nowheres," she says.

"I'm getting sick of people pushing me around. All I want is to get along with everyone, but they push and push until I can't take it anymore. Right about now, I feel like a soda bottle and that Billy Joe girl keeps shaking me up. One of these times I'm going to pop my lid and all this pent-up anger is going come spewing out all over her," I say. "Can't says that I blame ya for that," she says.

∞ ∞ ∞

The moment I step through the doorway of the children's section, the kids come charging toward me desperate for love and attention. They surround me from the waist down, pulling on my legs and arms. I can't move. They want the same thing as I do, to be loved, to matter, and to be recognized. As I kiss and hug each one them, I do it with the same love and sincerity I would want, but they are like hungry baby kittens, sucking me dry until I have nothing left to give. Like a deflated balloon, I feel as if all the breath has gone out of me. I need air. I need to get away from them. I break away and run into the cell, shutting the door behind me. I collapse on my little bed, and the tears that I've been holding back since I got here come flooding out. I cry hard into my pillow, so no one hears me. But nothing gets past Grandma Brown. I feel the edge of my bed go down, her hand gently patting my head. Grandma Brown doesn't say a word; she sits beside me rubbing her hand over my hair and hums a soothing tune.

Next thing I remember Mary is shaking me awake.

"Leave me alone," I tell her.

"Ms. Gore told me to come and get you," she says.

I sit up, then plop back down on the bed.

"Tell her I'm not hungry," I say to Mary.

"She's feeding the kids. You know if Ms. Gore has to come and get you, she's going to be mad at both of us. Come on, Con! I want to eat."

I work my way back up. When I stand, I feel like my legs are full of cement. I can hardly get myself moving.

Mary takes my hand and pulls me toward the dining area. The kids look up with messy faces and smile at us with food in their mouths. I look down at my plate and see roast beef, mashed potatoes with gravy, and string beans. My stomach growls, feed me, but I'm still having trouble getting myself to eat as much as my body wants to be fed. After we eat and cleanup, I head back toward the cell, but Grandma Brown tells me to follow her. She takes me through the same doorway that leads into the hallway we went through to go to the dance. Instead of going to the left Grandma Brown takes my hand and leads me the right.

"Lemme shows you what Mrs. Becker went and got done for yawl," she says.

She brings me to the doorway of that room that had all the Christmas boxes piled up in it.

"Oh my gosh! Is this for me?" I say, stepping inside.

"It be all y'alls whiles ya in this section," she says to me.

There's a small built-in dresser and closet to the right of the doorway, a single bed against the wall on the left side. Next to the bed under a window, sits a nightstand. The lamp that sits on top of it gives the room a soft glow. A desk sits across from my bed with my school books already sitting on top of it.

"I gets all you stuff whiles you was sleeping after school. I didn't have times ta puts yawl clothes away. I put yawl box of things on the dresser," Grandma Brown says.

I wrap my arms around her big waist and hug her. She folds her soft, pudgy arms around me, pressing me into her bosom. It feels good to be held by someone who seems to care about me genuinely. I long for someone to hold me, and even though I find it hard to trust love and kindness anymore, it feels harder to let go of her embrace.

"You are like my fairy godmother," I tell her.

"Oh, g'on with ya' now. It be Mrs. Becker you be wanting to thank. She be the one who makes all this happen for ya'."

"But I know you had something to do with it, too," I say as I give her a big squeeze.

"Ah, go with ya now and gets yo-self settled in," she says. "I gots ta get backs ta the babies now. Yawl needs anything ya' knows where's ta find me."

I hang the few clothes I have in the closet, put my underwear and socks in one of the drawers, lay the comb and toothbrush on the dresser. Looking at myself in the mirror, I'm all cried out, drained, tired, and even a bit thinner. I grab my pajamas and toothbrush, then head to take a shower. When I return, I braid my wet hair, grab my history book, and sit up against the headboard of my bed. I'm going to try and do well in school to get my grades up. As soon as I start to read my assigned chapter, it's as if the words go in one eye and out the other. Nothing seems to enter my brain, and the harder I try, the faster the words run away from me. I close the textbook, put it on the nightstand, and turn my light out, snuggling under the covers. The moonlight casts a shadowy glow through the window, and I lay there looking around at my room.

"God, it seems like as soon as I'm about to give up on you, something or someone comes along to give me a little piece of hope to hold onto. I get so angry lately. I feel like I'm going to explode. Hanging onto Your promise of a better life someday is getting harder to imagine ever coming true. As angry as I get with You, I can't stop holding on. Truth is, I'm afraid if I let go, I won't have anything left, and worst of all, I fear I'll lose myself as well."

"There is nothing to fear. I cannot leave that which is a part of who I am."

The Promise

Chapter 2 - December 1967

I said my goodbyes to Grandma Brown last night. I will miss her the most. She said I could come back here anytime I want to visit, but I know it will never be the same. I can't believe it's only been thirteen days that we've been here. It feels like months instead of weeks. I wish I were packing to go home. I knew if I stayed here long enough, I'd have to move out of my nice cozy private room and over to the Girls' Section.

As terrible as its been to come here, at least being in the Children's Section has helped me to adjust a little better. Now I'll have to get used to things all over again with a whole new environment and set of rules to learn.

"It be time to go," Grandma Cobb says as she stands in my doorway. "Now, come here and gives me a big hug."

"I'll miss you," I tell her.

"They ain't no reason why ya can't be coming back ta visit us," she says.

Grandma Cobb gathers all the little children around to say their goodbyes to us. As much as I've enjoyed being able to get away from them when I wanted some peace, I came to enjoy their hugs, kisses, and the funny little things they would say to me as well.

Kids aren't as mean to each other at this age as they are when they get a few years older. I love their innocence. Leaving them feels like all the other losses as if I keep cutting the strings of love that get attached to my heart. Sarah is gone. She left a few days after I got here. I haven't allowed myself to get that close to any of the other babies. But it's still hard to leave them.

Mrs. Jackson, the supervisors from the girl's sections, opens one of the gray double doors, and we step inside a stairwell. Another door straight across from us leads out to the first floor, but she directs us to go up the steps.

"This is the way to the dorm area," she tells us. "As you can hear, there's lots of commotion. Saturday morning is our cleanup day."

She opens the door for us to go in ahead of her. We stand before a long hallway that goes down the middle of the dorm. Mrs. Jackson gives us the tour. To our left are four big rooms, each designed to hold four beds. As we walk past them, we can see the girls stripping their beds, dusting, and sweeping the floors. There are three big hampers in the hallway, one for sheets, one for towels, and the third looks like it's for dirty clothes. Some of the girls give us a friendly wave. Others, like Billy Joe, stand in the doorway checking us out.

At the end of the hall is a glass-enclosed office where the supervisors work. Behind that is an apartment that was designed initially for house parents. Instead, they have supervisors who workday and night shifts, Mrs. Jackson tells us. There is another exit leading downstairs that takes you to the hallway to the infirmary and front offices at the entrance. As we proceed down the hall in the opposite direction, there are two rooms designed to hold two beds each. Billy Joe stands in the doorway of the second one down, and Wanda comes charging out from behind her, all bubbly and excited to see us. Right next to their room is a big bathroom with four shower stalls, two bathtubs, and no shower curtains or doors for privacy. There's a wall lined with sinks back to back in the middle of the room. One row is facing the showers and the other row facing the toilet stalls. At least there are doors on the stalls so you can have some privacy when you use the toilet.

Next to the bathroom is the "beauty parlor." It has a big mirror along the wall with a counter below it for putting makeup on or doing your hair. Mrs. Jackson points out all the hot combs and irons lying about with hair products to straighten the hair.

"I have never seen such things before," I tell her.

"These are the tools the girls use to make curls and straighten their hair. She shows me a long wand and says I could use it to create beautiful curls in my hair.

"I'll get the girls to show you how to use it," she tells me.

On the other side of the beauty parlor are two more rooms with two beds each. We head back to the third room on the left with four beds. "This will be your room from now on," Mrs. Jackson tells us. We stand in the doorway, looking to the left of the room are two stripped beds against the wall. On the same wall as the door are two built-in closets with a double wide dresser and a big mirror between them. My bed is the first one closest to the door, and Mary's is on the other side of mine near the windows. We both have a nightstand with a small lamp. The room is big and wide open, each side mirroring the other. The walls are white, and it feels cold compared to the cozy little room I just left.

Mrs. Jackson doesn't waste any time getting us into the flow of things as she hands us a set of flat white sheets and a gray wool blanket to make our beds. I know how to do it, but Mary needs a little guidance from Mrs. Jackson. There are no bedspreads, but everything looks in order with white sheets and dark gray wool blanket neatly tucked between the mattresses. I look up after making the last tuck and see Billy Joe still standing in her doorway, staring at me. Her right nostril flares, up, reminding me of a bull getting ready to charge. I've been able to avoid her so far, but I don't know how I'm going to do that here with her room right across from mine. What's to keep her from sneaking across the hall at night and choking me in my sleep?

"We have lots of new rules for you girls to adjust to," Mrs. Jackson informs us.

"Yeah, what're the rules on the other kids coming into your room?" I ask while I'm still looking at Billy Joe across the hall.

"We don't usually have a problem with that, as we try to respect the privacy of each girl's space. It is, after all, the only real thing you can call your own while you're here," she says.

"That's good to hear," I tell her.

"As for the rest of the rules, you probably won't remember them all at once, but it will be easy enough to follow along with all the others," she says. "Let's start with the morning routine: the wake-up call is at 6:00 am on weekdays. By 6:30 am, you are to be lined up along both sides of the hallway, dressed, and ready for school, with rooms picked up and beds made. We will take a headcount at this time, then say morning prayers before heading down for breakfast and then off to school at your designated times. You are to come straight back here after school, no dilly-dallying on the way home," she stresses to us.

"Showers before bed begin at 8:00 pm for the younger girls and bedtime is at 8:30 pm for them. Older girls shower at 8:30 pm and into bed by 9:00 pm," she goes on.

On weekends, wakeup call is 6:30 am, line up at 7:00 am, and breakfast follows. At 9:00 am we begin our chores up here, and after lunch, we go in shifts to the wardrobe room to pick your clothes out for the week. The rest of the day is for you to do as you please around here. At 8:30 pm, showers begin for the young girl's bedtime 9:00 pm. Big girls start their showers at 9:30 pm, and lights are out by 10:00 pm.

On Sundays, you can attend church if you like, and the rest of the day is once again to do as you please. Sometimes we have special activities or field trips these days. They are also visiting days for families," she says.

We head down into the lower part of the unit. The first doorway next to the stairway is the dining hall.

"What time is lunch?" Mary asks.

"At noon," Mrs. Jackson responds.

"What time is dinner?" Mary asks.

"At 5:00 pm," she responds with a smile. "Are there any other questions," she looks at us.

Most of the girls come down, walking past us. They're heading toward the sound of a TV that appears to be coming from the other end of the hallway. Billy Joe stands at the doorway that leads into the library, moving inside so we can peek in as Mrs. Jackson points it out to us. As we proceed to walk along following behind Mrs. Jackson, Billy Joe sticks her leg out the doorway just in time for me to stumble over it, almost falling on my face. The hairs on the back of my neck and arms are standing at attention. My skin feels red hot from the anger building up inside me. I stand there with my eyes locked on Billy Joe and ready to blow at any moment when I hear Mrs. Jackson's voice snap me out of it.

"What's going on between you two?" she looks at both of us.

"I was stepping out of the library, and she pushed right into me," Billy Joe lies.

"Don't you be telling no fibs girl," a high pitch voice comes from one of the other supervisors. She peeks her head around the doorway of the glass-enclosed office. As she steps out, I'm surprised to see a tough older woman with light brown skin and dark freckles. Short, tight, kinky, graying curls cover her head. She looks like a big chubby man in a baggy dress. Her mannerisms are very matter of fact with an air of confidence. She seems to be a mixture of everything: man and woman, black and white, vinegar and sugar. I'm not sure yet which part stands out the most. One thing for sure, she seems to have some street smarts, and no one is going to pull the wool over her eyes.

"You a liar," she says as she leans her face into Billy Joe's, almost touching her nose. "I saw ya' stick your foot out, so don't you be lying to me, girl," she says wagging her finger at her.

She tells Billy Joe to get the cleaning supplies out of the closet and get her lying behind to work on the bathroom right across from where we are standing.

"Don't you even think of coming out until I say so," she goes on.

She then turns to me and says, "Looky here, missy, you got to find a way to get rid of all that pent-up anger. I keep telling them we needs a punching bag same as the boys does ta release all them bottled up feelings, but they don't listen to nothing I say."

Mrs. Jackson tells me that this is Miss Betsey, and Miss Betsey tells her that she'll take it from here.

"I tell you what," she says, "how bouts you go down to the diner at the corner and fetch me a newspaper. The walk will do ya' some good," she says as she digs down between her breasts, pulling out a change purse. She clicks it open, raking her fingers across the coins and takes out a 50-cent piece. Here ya' go, missy, buy me a newspaper and get yurself something with the rest, I don't need no change back, ya' hear?"

I stand frozen for a minute, wondering if I heard her right, when she says, "Go on now, girl, and get yurself out of here."

Billy Joe peaks her head out the door, giving me an angry look. Miss Betsey yells at her to get her nasty face back in there and scrub them floors.

∞ ∞ ∞

I run upstairs to get my coat and use the other stairway that leads out to the front of the building. Miss Betsey said to go out the side doorway, but I pause for a minute, hoping I don't set off an alarm. I guess I'm safe enough since she said I could use it, and we go out this door every morning for school. I can't get Mr. Max and his keys out of my mind, the way he said, we're locked in for our safety. Closing my eyes, I push the bar down to open the door. All I hear is the gush of cold air as it smacks me in the face. I wonder why Mr. Max made such a big deal about us being locked in. Maybe he tells us that, so we don't try to escape. After the door shuts behind me, I'm curious to know if it's locked from the outside. Sure enough, it is. So, we're safe from anyone coming in but free to go as we please. Getting back in isn't as easy. I'll have to ring the bell at the front entrance so someone can let me in.

It's a cold crisp day, but the sun is out, and the skies are blue. The cold air burns my lungs, but being free energizes me. When I reach the diner and walk in, the waitress behind the counter greets me with a warm smile.

"What can I get you, honey," she asks.

"I'll take a cup of hot chocolate," I tell her as I rub my hands together.

I sit at the counter and twirl around in the seat as I wait. There are a few people spread out along the bar, but other than that, it's pretty empty. The waitress puts the hot chocolate down in front of me, and I take my time drinking it. A man a few seats down strikes a match and lights his cigarette. I love the smell at the first moment, the match, and the cigarette meet. It reminds me of my dad. I always knew that one day I would smoke. I couldn't wait until I was old enough. The first chance it was offered to me, I got hooked. I haven't had any since I've been here. Right now, smelling it is giving me a craving for one.

When I finish my hot cocoa, the waitress rings it up, I hand her the 50-cent piece, and she gives me 40-cents back. I go to the machine in the doorway and drop a dime in for the newspaper. A cigarette machine stands on the opposite side, and a pack cost 30-cents. I have the exact amount of money I need. I couldn't have planned it better, and this time I'm not going to waste the money trying to call Mom or my friends the way I have with the dimes I saved from my lunch.

I put the money into the machine and look for a brand I like; sometimes I smoke, Winston, Salem's, or Marlboro. "Winston tastes good, like a cigarette should," I hear the slogan in my head. So, I pull the lever, and the Winston's come out with a loud plunk. I look around sheepishly, but no one seems to be paying any attention. I grab a pack of matches on top of the machine and head out the door. I eagerly open the cigarette pack and sit on the curb to light one up. Striking a match, I bring its flame to the cigarette, and take a few puffs, until the tip lights up with red embers, creating a tail of white smoke curling upward. It makes me feel a little lightheaded at first, but after a few more drags, it's about the best feeling I've had in the past few weeks. I mosey on back to Stenton, wishing I had a stick of gum so that Miss Betsey won't notice the smell. Then I remember she had a cigarette burning in the ashtray at her desk when the incident happened. She won't even notice. I'll be smelling just like her.

As I hand Miss Betsey the newspaper, she looks pleased, and says, "Well, look at you all rosy cheeks and smiles. I knew that there walk would be good for ya. Now go on and get yurself some lunch before it's all gone.

Pulling out the tightly tucked sheet and the blanket, I climb into bed, drawing the cover-up to my chin for warmth. I hear the heavy breathing of Mary and the two younger girls across from me. They are already asleep. One of the girls still sucks her thumb, but it now lies on her pillow beside her open mouth. The dimmed fluorescent lights in the hallway buzz softly, casting a ghostly light into our room. I can hear the low whispers of the supervisors talking, and worst of all, the dripping water from a showerhead, echoing from the empty bathroom across the hall.

I wonder if I'll ever get to sleep between all the new noises and the fear of Billy Joe sneaking into my room. I'm hoping she won't get past the supervisors' watchful eyes. I'm also counting on Wanda. She doesn't miss a trick with Billy Joe, and since they share a room together, there's no way Billy Joe can pull the wool over her eyes.

This first day in the girls 'section has been a whirlwind of new things to do, learn, and remember. I hate the adjustments I have to keep making, but at least now, I know this will be a permanent one until I leave here.

Wow! Mrs. Jackson was right when she said we do everything together, even taking showers. It's hard enough that I'm so frigging modest, but being the oldest white girl here makes me even more self-conscious. I think it was pretty smart of me to figure out a way to get undressed behind the door in the toilet stall. But eventually, I have to take the towel I have wrapped around me off. I hang my nightgown on the hook outside the shower stall. I turn the water on, glance around to see if anyone is looking, then quickly hang the towel over my nightgown and step into the shower.

I wash quickly and grab my towel, drying off inside the shower. Then, holding my towel with my chin pressed against my upper chest, I try to put my nightgown on over my head. As my head goes up, the towel drops revealing my entire body, hands up in the air as I struggle to work my tacky wet limbs through the armholes. I hear a few giggles, but by the time I get it over my head, no one is there. Just thinking of it still makes me feel embarrassed. I hate it here.

My eyes are wide open as I lie on my side looking at the dresser and closet that is now filled with a weeks' worth of clothes. What a fiasco that was, trying to find something decent to wear at the same time as seven other girls who know exactly where to go for the best outfits! All I could do is watch and learn, and that's just what I did. Next time I'll be prepared. Monday, I get my ninth-grade graduation picture taken, and all I have to wear are a bunch of white oxford shirts and no makeup. It won't matter much what I wear or how much makeup I put on; there's no way I can hide how miserable I feel.

Looking at my doorway, I think about Billy Joe again and how anxious it makes me feel knowing there is nowhere to go to get away from her now that we are stuck in the same section. I don't know what's going to happen, but I can't ignore her any longer, and I'm afraid that one of these times I'm going to haul off and punch her in the nose. Man, as if we don't have enough to deal with here, why does she have to make it more difficult?

Turning on my back, I lie for a while in the quiet. My thoughts always find their way to God even if I don't want them to go there.

"You know me better than anyone, God. All I want is to get along with everyone. Why do you keep putting these people in my life who want to push me around? A person can only be nice for so long before they need to stand their ground. I don't like all the yucky feelings I have inside, but I don't know how to stop feeling them or how to get rid of them. I feel like I'm turning into the same Humpty Dumpty that Mrs. Becker compared Mom to, like I'm sitting on my own wall, minding my own business, and people keep coming along trying to

knock me off it. What if I fall off and crackup like Mom, God? Will you be there to catch me before I break open?

I lay in silence, waiting, listening for a response, but all I hear is the buzz from the lights.

∞ ∞ ∞

On Sunday, Mary, Gina, and I walk to the nearest Catholic Church after breakfast. Whenever I get outside the Stenton doors, I feel like a dog that is set free after being caged up. I want to run around like crazy and feel the freedom of nothing holding me back. I don't like going to church, but I've come along just so I could get out and smoke a cigarette.

When we get to church, I decide to go in anyway. I look through the prayer cards laying out and find one with footsteps in the sand. I stick it in my pocket. As we step across the threshold into the Church, I dip my fingers in the holy water and bless myself. I always think that maybe it will make me a little holier. We're early, but as usual, a few older women are holding their rosaries as their mouths move a mile a minute in silent prayer. They reminded me of my Dad's mother and his sister Honey when I used to see them in church. I thought they were the two holiest people I'd ever seen, especially when the light from the stained-glass windows shined on them praying in front of the Virgin Mary.

We can sit anywhere, but Gina walks to the front and sits in the first pew on the left. We face the statue of Mary sitting with Jesus on her lap. Joseph stands behind them. I like to think they're a happy family, but you would never know by the looks on their faces. Their expressions are as stone-cold as the statues that represent them. I look around at all the murals of saints and angels, and they look sad too. Then my eyes look up above the altar at Jesus hanging on the cross, and I think to myself if God didn't even help His very own son, then what hope is there for me? I'm overwhelmed by the sadness around me. It seems to magnify what I'm feeling inside. Suddenly I feel like I can't breathe.

"I have to get out of here," I say to Mary and Gina. "I'll meet you outside after church," I say, and run down the aisle and out the doors.

I stand on the corner, watching the cars pull into the parking lot. After it starts to fill up, I find a secluded spot at the back of the lot where I sit on the cold curb. At least the sun is shining, and I feel some warmth from its rays. I pull my cigarettes out of my pocket, and the prayer card with the Footsteps in the sand falls out. I pick it up to read. It says;

Footprints
"One Night,
a man had a dream.
He dreamed he was walking along the beach
with the Lord.
Across the sky,
flashed scenes from his life.
Each scene,
he noticed two sets of footprints in the sand;
one belonging to him,
and the other to the Lord.
When the last scene of his life flashed before him,
he looked back at the footprints in the sand.
He noticed that many times along the path of his life,
there was only one set of footprints.
He also noticed that it happened at the very lowest
and saddest times in his life.
This really bothered him,
and he questioned the Lord about it.
"Lord, you said that once I decided to follow you,
you'd walk with me all the way.
But I have noticed that during the most troublesome times in my
life, there is only one set of footprints.
The Lord replied,
"My precious, precious child,
I love you,
and I would never leave you during your times of trial
and suffering
when you see only one set of footprints,
it was then that I carried you."
Unknown Author

"Oh my gosh!" I say out loud as I bring the card up to my lips to kiss.
"You were listening to me last night, and You won't let me fall because You're holding me. I bet the only time You're not holding me is when I get stubborn and wrench myself out

of Your arms. That's no one's fault but my own. You never condemn or ask my forgiveness for doubting. You never even make me feel as if I'm a bad person. You pick me right back up, holding me with the same kind of love Grandma Brown gives, the way parents are supposed to love their child. I like You better out here, God. It seems like the God inside the church just wants to remind me of all the bad things I do, and if I don't watch it, I'm going to burn in Hell. Maybe someday I'll understand, but I sure like you better the way you love me right now. Thank You for that, and for always being there for me even when I get stubborn and try to do things my own way."

I light my cigarette, taking in all the familiar smells that give me a sense of comfort. It's strange in a good way how being out here on my own makes me feel like I'm in charge of myself. I wonder what will happen if they find out I didn't go to church, but then I think what does it matter? I can't imagine a punishment any worse than what I'm already going through. Besides, I get more out of being in the parking lot with God than I do when I'm inside the church.

"With all these good, hopeful feelings You've given me, I still don't know how I'm going to deal with Billy Joe. Maybe You could find her a foster home. Or maybe give my dad a hint of where we are so he can get us out of Stenton. I don't think I can turn the other cheek much longer the way You want me to. Billy Joe is going to keep smacking away at me until she wears me down or kills me in my sleep."

When the service is over, people start coming out. I walk over so Mary and Gina can see me when they come out. Mary comes running over and threatens to tell on me, but Gina says to her that sisters don't rat each other out.

At 7:00 pm, Mrs. Jackson turns the TV off.

"Okay, girls, it's homework time," she says.

We split up into two groups; the big girls, between the age of twelve and sixteen, follow Miss Betsey into the dining hall. Mrs. Jackson shepherds the six to eleven-year-old into the library room.

"You know the drill, girls," Miss Betsey says, holding the door open. "Spread yourselves out in the first four tables."

There are two girls to a table. Diane, the oldest, and her sister Sasha sit at the first table nearest the door. Gina and Wanda sit at the next table, then Sharon and Billy Joe, I'm stuck sitting in front of them.

"Okay, girls, you have an hour of quiet time. "No talking," she says in her high-pitched voice. "If you don't have homework, read a book or write a letter." As she moves away from the door, she puts a wedge in it, so it stays open slightly. She pops her head back in, "and if I hear any talking going on, you be getting an extra 15 minutes chocked onto this here hour. Do I make myself clear?" she shouts.

"Yes, Miss Betsey," we all say at once.

As soon as she's out of sight, Billy Joe switches places with Sharon, so she's right in back of me. The supervisors can't see us from their office.

I feel a kick against the back of my chair, making me jerk forward. I ignore Billy Joe, but she kicks harder.

"Knock it off, Billy Joe," I turn and say to her.

A shush from Diane in the back of the room makes Billy Joe stop, and things settle down. I open my math book and try to figure out how this new algebra formula works.

Another hard kick jerks me forward against the table. This time I fly up out of my chair and grab Billy Joe by the neck of her shirt, pulling her into the aisle. My face feels red hot with a wave of fiery anger as I pull her in closer.

"You got something to say, bitch, then to say it to my face. I've about had enough of your meanness." My mouth is flapping a mile a minute, calling her every name in the book, yet I don't feel like I have any control over what I'm saying. I see the fear in her wide-open eyes and my reflection. I don't like what I see, but I can't stop. She's become my mom, dad, uncle, aunt, my caseworker, Mr. Max, Nurse Jones, Ms. Gore, and everyone and everything that got me to this point in my life. My clenched fist is up and ready to fly right into her face when Miss Betsey grabs my arm in midair.

"Connie, let go of her," she's shouting.

I can hear her, but the anger has such a firm hold of me, I feel locked inside it, and I won't let go.

"Get her off of me, Miss Betsey! She's crazy," Billy Joe cries out.

Miss Betsey pulls a whistle out from between her breast and blows it so hard I snap out of it. When I see the disappointment on Miss Betsey's face, I feel that I've lost her friendship and trust now, too.

"Whatsa' matter with you, girl?" she screams at me.

I slump like a deflated balloon and go inside myself, feeling like the weak, defeated person I am.

"Look at me when I'm talking to you, girl," she says as she shakes me.

I move like a wet noodle with a blank stare.

"I didn't do anything to that crazy ass white bitch, Miss Betsey. She comes right after me for no reason," Billy Joe whines.

"What'd you say!" Miss Betsey's angry, squinted eyes turned toward Billy Joe. "You get you black ass up those stairs before I kick ya' up there. Go on with the rest of you, too, and finish ya' homework in ya' rooms."

Miss Betsey stands, looking at me with both hands still held tightly gripped to my arms. She shakes me, "Snap out of it now, girl," but I feel like I'm stuck inside myself. She shakes me a few more times, and there's still no response until she smacks me in the face, and I start to cry.

"I'm sorry, darling, but I hads to snap ya' out of it," she says as she pulls me in against her big bosoms. I'm crying so hard I can barely catch my breath.

"Lets it all out," Miss Betsey says to me as she pats my back.

When I finally calm down, she moves me aside so she can pull a pretty little hanky out from between her two breasts to dry my wet face.

I start to laugh hysterically, and Miss Betsey looks at me like she doesn't know what to think now.

"What else you got between those breasts of yours?" I ask, barely able to get the words out because I can't stop laughing.

"Girl, you gonna gives me a heart attack in this here place," she starts to laugh, too.

She takes my chin in her hands and looks me in the eyes.

"Well, girly, I don't think ya' gonna have to worry 'bouts, Billy Joe, bothering you anymore. You done scared the bejeebers out that one," she said with a bit of a smirk on her face.

"But I don't like being like that. I feel like people don't like the nice me, and they keep pushing me into being someone mean and hateful," I say.

"They ain't no ones who can makes you into anything; less ya' lets them. That like given all ya' gots ta someone else ta control and losing ya-self in the process," Miss Betsey says.

"I keep feeling like I'm slipping away, Miss Betsey, but as soon I'm ready to give up, God gives me another rope to hang onto, like you," I say.

"That be whats I here for; ta helps all ya' girls find a ways to hold on and sees something better in ya-self than being abandon and all alone. Ya' has to know ya' matter cause ya' ain't no good to anyone else if ya' ain't' good to ya-self first. That means, ya' has ta sometimes do the things ya' don'ts want's ta do, ta gets beyond it."

"You mean I have to get fighting mad like I did tonight?"

56

"No. I mean, ya' has to say what ya' needs to say before it gets that bad."

"But I don't like confrontation."

"Who does?" she asks. "But if ya' let all that stuff builds up inside, what's the better of the two? Confrontation or fist fighting? Ya' has to find a way to let it out."

"But can't I find another way to do it?"

"Maybe if ya' talks to someone like Mrs. Becker, she could help ya' think of some ways to let it all out. Sometimes just talking 'bouts it helps."

"I like talking to you, Miss Betsey. You're the first adult who listens to me," I say with tears in my eyes.

"Now don't you go crying on me again. You already done got my dress all wet with them tears," Miss Betsey says making me laugh.

"Thanks, Miss Betsey. I do feel a whole lot better," I say.

"That be 'cause you got all that pent-up stuff out. Ya' was like a hot water heater needing ta get some of that hot air out of ya pipes. Now ya' feeling the relief of it," she says.

"I think I'll tell Billy Joe, I'm sorry," I say.

"All I wanna say, girly, is ya' gots something special. Even I sees it in ya. Don't let no one takes that away from ya. It's who you is, and that's all ya' gots in this whole world is yo-self and God," she smiles at me.

"I sure wish I could see what you see in me," I say.

"Someday ya will," she says.

I run up the steps and tap at Billy Joe's door, peeking my head inside.

"Are you asleep?" I ask.

"Don't you come near me," she shouts.

"I just wanted to say I'm sorry!"

"Oh! Okay then! I guess I be sorry too," she says. "I thoughts you was gonna kill me in my sleep," she goes on.

"I thought the same thing when I first got here," I laughed.

"You is like a Jekyll and Hyde," Wanda chimes in, "and I hopes I don't ever see that Jekyll or Hyde, again. I don't knows which it is, but you sure was scary."

"I'm sorry, Wanda, I didn't mean to scare you. I guess I have a whole lot of hurt and anger stored up inside," I say.

"We all has the same feelings; you ain't alone," Wanda goes on.

"I guess that's all the more reason to stick together rather than fighting with each other," I say

"So, we friends?" Billy Joe asks.

"Sure! Why not!"

"See ya in the morning," she says.

"See ya then," I say.

"Me, too," Wanda says.

I walk across the hall to my room.

"What happened, Con? I heard you, and Billy Joe got in a fight," Mary says.

"Everything is going to be okay now, Mary. Billy Joe isn't going to scare us anymore.

"Did you punch her in the nose?" she asks.

"No, but I almost did before Miss Betsey stopped me," I say.

"I'm glad you're ok, Con, but I still hate it here. I want to go home," she says.

"Me, too, but at least maybe now it won't be so bad," I say.

Chapter 3 - January 1968

*M*rs. Jackson walks down the hallway ringing the morning bell.

"Time to get up," she says as she passes by each room.

"Happy birthday," Mary says to me.

"Thanks, but I don't know what's so happy about being in here on my birthday, Mary," I say.

"Oh, why do you always have to be so sad all the time," Mary says.

"Because today is Saturday, January 27th, almost ten weeks since we came here or saw Mom. It's eight weeks past the time we were supposed to be here.

"But Mom's coming to see us tomorrow for your birthday. Maybe we can talk her into taking us home with her," Mary says.

"We can try, but don't get your hopes up. Mrs. Becker said Mom isn't ready for us to come home yet. She's only starting to get back on her own two feet.

As we line up in the hallway for a headcount and morning prayer, Mrs. Jackson announces that it's my birthday like they do for everyone.

"How old are you today?" she asks me.

"Fifteen," I say.

"That mean I gets to punch you in the arm fifteen times," Billy Joe says as she gets the first punches in.

"Damn, Billy Joe! That hurt," I say. "You didn't have to wallop me so hard."

"Yeah, that means we all gets to punch her fifteen times, right, Billy Joe," Sharon says, giggling.

"There'll be no punching," Mrs. Jackson says.

I give Billy Joe a dirty look, but it doesn't faze her. She gives me that wide mouth smile of hers showing off her bright white teeth. "You gots fourteen more comings," she whispers in my ear.

"You punch me one more time, and I'll knock those pretty white teeth right out of your mouth," I tell her.

"Don't be making her mad again, Billy Joe. You remember what happened last time," Sharon says.

"Ah! I just kidding," she says as she pushes me lightly.

"We gots a plan for you after we done picking clothes out in the wardrobe room this afternoon. Meets us in the beauty parlor after ya' done putting ya' clothes away," Wanda says.

I thought it was nice that the girls let me pick my clothes out first in the wardrobe room. We didn't fight over any clothes. I know they're up to something. They keep running through the hallway, whispering.

"Don't come in the parlor until we tell you it be okay," Wanda says.

"After putting my clothes away, I pick up my school picture. I still can't believe how much it shows how I feel. I'm glad. Now when I give it to Mom, she can look at it every day and see what she's done to us. I pick up Kathy's senior picture that Mom sent to Mary and me. Putting the two pictures side by side, it doesn't seem fair that she's so pretty with Dad's blue eyes and straight teeth. Most of all, she's free of all this. I wonder if I'll ever have a smile on my face again.

"Ya can come in now," Wanda calls out.

As I walk in the beauty parlor, Diane is fixing her sister's hair as she yanks a big comb through it. It looks like it's all shrunk into tight curls after being washed. I sit upon the counter next to them and watch. Diane begins to section off her sister's hair using clips. I dip my finger in the goo she's using and ask Diane, "What is this stuff?"

"It's called pomade," she says. "It helps to relax the hair and gives it that nice sheen."

I pick the can up to read the label, "Royal Crown hairdressing. I never heard of it."

"Well, why would you?" Diane's sister Sasha says. "Your hair's already straight."

Diane dips her finger in the goo and spreads a small amount on one of the sections, then she takes the electric hot comb and smooths it out a few times until she gets nice and straight. She does this with each section. It takes a long time. Then she takes a hot iron roller and curls it under so it looks like a bob.

"Can I feel it?" I ask.

"It's so soft and doesn't feel greasy at all the way I thought it would," I say.

"I goes for the natural look cause I proud of who I is," Billy Joe says.

"Black is beautiful! Right, Billy Joe. That what the activist tells us to say," Sharon chimes in.

"That's what it says in the Ebony magazine," Diane says.

Billy Joe pulls the big-toothed comb she keeps at the crown of her head and starts to fluff out her 'Afro.

"Come sits here," Sharon says. "We gonna makes you beautiful on ya birthday."

"What are you planning on doing?" I ask her.

"I was gonna curl ya hair with this here, curling rod," Sharon says to me.

"I don't know," I say. "Can you use that on my kind of hair?" I ask.

"Sure, it just gives you a nice soft curl. Don't worry; I knows what I'm doing. I used ta do my mom's hair all times for she went out," Sharon says.

"Does she have hair like mine?" I ask.

"Nos, buts, I still knows how to use the curling iron," she says.

While Sharon plays with my hair, Wanda comes back in with something wrapped in a tissue with a little ribbon around and hands it to me, saying, "Happy birthday!" All the other girls gather around to watch me open the gift.

"Wow, a pair of gold post earrings," I say. "But these are your earrings, Wanda."

"I has more," she says.

"That's nice of you, but I don't have pierced ears," I say.

"We knows, the other part of ya present is we gonna pierce 'em for you," Sharon says.

"How you gonna do that?" I ask.

"With this," Billy Joe says as she holds up a big diaper pin.

"I don't think so," I say.

"Why not?" Sharon asks. "That how the rest of us had ours done."

"Maybe not with a diaper pin," Diane says, "but with a big needle, that's just about the same size."

"Don't you want them pierced?" Wanda asks me.

"Yeah! But my mom would kill me if she saw I had pierced ears. She always says, if God wanted you to have holes in your ears, He'd have put them there in the first place."

"Are you gonna tell me you care what ya mommy think when she done put you in this place?" Billy Joe asked.

I thought for a moment and said, "Yeah, you're right, Billy Joe. I don't care. Let's do it."

Sharon tells me to rub my earlobes tight between my fingers to make them numb. Billy Joe takes a match and burns the tip of the diaper pin to sterilize it.

"I even gots some alcohol cotton balls from Nurse Jones. Told her I needed them cause my earlobes was feeling sore," Wanda says, giggling.

Sharon takes over, rubbing my earlobes even tighter between her fingers.

"You okay?" she asks me.

"Yeah. Just let me know when you're ready to poke me," I say.

"I already dids," she laughs.

"I didn't even feel it," I say.

"Looky how pretty that there earring looks," Wanda says to distract me.

"We all done," Sharon says while she wipes my earlobes down with the alcohol cotton balls.

I go up to the mirror with my hair tucked behind my ears.

"I love it," I tell them. "You've made my day more special than I ever expected it could be in here. Thank you."

"Now you gots to keep turning them throughout the day," Sharon says.

"And you gots to keep putting the alcohol on till they heals up," Wanda says handing me the ones she got from the infirmary.

"What do I do when I run out of cotton balls?" I ask.

"Just tell Nurse Jones ya needs them for ya ears, she ain't gonna think nothin of it," she says.

"I don't know about that, but I'll give it a try," I say.

They sing "Happy Birthday" to me, and after all the nice things they do for me, they end my celebration by punching me in the arm for good luck.

"I don't think I like this tradition," I say, rubbing my arm. "I'm not sure what hurts worse, my arm or my earlobes," I say.

∞ ∞ ∞

"Your mother's here," Mrs. Jackson tells us.

Mary shoots out of the door of the girls' unit before I'm up and out of my chair.

"Good luck," Diane says. She hardly ever talks to me.

"Don't forget ta keep ya ears covered, so as ya mamma don't see ya new earrings," Wanda says

As I walk out the door, I want to run to Mom as well, but the hurt and anger I feel toward her hold me back. Walking around the corner, I see the two of them together, Mom hugging and kissing Mary with that special love they hold for each other. As Mary cries, Mom wipes away her tears. I feel my tears welling up in my eyes. I wipe them away as quickly as they come, take a few deep breaths, and stuff my feelings deep down inside me

Mom looks up from Mary and sees me standing outside the doorway of the visitors' room.

"I always forget how much you remind me of your father," is what she says to me. Not, "Come here, honey," or "I've missed you," but that thing she says that always reminds me of how much she hates me.

I'd rather look like him than you, any day of the week, I think to myself. I have to bite my tongue to hold the words back.

"Come here, give me a hug," she waves me toward her.

I dutifully go to her and let her hug me, but I can't bring myself to hug her back.

"Are you all right?" she asks.

Once again, the tears begin to well up in my eyes.

"No! I'm not fine," I say as I quickly wipe the tears away. "You said we would only be here for a few weeks, and now it's been a little over two months."

"Oh, don't start in on me now, Connie. I'm doing the best I can," she says. "I've come to take you out and celebrate your birthday. You should be grateful I was able to come at all. Now let's go out and enjoy the time we have together."

I walk behind Mom and Mary as we go out the door. They look so happy, mother and daughter walking down the street hand in hand. I wonder if I wasn't in the picture whether Mom would have found a way to keep Mary with her. Maybe even now, she would take her if I disappeared.

We go to the diner, the same one I go to when Miss Betsey sends me out for her newspaper. The waitress Martha recognizes me and says, "Is this your mom?"

I shake my head, yes, and her smile disappears as she sees I don't look that happy. She doesn't say anything else. I don't want her to. I'm afraid if Mom finds out that I come here every day, she'll think I'm running all over the place on my own. Then she'll say something to Mr. Max, and I'll lose the little bit of freedom I get each day.

"I bet you girls haven't had a good hamburger and fries in a while," Mom says.

"And can we get a chocolate milkshake to go with it?" Mary asks.

"Sure, sweetheart," she says to Mary.

Mom orders two hamburgers, fries, and milkshakes for Mary and me.

"Don't you want anything, honey?" Martha says to Mom.

"No, just a cup of coffee will be fine," she says.

"Why aren't you eating, Mom?" Mary asks.

"I ate a late breakfast this morning. I'm not feeling hungry yet," Mom says.

"So, what are we going to do after this?" Mary asks.

"I don't have much," Mom says, pulling her wallet out, "but I thought we could go to the 5 & 10 stores so Connie can pick something out for her birthday," she says as she hands me $3.00.

"I don't want your money, Mom. I just want to go home. That would be the best birthday present you could ever give me," I say.

"I can't take you girls home until I have a decent place to live and make enough money to put food on the table," she says.

"Who won't let you take us home?" I ask.

"The Department of Child Welfare. I didn't know how hard it would be to get you girls back once I gave you up. I've been trying now that I'm feeling better, but I have to meet their requirements. They're trying to help me get some better training so I can get a decent job and make more money. All I can afford right now is a room in a boarding house," she says.

Martha brings our order, sensing the tension between Mom and me.

"Anything else I can get you?" she asks.

"I could use some catsup," Mary says.

"I need to use the bathroom," I say.

"Your food's going to get cold," Mom says.

"I'll be right back," I say, scooping up the $3.00 as I pull myself out of the booth.

I sit in the toilet stall and light a cigarette. I don't care if Mom notices the smell on me. She can't do anything worse to me than she already is doing. I look at myself in the mirror. Tuck my hair back behind my ears. I don't even care if she sees my pierced ears. She gave us up; now my life's my own to do with as I please, and she can't do anything about it anymore.

I go back to the table and nibble on my burger and a few fries. Mom notices my ears right off, but she looks away. I'm surprised she doesn't challenge me on it.

"Can I buy something too at the 5 & 10 stores?" Mary asks Mom.

"Yes, I have an extra 50 cents for you too, but that's about it, Mary," she says.

"That's okay. I can buy a nice bag of candy with 50 cents," she says.

"Is there anything else I can get you today?" Martha asks.

"No, just give me the check," Mom says.

"But it's Connie's birthday. Aren't we going to have any cake to celebrate?" Mary asks.

"That's okay, Mary, I don't want any cake," I say.

"But I do," she says.

"Well, you're in luck," Martha says. "It's on the house when it's your birthday. I'll be right back," she says.

Mom is getting that faraway look in her eyes, and I can see the irritation forming on her face. Her skin goes taut, pulling her features back like an angry cat hissing at you. It's the face of unpredictability that scares me most of the time. What will she do next? I never know, but it's the face that tells me I'm better off if I try to play dead like a possum or the invisible man.

"I love you, Mom," Mary says, leaning her head on her. That's all it takes for Mom to snap out of it. Mary is good for her that way. She doesn't even know it, but she has a way of melting Mom's heart.

Martha brings us an extra-large piece of cake to share with a candle in the middle. She puts it down in front of me with a wink that only I can see. Then they all three sing "Happy Birthday" before Mary dives into it.

When we leave for the 5 & 10 stores, I stay behind them looking in the windows of the stores we pass. As much as I want to be loved by Mom the same as Mary is, I know it can never be that way for me. It gives me the shivers all over, even thinking of her touching me the way she dotes all over Mary.

I walk off inside the store, and they don't even know I'm not with them. I have $3.00. I know what I want to buy, but browsing around looking at all the things I can get with my money is fun, too. We have never had much money, and I always saved my penny's and nickels. They do add up after a while, so I want to make every penny count. I won't just buy anything. There are lots of mascaras, but I like Maybelline, and it's $1.00. I also love the same brand of eyeliner, the ultra-cake liner that you apply with the little paintbrush. That's a $1.00, too. It will be $2.12 with tax. That leaves me with me 88 cents to add to the money I've been saving from lunch.

We get back to Stenton around 3:00 pm. Mary starts to cry, holding onto Mom, begging her not to leave her. I get it because I feel the same way, but what's hardest for me to understand is how she can leave Mary behind. I don't know; I'm starting to think a lot more about how Mary would be better off without me around. I'm sure Mom would be able to afford to take one of us.

"Come here," Mom says to me. "Give me a hug." I can barely stand getting near her. But I do, because I know it's the right thing to do. We barely touch. I'm not sure if it's her or me not trying. It just feels phony. How can you want to be loved so much yet push yourself away from it at the same time? I sure don't understand love, that's for sure, yet I long for it somewhere deep down inside me.

"Come on, Mary, let's go," I say as I pull her away from Mom. She cries hard the whole way back to our room. As soon as we get inside the girls' unit, Mary turns the tears off. She sits by herself away from the other girls who are watching TV. She opens her bag of candy and dives into it while she laughs at something she sees on the TV. I don't know how she turns her feelings off and on like that, but it seems to be how she gets through the worst of things.

"I'm going upstairs," I tell Miss Betsey.

"You okay?" she asks me.

I tell her what it's like to be around my Mom, how I can't say anything without Mom biting my head off. All I want is to understand why this is happening to us, how I want someone to tell me the truth instead of lying all the time. I tell her how much it hurts to see the way she loves Mary and that I wish she loved me too.

"What am I doing so wrong that no one loves me, Miss Betsey?"

"You ain't done nothing wrong, sweet girl," she says.

"It hurts so bad in my heart that sometimes I think I'm going to die from the pain," I tell her.

"Now listen here, girly! There ain't much you can do 'bouts how other people gonna treat ya.' But ya gots ta go on loving people the ways you wants to be loved. You gonna see, someday, all that love you gives is gonna come back and dump itself all over you. And you ain't gonna know what hit ya' till it all sets in."

"Sometimes, you sound just like the God I hear inside me."

"Maybe that's cause we be talking to the same God," she says.

"You always make me feel better," I tell her.

"You go on upstairs now and sees what the other girls are doing. I bet they want to see what you gots there in that bag."

"I love you," Miss Betsey!

"Go on now. I be needing a cigarette after all this mushy talk."

Chapter 4 - February 1968

"Something smells good," I say as we walk toward the gym. What's the occasion?"

"We gonna eat some soul food," Wanda tells me. "Ain't you ever had no soul food?"

"I don't think so. Is it like Thanksgiving? Sure, does smells like it," I say.

"It's kind of like an African-American heritage Thanksgiving," Ms. Gore's voice comes out of nowhere.

"Whatcha doing here, Ms. Gore?" Wanda asks her. "I thoughts ya spose to be with the babies."

"I'm filling in for Miss Betsey tonight over in your unit," she says.

"Is everything alright with Miss Betsey?" I ask.

"You need to mind your business," she snaps at me.

"Bitch!" Billy Joe whispers in my ear. "She ain't nothin, but a bitch is all I saying."

I don't even want to go there with how I feel about her.

"So, tell me more about this soul stuff. I know about soul music," I say.

"Yeah, we gots all kind of soul-stuff going on, like soul brothers, soul sisters, soul music, and soul food," Wanda says.

"And the soul train, too," Sharon says.

"I might be white, but I got a soul, too," I tell them.

"You one of our soul sisters for sure in here," Wanda says, putting her arm around me.

Billy Joe curls her nose up to one side, shaking her head with no other comment.

"But what are we celebrating?" I ask as we approach a table where Mrs. Becker sits.

"February is black history month," she tells me. Behind her are posters of African tribes such as I've seen in the National Geographic magazine. Another poster says "African American Heroes' with pictures of people I never heard of, like Rosa Parks, Booker T. Washington, Marian Anderson, Satchel Paige, and Martin Luther

King Jr. I never even knew there was a particular month that they had all their own. But I never knew much about the people of color at all before I got here.

As we walk past Mrs. Becker, we reach the long table filled with soul food. I follow Billy Joe into the food line. We take a plate and work our way down the table. I recognize the candied yams, cornbread, macaroni & cheese, fried chicken, and fish.

"What's this," I ask.

"That be ham hocks and black-eyed peas, this chitlins, and that be collard greens," Wanda says.

"Here, has some of this," Billy Joe holds up the foot of some animal.

"No way! What is that?" I ask.

"It pigs' feet," Sharon chimes in with a giggle.

"It be good," Billy Joe says as she tries to put it on my plate. "If you was a real soul sister, you'd eat it," she says.

"No, thanks," I say.

At the end of the line are fruit pies and cobblers.

Mrs. Becker comes over to our table and asks us how we all liked the food.

"I'm so full, Mrs. Becker, I can hardly move," I tell her. "I liked everything except the collard greens."

"And the pigs' feet," Billy Joe reminds me.

Chapter 5 - March 1968

*M*rs. Becker drives Wanda, Gina, and me to her church. Mrs. Jackson, our supervisor, pulls up, parking behind us along the street, and Billy Joe, Sharon, Diane, and her sister Tasha all get out. We walk together toward the small red brick building on the corner. It's a slow movement as one passerby greets Mrs. Becker after the other. They sure do love her. There's no way we could miss where we're going. All we need to do is follow the banging drums, a whining electric guitar, and the organ in the background. I don't know how they put the three together, but it works. When you walk inside, people aren't kneeling and sitting quietly. They're standing, clapping, singing, and swaying to the music, and it feels as if the spirit of God swoops your soul up and starts dancing with you before you even have a chance to sit down.

There's a sea of fancy hats decked out in flowers, feathers, ribbons, and bows moving and swaying to the music as the women dress in their Sunday's best. With white-gloved hands, they wave their fans to cool their faces. Men wear crisp white shirts with skinny or fat ties. Some wear suit coats, and some don't. They wipe away the beaded sweat from their brows with white handkerchiefs.

The choir stands in their golden robes as the preacher arrives. One of the members leads them in the song "Amazing Grace." I never heard it sung with such passion. It brings goosebumps to my arms.

The preacher stands dressed in a black robe and shouts, "Hallelujah."

"Praise the Lord," a woman shouts, jumping up from her seat. The music starts up again, and the preacher claps along. A few women can't contain themselves and start praising the Lord from the aisles, with their hands stretched to the heavens. When things settle back down, the preacher shouts, "Amen!" Da-dum, the drum goes. I could never imagine dancing in the isles at a Catholic Mass or praising God out loud. Everything is the same way each Sunday. Our prayers are said together, we kneel together, and we sing together, but no one yells, amen, all by themselves. It would be considered disruptive. I like the freedom here the way the people stand and sit and sing and sway and clap. It feels freeing, and if I had the nerve, I'd shout out loud myself. I never felt anything like this.

"God, I was thinking for a few minutes that I could go to a church like this, but then the preacher started shouting that we were all sinners. All that hell and brimstone stuff changed my mind. He said unless we are born again and accept Jesus Christ as our savior, we ain't never going to get to heaven. He went on to say that you must give up yourself and follow Jesus Christ. But it doesn't make sense to me. Why would You go to all the trouble to make each one of us special, if You didn't want us to become who You created us to be?"

"Would it be so bad, so follow in Jesus' footsteps?" God asks me.

"I guess not I mean all the stories I heard about him; he seems to love us as much as you do, God. The thing is, my curiosity wants to know where we are going and what I'm supposed to do along the way. How can I do that if I have to give up who I am?"

"I've never asked you to give up who you are. I promised you that one day you could make your life the way you always dreamed it could be," God says to me.

"God, I wish all the people in the world could experience You the way I do."

"They do but in their own way," He tells me.

"Yeah! It would have to be that way because you made us all different for a reason."

∞ ∞ ∞

I'm standing in line with my breakfast tray when I start to feel a little woozy. As I sit down it gets worse except it feels pleasant and relaxing. The girls at the table are talking to me, but with my fork in hand about to dig into my scrambled eggs, I stare off into space. "Connie, what's wrong with you?" one of the girls says as she shakes me. I look at the girl and start to laugh hysterically.

"What you up to now, girl?" Miss Betsey yells at me. "You better not be taking no drugs!"

I crack up laughing again, "I'm not taking no drugs," I say with a slur.

She grabs me by the sleeve of my shirt and drags me down to the infirmary. "Nurse Jones," she says, "what's wrong with this here girl. I send her down to get her meds, and she come back, acting all high as a kit."

"Are you taking drugs?" Nurse Jones asks as she shines a light in my eyes.

I laugh again, saying, "No! The only drug I took was what you put in my medicine cup this morning."

They look at each other like they don't know what's going on. "Maybe you done mixed the pills up," Miss Betsey says to Nurse Jones.

"No, I'm very careful that they get the right pill." Don't blame this on me. She looks down at Miss Betsey.

"Maybe one of the other kids moved them around when you weren't looking," Miss Betsey said.

"But I don't know what could have made her get high like this," Nurse Jones says.

"Ya never knows what these here kids could be bringing in," Miss Betsey says as she looks at me.

I start laughing hysterically at the thought of it, and Nurse Jones takes me into one of the sick rooms and makes me lie down. "I'm fine!" I jump back up like a jack-in-the-box. I can't sit still; I'm laughing so hard.

She tucks her fat fist into her waist, "You better lie down, or I'm going to tie you to that bed, you hear me."

I lie down, and my mind is going a mile a minute as I go from happy to sad. "I hate it here. I want to go home," I start whining out loud. Miss Betsey comes in and sits on the edge of the bed. "Now, you just try and gets some rest while we gets to the bottom of this," she says.

I push my face into the pillow as I sob in silence, not wanting Nurse Jones to hear me. Eventually, I cry myself to sleep. A few hours later, when I wake up, Nurse Jones sends me to Mrs. Becker's office. She has one of those stupid troll dolls standing on the end of the desk staring at me. I pick it up and wrap the purple hair around my finger over and over again.

"So, are you feeling better?" she asks.

"Yeah, can I still go to school?" I ask her. "I'd rather be at school than sitting around here all day."

"After we talk," she says. "Then I'll drive you if you still want to go.

"It seems that it's taking longer than we hoped for your Mom to get better. So, we were looking into foster homes for you and Mary, but your Mom doesn't want that. She wants you to go under the Catholic social services care."

"What does that mean," I ask.

"It means you'll be going to a place called St. Joseph's of Gonzaga Catholic Home for Girls," she tells me.

"You mean with nuns and all?"

"Yes, it's very nice. It's been all newly renovated. The home is just waiting for two beds to open up so you and Mary won't have to be separated."

"Will I have to go to Catholic school?"

"Yes, of course," she says.

"But, what about my grades? I can't go to Catholic school. They'll hold me back. I know they will," I say.

"Let's not jump to any conclusions. We don't know that they'll do that for sure," she says.

My heart sinks into my stomach at the thought of it. It feels like I'm a prisoner, and they've added another year to my sentence before I'm free to live my life.

"Can I go to school now?" I ask.

I get to school in time for music class. We are listening to Beethoven's Fifth Symphony while following the score. I like listening to music. It sometimes sounds the way I feel. I hear the highs and lows, the horns, violins, piano, and drums, but to read the music is like a foreign language to me. It feels the same as it would be walking into a third-year Spanish class and being expected to pick the language up right away. That's what happens when you go to so many different schools; you always feel you're trying to catch up. It doesn't matter how hard I study; everything goes in one ear and out the other. The harder I try, the more I don't understand. My mind goes blank. I get frustrated. I feel stupid. Most of the time, all I do is sit and daydream. Now I can't get what Mrs. Becker told me out of my mind. I can't go to the Catholic home, and I don't know what I'm going to do to get out of it.

The cafeteria smells like Italian food today, probably spaghetti. I open my brown paper bag lunch. I wonder what surprise I'll find today between the two slices of bread. As I peel it apart, it's liverwurst, cheese, and mustard. Yuck! Dad used to love this, but I don't know how anyone could eat anything so disgusting.

I munch on my apple, waiting for my friends Karen and Jennie to join me. I was so happy that they came over and sat with me a few days after I first got here. They wanted me to hang out with them after school, but when I said I couldn't, they wanted to know why. When I told them where I lived, they wanted to take me home to live with them. I did finally go home with Karen one day after school. She introduced me to her mom and tried to talk her into keeping me as if I was a lonesome dog she found on the street. Mr. Max scolded me for being an hour late when I got back to Stenton, but he didn't punish me. He just told me not to let it happen again.

"We missed you this morning," Karen says as she puts her tray down on the table.

"Yeah, how come you came in so late?" Jennie asked.

"They mixed my medication up, and I got high on someone else's. I don't know what it was, but I was having a good time until Nurse Jones made me lie down and sleep it off."

"Oh my God, we got to get you out of that place," Karen says. "I keep trying to talk my mom into letting you stay with us, but I can't get her to budge on the subject," she says.

"Your mom is nice. I liked meeting her that day I went home from school with you. I appreciate your effort. If I weren't in Stenton, maybe it wouldn't be as hard. My brother moved in with his friend's family, but he was sixteen at the time and not a ward of the Philadelphia Child Welfare system like I am. Who knows what could happen to your mom if she took me in?" I say.

"There is a place not far from here that takes in homeless kids like you. I think it's called Carson Valley School," Karen says.

"Yeah, my brother has a friend who lives there," Jennie says.

"I heard they have houses all around the property, and that's where the kids live, so it's just like living in a real home," Karen says.

"Yeah, I remember my brother's friend saying how much he likes his house parents. I remember him asking my brother if he wanted to come and see the horses they have there," Jennie says.

"Maybe you could ask your brother's friend how I can get in there? It would have to be soon, though, because Mrs. Becker told me today that my sister and I are going to a Catholic home as soon as two beds open up for us," I say.

"Maybe that won't be so bad," Jennie says. "At least better than where you are."

"I can't go there. They'll put me in Catholic school, and then I'll get held back another year because my grades are so bad," I say.

"That would be awful," Karen says. "It would mean you'd have to live there another year before you could be on your own."

"I know! And there's no way I'm going to let that happen," I say.

"I haven't seen my brother's friend for a while," Jennie says.

"I think you should run away and go there," Karen says. "I bet when they see how desperate you are, they'll take you on right away."

"We could help you get there," Jennie says.

"Yeah, we can knock off school one day and walk there," Karen says.

"Hm! That sounds like a great idea, but I need to think about it," I say.

"You say the word, and we'll lead the way when you're ready," Karen says.

The Promise

Chapter 6 - April 4, 1968

Sitting at a table in the library room, I begin my letter to Donna by writing, April 4, 1968. Before I even have a chance to write Dear Donna, I'm distracted by all the screams and commotion coming from the TV room.

"Oh, my God! Oh, my God!" I hear Miss Betsey and Mrs. Jackson scream. I run out to see what's going on, and Walter Cronkite is on the news making the announcement that Martin Luther King has been shot and killed. They saw two white men running from the scene. Lots of rioting is going on as a result. President Johnson came on saying how shocked and saddened America is by the brutal slaying of Dr. King. He asks citizens to reject the blind violence that has been stoked by Dr. King's death because he practiced non-violence.

As I stand in the background watching my poor Miss Betsey howling a cry of sorrow, Mrs. Jackson holds some of the girls and cries softly. Many of the girls have tears rolling down their cheeks. Gina, Mary, and I stand together, not knowing quite what to do. It feels kind of like it did when President Kennedy died, but I realize I don't know hardly anything about Martin Luther King. I hear bits and pieces about the civil rights riots, the Vietnam protesters, and all the soldiers getting killed, but I don't pay attention to what's going on in the world. I have a hard enough time dealing with what's going on in my own little world.

"Ain't you even sad?" Wanda whines to us.

"Why you expecting them to be sad," Billy Joe says. "They don't care, Wanda. They just like the white man who shot Dr. King." I feel all their eyes on us, and that creepy feeling I had when I first got here comes back.

Miss Betsey screams out, "Now we'll have none of that! He ain't here no more, buts we have a duty to carry on his message right here, right now in this here place. We has to all learn to get along, or none of us gonna be free to live in peace. I won't's hear any more of this! Do I makes myself clear!" she shouts out.

"Yes! Miss Betsey," we all say a once.

I go back to the library to finish writing my letter. I can't say anything about what's happening here, so I write 8:00 pm next to the date. Little clues that I hope people pick up on when they read my letters. Like, wow, that this was the day of Martin Luther Kings' assassination, and she was writing just a few hours after its announcement on TV. Most of my friends haven't a clue of what it's like living here. I can't blame them. I write as if I'm fine all the time. I wish I could tell them. Miss Betsey gave me a marble book to journal in, but I can't even write the truth in that without someone grabbing it away from me and reading it out loud. Someday I'll write about it, because even as I live through it, I find myself asking, is this for real?

∞ ∞ ∞

I'm so glad my Mom is coming today. It's been a little over a week since Martin Luther King's assassination. Billy Joe's back to picking on me again, and Sharon and Wanda are all ignoring me. It feels like none of it matters anymore that we're all in the same boat here. That color thing always finds a way of coming between us. I didn't shoot Dr. King. I think they have just as much right as anyone else to live in this world as free as the rest of us. Even when I walk up to get Miss Betsey's, newspaper the black kids on buses and in cars yell out to me, "White trash."

Maybe if I tell Mom how bad the racial issues are here, she'll take us home with her. She did say in her last letter that she was going to do what she could to bring us home soon, but Mrs. Becker said we were going to that Catholic home to live as soon as they have space for us. I wonder if Mom knows about that?

"I thought it would be fun to take you both to the hairdresser to get your hair done for Easter," Mom says.

"Mom, I need to talk to you about what's going on here."

"We can talk later," she says. "We're going to have a fun day together, and I thought we'd get you both a nice Easter outfit to wear to church tomorrow."

Wow! She must be doing pretty good if she can afford to do all this for us. Maybe she is going to surprise us at the end of the day and tell us she's taking us home after all.

The hairdresser plays with my hair asking me how I'd like it cut.

"I don't know. I was thinking of going a little shorter," I say.

"Oh, I know just what I want to do with it then," the hairdresser says.

I feel kind of excited because she seems hip. I'm sure whatever she does will be cool.

She pulls my hair back in a ponytail and cuts it as close to the ring as she can get.

"I didn't want it that short," I tell her.

"Oh, don't worry, honey. By the time I finish your hair, you're going to love it," the hairdresser assures me. All I hear is the clip, clip, clip of the scissors as I watch my hair getting shorter and shorter. My pretty long hair is gone, and it's the only real good thing I had going for me. After putting the rollers in, she sets me up under the hairdryer. Mary jumps up in the chair. Mom tells the hairdresser only to trim Mary's hair. By the time she's finished with her, Mary's hair looks nice and can still be pulled back into a ponytail. I wish she would have gone before me. I would have told the hairdresser to do the same thing for me.

As I return to the chair, the hairdresser starts pulling out the rollers, brushing the puffy curls out, then teasing it into a beehive. She finishes it off by spraying so much hairspray that it feels more like a helmet than my actual hair. She hands me a mirror and turns the chair so I can see the back.

"You look all grown up now," she says, "like a real lady."

I hate it but don't want to make her feel bad, so I don't say anything. I see in Mom's face that she doesn't know what to think. Mary doesn't hesitate to say what she thinks out loud, "You look funny, Con."

Mom burst out laughing, then swallows it back as quickly as it comes out of her mouth.

"Now, it doesn't look so bad. We're just not used to seeing you with short hair," Mom tries to make light of it.

"It makes you look even taller," the hairdresser says. "You're going to love it once you get used to it being short. You'll never want to go back to long hair again."

I doubt that.

"Listen, girls, "Mom says, "I didn't think it was going to cost that much to get your hair done. I don't have enough to buy you an outfit now, but we can go to the 5 & 10 stores. Here's $3.00 each. You buy yourselves something nice."

Every time I walk past a window, I see my reflection. I try to flatten my hair down with my hands, but it bounces right back out. The first thing I look for is a brush. Maybe some barrettes or a headband will help. Maybe I should get a scarf and cover it all up. I buy all four things and head straight for the bathroom.

"I'll be out in a few minutes," I tell Mom. I can barely get the brush through my hair. I'm afraid I'm going to pull it all out. Brushing didn't help much. It's still all puffed out. I try barrettes, the headband, and end up tying the scarf under my chin to hide the whole mess.

"What'd you do with your hair? I paid a lot of money to get it done, and now you go and hide it. Give me that scarf," Mom says, yanking it off my head. I smooth it back with my hands, putting what's left of it behind my ears.

"Where we going now?" Mary asks as we stand at a bus stop.

"I'm taking you to see where I live so you understand why I can't take you home with me yet," Mom says.

We go past St. Joseph's of Gonzaga home for girls, and Mom points it out to us.

"That's where you'll be going soon. Mrs. Becker says it's a nice place, better than where you are right now."

"But I don't want to go there," I tell her.

We get off the bus to transfer to another one. While we are waiting, I feel as if my head is spinning around with all the things, I wanted to tell Mom, but she won't listen. She never listens, and she has no idea what it's like for me.

"I don't understand, Mom. If you have all this extra money to spend on us, then how come you can't afford a bigger place to live so we can come home?"

"You're an ungrateful little brat," she yells at me. "You're just like your father. You don't care about anyone but yourself. Get out of my sight."

"Fine!" I say. "And just so that you know, I'd rather be like Dad than you anyway."

She takes Mary by the hand and gets on the bus, and I stand there watching it leave without me. I'm so angry I don't care. After the bus disappears, I realize I'm all alone. I have no more money left. I spent it all on stuff to fix my hair. I look back the way that the bus brought us and thought I could find my way to Stenton Avenue. From there, I could find my way back to Stenton Child Care Center, but it might be too far to walk. I look around at the people waiting for other buses and wonder if they saw what happened. A black woman walks past me to get on the bus and hands me a quarter.

"Maybe this will help you get home," she says.

"Thank you," I say.

I sit on the bench for a while, trying to figure out what to do. Maybe I could ask some other people for a dime or quarter to help me out. I take a deep breath and walk up to a man who looks like he could be a dad.

"I was wondering, do you have an extra dime you could spare me?" I ask.

He hands me a quarter. Hum! That was easier than I thought. So, I ask a few more people until I have four quarters. I have plenty now to get a bus and maybe a hot dog.

I go into the store in front of the bus stop and look around for something to eat. I buy a hot dog and coke for 25 cents. As I'm going out the door, I see a cigarette machine. I put my coke and hot dog on top of the machine and dig through my money for the right change. I get a pack of Winston's, and I quickly stuff it in my coat pocket with a pack of matches. I lean against the wall outside the store, eating my hot dog. I think I'll save the rest of the money I have and walk back to Stenton. I'm not in any hurry to get back anyway. If I get too tired, I can catch a bus along the way.

I find my way to the St. Joseph's of Gonzaga Catholic Home for Girls. I stand in front of the big chain-link fence that goes around it. It appears old, but Mrs. Becker said it's all redone inside. I don't care. There's no way I'm going to step foot in there. The idea of running away to Carson Valley School sounds much better. I have a little more money back at Stenton. Yep, I think it's time.

I can't believe how good I feel. It doesn't even bother me anymore that Mom left me. I feel kind of free of her. I know that whatever happens to me is up to me now. It's exciting and scary all at the same time. Maybe with me not around anymore, Mom will be able to afford to take Mary home with her too.

∞ ∞ ∞

As I'm walking toward Karen and Jennie, I can tell they are talking about my hair and how bad it looks. It's the way they look at me and try to hide what they're saying to each other.

"I know, I can't get used to looking at myself in the mirror either," I say as I approach my friends.

"The good thing about hair is it always grows back," Jennie says.

"So, what'd you bring with you to run away with?" Karen asks me.

"My lunch," I say, holding up the bag. "Let's see, I have a ham sandwich, an apple, and a brownie," I say. "It was nice of them to send me off for the last time with a decent lunch for once." I swipe my hand across the bottom of the bag until I find the dime. Then dig in my pocket for the rest of my change. "Looks like I have one dollar and 10 cents."

"Don't you have a pocketbook to put that in?" Karen asks.

"Nope, but I have everything I need in my pockets. Here's my cigarettes, my makeup, and a comb. Oh, and a pair of underwear in case I need them."

"What'd you bring, Karen?" I ask.

She digs through her purse and pulls out a green Girl Scout knife. "I thought this might come in handy. I learned how to use it when I went to Girl Scout camp. Look, it has a blade, can opener, bottle cap opener, and a leather punch.

"Cool, you think of everything, Karen," I say. "What else you got in that big pocketbook of yours?"

"I have cigarettes, $2.00, my makeup, a brush, and some hairspray so we can make sure we look good when we get there. I'll play around with your hair and fix it up for you," Karen tells me.

"No, thanks," I tell her. "I have nightmares of what I looked like the last time I let anyone touch my hair."

"What did you bring to eat?" I ask her.

"I have a baloney sandwich, chips, apple, and some snickerdoodles my mom made.

"What about you, Jennie?" Karen asks.

"I have a peanut butter and jelly sandwich, carrot sticks, and a small box of raisins." Jennie opens her purse and digs around, "Let's see, I have cigarettes, lipstick, powder compact for touch up, a brush, and $1.64."

"We can stop at a corner store along the way and buy some pops to drink later," Karen says.

As we're walking past this secluded parking lot, I notice a big box toward the back of it. "Does anyone else see a pair of feet sticking out of that box up there?" I ask.

"Oh my gosh, do you think it's a dead person? Jennie asks. We walk a little closer and see the feet move.

"Na, it's just a bum, this is where the bums always sleep at night. There's a lot more in the summer. I guess now that it's getting a little warmer, they'll start coming back," Karen says.

"So, if you ever run away again and have nowhere to sleep, all you have to do is find a big box to keep the cold out and curl up inside it," Jennie tells me.

"Are you kidding? I'd never do that. I could get killed or raped," I say.

"I never thought of that," she says. I guess there's a lot more to think about than you realize before you run away."

"Yeah, I ran away a few times before I went to Stenton. I hid in the garage our landlord used for storage behind our house. My girlfriend told her parents she was sleeping over at my house and we sat in these chairs and talked and smoked cigarettes all night. My Mom must have called my friend's family because her father eventually found us in the morning and took us both back to their house for a lecture on how dangerous running away is. Another time my friend hid me in the attic that was right off her bedroom. I sat at the foot of the stairs waiting for her parents to go to sleep so I could come out. It was dark and smelled dirty and musty. I started imagining all kinds of things, like what if someone had died in this old house and there was a ghost up at the top of the stairs. There had to be lots of spider webs. Old attics always have spiderwebs in the movies. I remember how I kept getting creepy feelings running up and down my back. I couldn't take it anymore. I had to get out of there. As I pushed the door open, the hinges creaked like stiff old bones. My friend was sleeping, and I could hear her parents snoring in the room right next to hers. I slowly made my way down the stairs and out the back door. I snuck in my house and slipped into bed beside my sister Kathy. She never even woke up. Another time I ran away, I hid behind the Knights of Columbus house across the street from where I lived. I sat up against the building all night. It's funny how your eyes adjust to the dark and your ears to the sounds around you. It's like your senses go into high gear. It makes you think what it must have been like in the cave days when you had to be afraid of lions, wolves, and bears. I was more afraid of some weirdo coming along, though."

"What did your mom do when you finally went home?" Jennie asked.

"She'd yell and sometimes smack me around, but she started to catch on that if she did that, I'd just run away again. She had my aunt talk to me. I like my Aunt Tee. She understands how difficult my mom can be, but at least she listens and tries to help me find a way to cope with things. That was the last time I ran away. I decided to try to hang in there, thinking at the time that I had only four more years to go before I could go out on my own and make my life the way I wanted. I mean, I had nowhere to run away to, and the running didn't change anything."

"But things are different now for you," Karen says.

"Yeah, I feel like things are only going to get worse now that I know for sure my mom isn't going to bring us home."

"Why would you want to go home with her anyway after the way she treats you, especially after this last time when she left you standing there with no way to get back to Stenton?" Jennie says.

"I don't know. At least if I was with her, I could come and go as I like and be better able to take care of myself until I could get out on my own. Or maybe I could even find someone to live with the way my brother did. As long as I'm in Stenton, I feel like a prisoner," I say.

"I wish my mom would let you come live with us," Karen says.

"I know. I appreciate all you're both doing for me now. I hope you don't get in too much trouble for this," I say.

"My mom will ground me for a week, and after a few days, she'll let me off. Plus, she likes you, so she might understand why I'm trying to help you out," Karen says.

"Your mom is cool, Karen," I say.

"My parents will ground me for a week, but they won't forget or let me off," Jennie says. "But it's okay if it means what we're doing will help you out."

"You two are the best. I don't know what I'd have done without meeting you. I'm going to miss you both."

"Yeah, but see, once you get into Carson, you'll be able to come and hang out with us whenever you want." Karen reminds me.

"I'm so excited; I can't believe how free I feel since my mom left me stranded at the bus stop."

"I still can't believe she did that to you," Karen says.

"It reminds me of a documentary we watched at school one time where the mommy or daddy bird pushed the baby bird out of the nest so it can fly free," Jennie says.

"Yeah, that's the way I feel, like I'm flying free. But my mom didn't do it to help me be free. She did it because she hates me. I don't care anymore, and that's what feels good, the not caring part," I say.

"Do you feel bad about leaving your sister?" Jennie asks.

"No. I figure if I'm not there, maybe Mom will be able to afford to take her home. If not, then at least without me, Mary will be able to get in the Catholic home faster. I think that place will be good for her. We've been walking for a long time. Are you sure you two know where we're going?" I ask.

"Yeah, but we're going to have to walk through this wooded area if we want to get in from the back way," Karen says. "Once we get through the woods, it should open into a field, and we'll look for the big barn where they keep the horses."

"Then what?" I ask her.

"I don't know yet; I thought that maybe we'd run into one of the kids who live there and ask them to help us," she said.

"That sounds like a good idea," I say.

It is one of those unusually warm days in April, and after walking in the sun all morning, it feels good to be in the coolness of the woods. We decide to stop and eat our lunch before we go out into the open field. We lay our coats out and sit on them, opening our lunch bags and eating like we are having a picnic. We decide to waste some time, thinking that none of the kids would be home from school until after 3:00 anyway.

"What do you want to do when you graduate from school?" I ask them both.

"I want to be a nurse," Karen says.

"I want to open a daycare for little kids. I especially love babies," Jennie says.

"How about you, Connie, what do you want to be when you get out on your own?" Jennie asks.

"I don't know for sure. I've been so busy just trying to survive; I never thought much about what I'll do when I graduate. I guess I'll get a job in a store like my sister did at first. I don't want to end up like my mom, who didn't have any skills except sewing. I might become a secretary. I'd love to be a counselor, but I don't think I'd be able to pay to go to college or be smart enough to go. What I want the most is to be happy and loved by somebody," I say.

"Ah, we love you, Connie," Karen says.

"I love you guys, too," I say. "But it's been this dream-like promise from God that keeps me holding on, that someday my life will be the way I believe it can be."

"I do not doubt that someday that will come true for you, Connie," Karen says.

"I believe it will, too," Jennie says.

When we get to the barn, we sneak up beside it. We can hear a guy talking. It sounds like he's saying something to one of the horses. There's a small knothole, and while we're taking turns trying to get a good look inside, the guy walks around surprising us.

"You know I could see you all standing here between the cracks in the boards," he laughs at us. He's a kid about the same age as us. "What are you doing out here?" he asks.

Karen tells him my story and why we have come.

"I have great house parents. I'm sure they'd take you in or get you into one of the other houses. In the meantime, I should hide you until I get back," he says. He takes us up to the loft, hiding us behind a few bales of hay. "If anyone comes, get under the pile of hay so no one can see you.

"He sure is taking a long time," Jennie says.

"Yeah, I have to pee," I say.

"I'm getting hungry again," Karen says.

"I sure wish we could have a cigarette," Jennie says as she gets her pack out. "You think we could light one up if we're cautious?" She asks.

"NO!" Karen and I say at the same time.

"That's all we need is to start the barn on fire," I say.

"Shush," Karen says. "I hear someone coming." As they begin to climb up the ladder, all three of us dive under the hay.

"They're over here," we hear the kid's voice.

"Come on out, girls," a man says.

He sits on one of the bales of hay and reaches his hand out to each of us, introducing himself. "My name is Jim, and I'm one of the house parents here. Kevin tells me that one of you is from Stenton Child Care Center."

"That would be me," I say. "Is there any way I could stay here? It sounds like such a nice place. I have to get out of Stenton, Mr. Jim. They hate me there because I'm white. They're going to send me to St. Joseph's of Gonzaga Catholic home for girls and hold me back a grade, and I'll have to stay there another whole year before I can graduate, and my mom hates me, and I don't have anyone who cares about me."

"Slow down," he says as he takes my hand. "What is your name?"

"Connie."

"First of all, St. Joseph's of Gonzaga's home for girls is a nice place. I don't know why you think they'll hold you back a grade. I'm sure they'll help you in any way they can to be the best person you can be," he tries to reassure me.

"I've been told all my life if I ever went to a Catholic school that they'd hold me back because my grades are so bad," I say. "Can't I just stay here where it's more like living at home?"

"It sounds like you're under the Catholic Social Service, and once they put you in their care, there isn't much we can do to help you out. Plus, this isn't the way to do things. You can't just show up here and expect us to take you in as much as we'd like to. I bet you're hungry. How about if I take you girls out to eat and we can talk some more? But first, I'll be needing to call your parents and Stenton to let them know you're all right."

∞ ∞ ∞

When I get back to Stenton, I have to get another entrance bath by Nurse Jones. She gives me a blue sweatshirt and pants to wear. Then she walks me to the cell room, the one I stayed in when I first got here. Only this time, she locks me in. My hair is wet and feels like straw again. I have no comb, but I don't even care. It's just like being in a real prison where they take everything away from you. All I have are the clothes on my back and a bed to sleep in. I look out the small window in the door. I can't see anything but the soft light from the hallway. They've shut the doors between the nurse's station and the kids' area. It's as if they are putting me in a state of solitary cut off from all life. I turn the bright light off and lie on the cot facing the big caged window. The glow from the hallway across the courtyard brings a gentle softness into my prison cell. It brings out the shadowy indentations of the few names that others have dug into the walls, names they've tried to hide by painting over them. I wonder how many other kids have been locked up in here as I rub my fingers across their names.

"Well, God, it looks like I screwed up this time. They want to break my spirit by putting me in here. But it makes me even more determined to get out on my own. Next time I'll have a better plan."

As the sun comes streaming through the caged window hitting white walls, it's as if someone turned on a bright fluorescent light. Even though I have my eyelids closed, I see the color red shining through them. I pull the covers over my head. All I want to do is sleep and live inside my dreams. I don't have nightmares anymore. It feels like I'm living in one. I like the world I live in when I'm sleeping. Sometimes I dream that Dad finds me and takes me home. I go to dances with my friends. I kiss my last boyfriend, Luke. When I'm awake, I want to go back to sleep, and when I can't, all I want to do is go looking for the things I dream of having someday.

I hear the familiar cough and hacking outside my door as Grandma Cobb unlocks it. I peek from under my covers, and she says, "Good morning, sunshine! I bring ya some of them grits ya like with bacon, eggs, and toast. I knows ya' gots to be starving after that adventure ya' went on yes-ta-day."

I don't move, so she sits on the edge of the cot and puts the tray on the floor. Then Grandma Cobb starts patting my back, and the tears come barreling out of me. No matter how hard I try to stop them, I can't. It is like a dam has broken loose, and all you can do is let the tears flood out. Her touch melts away my hardness, and I lose all sense of control of my feelings. She wraps her arms around me, holding me close, letting me cry until there's nothing left to come out.

"Ya gonna be alright, girly, yes ya is," she says just like she always did before. "Now sits ya' self-up and eats something. It be making ya' feels better in no time," she says as she hands me a wad of tissues from her pocket.

"Now blow ya' nose and get to eating. I be back soon, so we can gets ya' cleaned up," Grandma Cobb says.

I take the lid off my food. The smell makes my stomach growl a couple of times. There's nothing like eating comfort food after a good cry.

As I'm finishing, I see the girls from my unit across the courtyard walking through the hallway. They're leaving for school. I jump up to wave at them. They wave back, shaking their heads as if they're sorry I got caught. Hum! Maybe they do care about me.

I was starting to feel a little more hopeful and cared about until Ms. Gore came on duty in the afternoon. She and Nurse Jones kept coming by every once in a while, looking at me through the small window in the door. It's creepy. No one talks to me, not even Mrs. Becker. They bring me food and let me out to go to the bathroom.

"Can I have a pen and paper?" I ask Ms. Gore.

"Ha!" she laughs. "You don't get nothing when you're in punishment, girl."

"How long am I going to be in here?" I ask.

"Word is the rest of the week," she says with a smirk. "You know you're lucky you're in here and not at some juvenile hall where they send most kids that run away."

"Juvenile hall is for bad kids," I say.

"What do you think you are? You been trouble since you got here. If it were up to me, you'd be in that juvenile hall for sure. Then you'd learn some lesson on how to behave."

That's it! The first chance I get, I'm running away again. I have to get out of here. They make me feel hot then cold, up then down, happy than sad. I feel like a yo-yo all the time. Besides, they don't scare me. If they put me in juvie, I'll find a way to run away from there, too. I'm going to run and run until I find a place to live where they'll never find me again.

Chapter 7-May 1968

I'm sorry we had to put you in punishment," Mrs. Becker says as she walks me back to the girls' unit.

"Then why'd you let them put me in there so long?" I asked.

"It's not all up to me. We have a committee that decides these things, which brings me to something else. I think it will make you happy. Come see me after you get cleaned up."

As I walk into the unit, Miss Betsey says, "Well, look who we got here. Um-um girly, you done got yourself in a heap of trouble this time, didn't ya? Come on over and gives Miss Betsey a big hug. Eww-ee, you be smelling ripe about now and looks at your hair sticking up all over the place. Didn't they let you get a shower over there?"

"No. Grandma Cobb let me wash up as best I could at the sink each day, but other than that, I wasn't allowed to do anything."

"Um-um! That ain't right," she says. "Go on upstairs and gets you self-cleaned up."

"Welcome back, jailbird," Billy Joe laughs. "Ya knows, next time they be putting ya' in juvie. Ya know what's they be doing ta ya in juvie, don't ya? I hear they rape ya."

"How's a girl rape a girl, Billy Joe? That's the stupidest thing I ever heard," I say.

"I hear they use hot dogs," Sharon says with a serious face.

Billy Joe cracks up, laughing, "That be right, Sharon. I might hear the same things."

"Go on with ya girls, and stop making up stories ya don't know nothin bouts," Miss Betsey says.

I don't usually stand in the shower for longer than I have to, but today it feels so good to let the warm water wash over me. When I'm all cleaned up, I go to Mrs. Becker's office and sit down.

"Are you feeling better after getting showered?" she asks.

"There isn't any amount of cleaning up that's going to make me feel better when I remember I'm still here," I say.

"Are we that terrible here?" she asks.

"Some people make it feel so," I say.

"Who might that be?" she asks.

"You know if I tell you anything, it just makes it worse on me here."

"Well, it is the people here who voted to make you May Queen for our celebration this year." She says.

"What the heck is a May Queen? I ask.

"You get to wear a pretty blue gown and a sparkling crown," she says. "Then, we parade you through the celebrations we have here."

"Are you kidding me?"

"Now, why'd I do something mean like that?" she asks.

"I don't understand you people here. First, you put me in a jail cell for a week. You don't let me read, write, talk to anyone, or take a shower. Then you turn around and want to make me your May Queen, and that's supposed to make me happy?"

"Maybe we just wanted you to know that we do care about you," she says.

"Is it true that the next time I run away, you're going to have me sent to juvenile hall?" I ask.

"We would never do that to you. Who would put a thing like that in your head? We all know you're not a bad kid. You're just hurt and angry," she says.

"You've always been nice to me, Mrs. Becker, and I thank you for wanting to do something nice for me. I don't feel like I'm up to it, and I don't think it's fair to the other girls. Why not pick Wanda?"

"She's already been May Queen," she says.

"Maybe you should pick Billy Joe. She'd be mad anyway if I became May Queen. She'd say it's just because I'm white. Or pick Sharon. They feel just as unloved as I do, and it might make them feel really special."

"See what I mean. That's what makes you special. You always find the good in others even if they are the people who cause you the most trouble," she says.

"No, I don't. I'm only thinking of myself. I don't even think of Mary. I only think of what I need to do for me. Stop trying to make me into a nice person. I'm not nice."

"Our celebration isn't for a few weeks. Maybe by then, you'll change your mind. We want you to be our May Queen," she goes on.

"Can I go now, Mrs. Becker?"

"Go on, then. We'll talk some more in a few days," Mrs. Becker says.

Sorry Mrs. Becker, I wish I could tell you, but I won't be here in a few days. I'm taking the first bus I can get on Monday back to my old neighborhood. One of my friends there will help me out. I'm sure of it.

Ever since Martin Luther King died, the relationship with the girls at Stenton has changed. They don't want anything to do with me anymore. Wanda has tried to pull us back together, but I tell her it's okay. As we walk to get the bus for school, I tell her that I want to be alone right now. I watch as the girls get on the city bus that takes them to school, then wave goodbye to Wanda. She shakes her head and waves back at me.

I walk in the opposite direction to catch a bus that will take me back to my old neighborhood. Several busses sit idling, waiting for their proper time of departure, creating the heavy scent of exhaust in the air. That, mixed with cigarette smoke and the cold damp pungent smells seeping up from the pavement, stirs excitement in me. I don't quite understand why until I find myself sitting on the bus looking out the window. I close my eyes and lean my head against it, and I'm back on the Greyhound bus that took us from California to Pennsylvania. The window vibrates against my head as the bus rocks up and down like a restless horse at the starting gate, anxious to be set free so it can run the race.

It's funny how one thought leads to another, taking me back to that day. I wanted to stay with my friend in California in case Dad came back looking for us. Leaving on that bus meant I was leaving behind any hope of ever seeing him again. Where else would dad look for us but though mom's family. I thought I saw him once standing across the street from our house as if he was trying to figure out which house was ours. But when I looked at the man long enough, I realized it wasn't him. I'm not sure I remember what he even looks like anymore, but I'd know him when I looked in his eyes. I sometimes wonder if he's dead. But then as long as I don't know that for sure, there's always the chance that he isn't. Besides, I'd feel it inside if he were dead. No, I believe we'll find each other one day, and sitting in Stenton waiting isn't going to make it happen any faster.

When I get to Somerton, there's not much to do until my friends get out of school. I go into Betty's Restaurant, where we all used to hang out after school. Betty is the mom of two of my friends. She's the kind of mom any kid would love to have. Not only is she soft and cuddly to hug, but she makes all the yummy things you like to eat.

"Where you been?" she asks as she wraps her warm, chubby arms around me.

"Oh, we had to move away," I say. I can't tell Betty where I'm living now, or she might make me go back.

"Don't you have school today?" she asks.

"No, we have off for a teachers' conference," I say — another lie. I hate lying to people. Once you start one lie, it leads to another. Plus, I don't do it very well. I wonder if she can tell by the way I avoid eye contact with her.

"Can I get you anything to eat?" she asks.

"I don't have much money," I say. "But I can afford hot cocoa."

She brings me the cocoa and a big slice of apple pie. "It's on the house," she says with a smile.

"You don't have to do that, but I sure do appreciate it. Maybe I could wash some dishes to help you out until the girls get out of school?" I ask.

"Sure, I could use some help in the back," she says.

I work hard enough to earn myself lunch, too. When Betty's daughters arrive after school, I tell them the truth about where I've been and how I've run away. They want to tell their mom because they think she'd take me in a minute, but then they realize that wouldn't be a good idea. They were struggling enough to keep the restaurant. There was no way their mom could afford to take in another kid. My friends Jane and Barb come in next. I haven't seen them since I went into Stenton. I know Barb can't help as much as she'd like to; her mom's as mean as mine. So, Jane tells me to come home with her. Jane's mother died a year ago, and it's just her and her brother living with their dad. He works all day and doesn't pay a lot of attention to what they do. We hang out in her room, trying to come up with a plan of how she can hide me from her dad when he gets home. Jane and I rearrange the bed catty-corner. I practice slipping behind the headboard and ducking out of sight.

"It's tight and uncomfortable, but I can make it work for a little while if I have to," I say.

"It would only be until my dad goes to bed," she says.

We made it through the night, and in the morning, June tells her dad she doesn't feel right so she can stay home from school.

We hang out at her house listening to music, singing out loud, eating popcorn with lots of butter, and watching old movies.

"I don't think this is going to work, Connie. I mean, as you can see, there's no way I can hide you here forever. Isn't there anyone else you can think of who might be able to take you in?" she asks.

"Yeah, I know. I need a better plan. I can call my friend Mary Faith. She should be home from school by now. She drives now, and I think she'll come to pick me up," I tell her.

When Mary Faith picks me up, she suggests that we stop to talk with Rick and Moriah. They used to be our neighbors, and they were always giving us good advice in the past. Maybe they would take me in or give us some sense of direction. They were both super happy to see us, but when I told them my situation, Rick said it would be against the law for them to harbor a runaway and that he couldn't put Moriah in that kind of situation. They both said they wished they could help, but just like Mr. Kevin said to me when I ran away to Carson Valley School, this wasn't the right way to go about it.

Mary Faith takes me back to her place. They live in a nice apartment building with a pool. She tells me to stay in the laundry room down the hall from her until we figure out what to do next. After her parents go to bed, she sneaks me into her bedroom. The next morning when her mom discovers I'm there, she sends me back to Stenton.

As soon as I get back, Mrs. Becker is waiting for me in her office.

"What are we going to do with you?" she says.

I sit there looking out the window. My eyes are filling up with tears. I realize now I have nowhere to go.

"Connie, I know you're not happy here," she says.

"It's not so much this place, Mrs. Becker," I say, "It's that no one wants or cares about me."

"You go on back to the girls' section now. I'll let Miss Betsey know you're on your way back," she says.

"No bath or prison cell this time?" I ask.

"No, not this time. We're going to try to work this through together, you and I. How does that sound?" she asks.

The Promise

Chapter 8 – Summer of 1968

I've made it through the rest of the school year without running away again. I don't know what I'm going to do all summer stuck inside this place. Mrs. Becker says they have lots of fun things planned for us this summer. I'm biding my time, saving what little money I get from Miss Betsey when I go for her newspaper.

Last night, Mrs. Jackson called me into the supervisor's office, the one they sit-in at the end of our dorm while we sleep at night. She said that she'd noticed I haven't asked for any sanitary napkins since I've been here.

"That's because I haven't gotten a period since I got here," I told her.

She told me sometimes that happens when a female is going through a lot of stress.

"It's been kind of nice not getting it. If I never got it again, it would be all right with me," I said.

She said it's not quite that simple, that something else might be wrong, and they need to be sure. So, now I'm on my way to see Nurse Jones about it. I hate that woman.

"Let's see," Nurse Jones says as she looks at my chart. "You got here in November and told me then that your last period was a few weeks before that. It's June now. That makes it eight months late."

She makes me lie down on the exam table and presses all around my lower abdomen.

"You been sexually active during any of your runaway escapades?" she asks.

"No!" I say.

"Have you ever been to a gynecologist?" she asks.

"What's a gynecologist?" I ask.

"It's a doctor who deals with female issues. They'd be able to figure out why you're not getting your menses," she says.

"How do they do that?" I ask.

"What they do is have you lie on a table like this one. Then you put your feet in these side stirrups at the end of the table. You slide yourself forward toward your feet and open your legs. The doctor slides an instrument into your vagina, to open it up and get a look at what's going on inside there," she says.

I look at her, wondering if she's kidding around with me or being serious, but Nurse Jones doesn't kid with me.

"There's no way I'm going to a doctor like that," I say as I jump off the exam table.

"It's not as bad as it sounds," she says.

"I don't think it could sound any worse," I say.

Nurse Jones crosses her arms over her fat belly. "You know for someone who wants to be off on her own in the world; you sure have a lot of growing up to do," she says.

"Can we please give my period a little more time to come back? I've been feeling a lot of cramps lately. I'm probably going to get it any day now," I say.

"I'll give it until the end of the summer. If you don't get it by then, I'm going to have to take you to the doctor," she says.

My list of reasons for running away is starting to add up. Maybe I could go to Ohio and live with my sister Kathy and her new husband. There has to be someplace I can find to live.

∞ ∞ ∞

As I leave the dispensary, I notice a bunch of people carrying things into the gym. One of the guys sees me standing in the hallway and comes walking toward me.

"Hi!" he puts his hand out, "My name is Dan. I'm one of the tutors from La Salle College."

"Hi!" I say, looking him in the eyes, scanning his chiseled face, blonde hair, and blue eyes.

"You do have a name, don't you?" he asks.

"Connie," I say, looking down. I can feel the heat of redness going up my neck, over my cheeks, and up to my forehead. To make matters worse, I get embarrassed about getting embarrassed in the first place. I can feel my face glowing like a neon sign now.

"Hey Morin, this is Connie," Dan says. "Morin is one of the tutors too. She'll be working a lot with you, girls."

"It's great to meet you," she says, shaking my hand. "Are you ready to have some fun this summer?"

"More than fun. We're going to have a blast," Dan says.

"What do you mean fun?" I say. "Who could have fun in a place like this?"

"Well, that's why we've come to make things a little brighter by doing lots of fun things with you this summer," Morin says.

"Like what?" I ask.

"Things like field trips," Dan says.

"And arts, crafts, and games," Morin adds.

"Come on, can't we get a little smile from that pretty face," Dan teases as he brushes my cheek with his hand.

I smile, blushing again. Maybe this isn't going to be such a bad summer after all.

"Look at that smile, Morin. I knew she had one hidden inside her," Dan goes on.

"All right, come on, Dan. We have a lot of unpacking to do. It was nice to meet you, Connie. We'll be seeing you later today."

"Bye, Connie," Dan says.

"See ya'," I wave as I head back to the girls' unit.

∞ ∞ ∞

Stepping onto a yellow school bus, I head toward the back with the rest of the girls from my unit. Dan comes walking down the aisle, saying hi to everyone, and stops to chat with me. I smile and blush, now every time I see him. It's like wearing your feelings on your face. The girls start teasing me in front of Dan.

"Ah, look, she's getting all red," Sharon says.

"Yeah, it cracks me up," Billy Joe laughs. "On white peoples, it be like a bright neon sign."

"Don't black people blush too?" Dan asks.

"Sure, we does," Wanda says. "See, the funny thing is we can see it on you, and we can see it on each other, but you can't see it on us, less you looking real close."

"Hm, that's interesting," Dan says. "You learn something new every day. That is if you keep your mind open to it."

When we get to the public swimming pool, I stand a few feet away from the edge. Dan comes up beside me.

"Aren't you going in?" he asks.

"When I look out at the pool, it reminds me of a fish tank full of black mollies swimming in clusters. The few off-color fish stand out against the black backdrop. I've learned what it feels like to be on the other side of things, how lonely and isolating it can be. It was hard in the beginning, but in the past eight months, we've done everything together. I've never thought of myself as being prejudiced. Right now, though, getting in that pool with them feels kind of creepy, and I'm not sure where it's coming from."

"Do you think you're going to turn black if you go in the water with them?" he asks.

"No! Don't be silly, Dan," I say.

"Maybe it's because of all the oily things they put in their hair and on their body. I imagine it coming off their skin and floating all over the water. I don't know," I say.

"How is that different than the people lying out here who put suntan lotion on?"

"I never thought of that," I say.

"See, you learn something new every day if you keep your mind open to it," he reminds me.

He takes my hand and says, "Come on, we'll jump in together."

As my head pops up from the water, I look around for him. He waves from the middle of the pool surrounded by all the other kids, and I float at the edge of the pool watching him. I wonder how old he is, maybe twenty? I don't care. I think I'm in love.

∞ ∞ ∞

Sitting in the gym, I look at the wall of posters we painted throughout the summer. They represent what peace looks like to each of us. For a short time, they made us feel as if we were away at summer camp. The posters are a colorful collage of our moments of happiness captured.

With folded arms on the table, I lay my head down, closing my eyes, trying to find the color in what's ahead for me. If I were to paint a poster today, it would be full of darkness.

Looking forward to the days the college tutors come has been the only thing that's kept me from running away. It's been like hanging out with friends again, and today is our last day together. It feels as if every time something good comes into my life, I wake up one day, and it all seems like it was only one of my dreams.

I still haven't gotten my period. School starts in a few weeks. I'm scared to go to Germantown High School, hearing how rough the kids are there. I haven't seen Mom since that day she left me standing at the bus stop. She's come to visit, but I refuse to see her. She always acts like nothing ever happened. When I try to talk to her about things, she either doesn't remember it or says, "Oh, that's water over the dam." At this point, I'd welcome going to the Catholic home to get out of here. Who knows how long that will take for Mary and me to get an opening at the same time? Mary would have a better chance of getting in there without me around, holding her back.

"Don't you feel good?" Dan taps me on the shoulder. I raise my head. It's like I've woken up from a bad dream, and there he is smiling at me. Sometimes I can't tell what's real. Am I living the nightmare, or am I having a nightmare?

"Everyone's getting on the bus. Come on, we don't want to miss a minute of this beautiful sunny day ahead of us," Dan says.

He has this effect on me that makes me smile, even when I don't want to.

"Where are we going today?" I ask.

"To the Schuylkill River Park," he says.

Dan is with the boys most of the time, the same way he's been all summer. Morin has been the female tutor I connected with the most. I often look off in the distance at Dan. Sometimes I see him looking back at me. It's probably all in my imagination, but I don't care. It feels real to me that he likes me, too.

After our picnic lunch, we all sit around together, talking about what our favorite part of the summer was. Kids shout out, "Going to the zoo, the pool, Valley Forge, the Liberty Bell, and Betsy Ross's House, too."

"Yeah, and the best part was when we jumped in the fountain after walking in the heat all day," I say.

"Which you weren't supposed to do!" Morin says, laughing.

"What about the apartment we fixed up for you girls in your unit to make it feel more like home?" Morin asks.

"It's nice, but to be honest, nothing about being away from home could ever feel like home to us," Diane says.

"Yeah, but it be nice when we gets to make popcorn and watch movies," Wanda says.

"Who's ready for a walk along the river?" Dan asks.

"I am," I say.

We start off walking as a group, but it's not long before Dan, and I find ourselves lagging behind the others.

"So, what are you going to do with yourself for the rest of the summer now that we won't be here?" Dan asks.

"I don't know for sure," I say. "I'm thinking about running away again."

"Don't do that," he says. "It's too dangerous out there. You don't know what could happen to you."

"I can take care of myself," I say.

"Now I'm going to worry about you," he says.

"No, you won't. You'll go on with your life like everyone else and forget about me," I say.

He hands me a slip of paper with his name and phone number, telling me to call him if I ever need to talk. I wrap my arms around him. I know I shouldn't be hugging him. So does he, but he hugs me back, and we quickly break apart from each other. Looking out at the river, I try to hold my tears back. He talks to me now, like all the other adults do, to try to reassure me that everything is going to be all right. He tries to convince me of all the reasons why I shouldn't run away. Now I don't even want to be around him. There is nothing anyone can say that would give me a reason to stay. I have to figure this out on my own, and I have no idea how I'm going to do it. I only know that I have to keep trying.

Chapter 9 - August 1968

*I*t's easy enough to disappear after breakfast. Everyone scatters throughout the unit, girls watching TV downstairs, some in the apartment upstairs, or the beauty parlor or the library. I think the supervisors are ready for us to go back to school since the summer activities with the college tutors have ended. Everyone seems restless and bored, and I'm ready to escape it all.

I wait for the perfect moment to slip down the stairs. I walk across the hallway that opens to the courtyard between the girls and the children's section. I glance at the caged window of the cell, knowing the nurse's station is on the other side of it. None of it scares me anymore. The closer I get to the doorway, the more excited I feel. A warm breeze hits me the moment I open the door. I step out and think how easy that was and how afraid I was when I first came here. Mr. Max's keys jingling from his belt, the thought of always being locked inside, and never being able to walk out scared me. Eventually, I learn that I could leave anytime I wanted.

I go up Tulpehocken Street to Stenton Avenue. My heart is beating fast, not just because I'm moving quickly, but from the thrill of my courage. Then all the familiar smells come into play, of the bus, the cigarette smoke, and the pungent smells that drift up from the morning dew on the sidewalks. You can feel the humidity. It's going to be a hot one today. That's good. If I have to find a place to sleep tonight outside, it won't be so dreadful.

I set near the back of the bus and pull all the stuff I have crammed in my pockets out, laying it on the seat beside me. I unfold the paper bag with all the change I've been saving over the summer. I have a little over $10.00 in change. That should last me as long as I'm careful about what I buy. I even brought a change of underwear. I stuff them in the bag with the money. I open my window and light a cigarette letting the air blow on my face as I lean my head back against the seat and start to wonder what I'm going to do next. I don't want anything to spoil how good I feel right now. I'll deal with each step as it comes.

As I approach my old neighborhood, I wait to see Betty's Restaurant before pulling the cord for my stop. It's mid-morning, and hardly anyone is there. Sue is behind the counter working, and Pat is wiping tables when I walk in. Betty's two faithful daughters are doing what they can to help their mom hold onto the restaurant. I've never once heard them complain about helping her. Betty comes out from the kitchen to see what all the fuss is about as the girls express their excitement to see me. She gives me one of her big momma hugs and tells her girls to take a short break before the lunch crowd comes in. We sit in the booth at the back of the restaurant, drinking cold fountain cokes.

"Did you run away again?" Sue asks in a low voice.

I shake my head, yes.

"What's your plan? Where are you going to go?" Pat asks.

"I don't know yet. I want to find a job," I say.

"You need working papers at our age to get a job," Sue says. "And you need your parents' permission to get them."

"Oh, I didn't know that," I say. "I wonder why the adults make it so hard for us to grow up and be independent. You'd think that's what they'd want us to do."

"Well, for tonight, you can stay at our house. It's Sue's birthday, and we're having a slumber party," Pat says.

"Mom will never think anything of you staying over, too," Sue says.

"Cool! It's like a sign that things are going to work out this time. You two are the best, thanks," I say.

"At least it's one night down for you," Sue says.

"So, what are you going to do with the rest of your day?" Pat asks.

"I was hoping to meet up with a few other friends hanging out here. Where is everyone?" I ask.

"They all hang out at the pool down the road and the Custard Stand in the summer," Sue says.

"I'll head on down to the Custard Stand and see if anyone I know comes along. I have a friend to visit along the way too, so I have plenty to do. What time should I meet you back here?"

"Mom has help coming in at 4:00, so we can go home and get our place ready for the party. Meet us back here then, and we'll take you home with us," Sue says.

∞ ∞ ∞

As I walk up the steps to Donna's house, I remember what a happy family it is that lives here. She has a stay-at-home mom, a caring dad, a few brothers, and a little sister. To me, they always seemed like the perfect family. Donna holds her mouth wide open when she sees me.

"I can't believe you're standing here," she says. "How long has it been since we saw each other?"

"Nine months I've been gone, and you've been the one faithful friend writing me letters," I say.

"Are you back with your mom?" she asks.

"No, I ran away again," I say.

She closes her front door and steps out onto the porch, whispering to me, "My dad's a cop. I don't think you should be here."

"I forgot about that. Can you come down to the Custard Stand and sit with me for a while? I ask.

"You go on ahead of me, and I'll meet you down there," she says.

As I continue walking down the road, I start to envision my runaway picture tacked to the wanted board in the police station. Man, they could be looking for me right now — all the more reason to keep out of sight.

I walk past a few houses until I get to the Knights of Columbus building and stop. Across the street is the first apartment house we lived in when we moved to Pennsylvania. Looking up at the second and third-floor windows, the part of the house that we occupied, I remember what a perfect place it was for the five of us. It was small but met our needs. Mom and Mary shared one room, Kathy and I, the other, and Johnny had the whole attic to himself. It was our first winter in Pennsylvania, discovering how much fun it was to play in the snow, sled downhills, and ice skate on frozen ponds. Meeting Mary Faith two houses down was the best thing that happened to me. It was just the two of us, and four guys — Jimmy, Gus, Nace, and my brother Johnny.

I miss that time in my life. It seemed like when I was with my friends; I didn't think about how difficult it was at home.

At the Custard Stand, I order a fountain coke and sit under a shade tree waiting for Donna. A girl gets out of a car and comes running over to me. It's Jane, my friend, the one I stayed with the last time I ran away. She's with her boyfriend and doesn't have time to talk right now, but tells me to come to her house tomorrow, and we can hang out.

After spending the afternoon with Donna, I head back to Betty's Restaurant. When I stand up to leave, I get terrible pelvic cramps that make me double over in pain.

"Are you all right?" Donna asks.

"I feel like I'm going to throw up," I say.

"Maybe it's the heat," she says.

"I do feel awfully hot and sweaty all over," I say.

"Do you think you're alright to walk back to Betty's?" Donna asks.

"Yeah, it's passed for now. You know, I haven't had my period in all the time I've been at Stenton. I wonder if I'm getting it now?"

"What a time to get it when you have nowhere to go," Donna says.

"I know," I say.

As soon as I get to Betty's, I run into the bathroom, and my fears are confirmed. *Oh, God, why now?* I put a dime in the sanitary napkin machine, and then I buy an extra one for later.

"Are you all right?" Pat asked, "You look kind of pale."

"Can you think of anything worse happening when you run away than getting your period?" I ask.

"Oh no," she says.

"The thing is I haven't had it in the past nine months that I've been in Stenton. I'm glad to get it finally, but not this way," I say. Do you think I could wash up at your house?" I ask.

"Sure," Sue says, and we'll give you a hot water bottle for your cramps."

They are both much bigger than I am, but they find a shift I can wear while I put my clothes in the washer.

"Go ahead and lie down while we get ready for the party, and hopefully, you'll feel better by the time everyone gets here," Sue says.

I fall into a deep sleep until I feel Pat tap me on the shoulder.

"Connie, Connie. It's time to wake up the party is starting," she says.

My washed clothes sit at the end of the bed. The moment I get up, I feel a gush of flow filling my pad, reminding me what an awful time it is to have gotten my period.

"Do you have any extra pads?" I ask Pat.

"We don't use pads, but we have tampons," she says.

"I never used one of them before. I don't even know how to put it in," I say.

"It's not hard; just follow the directions on the box," she says.

I try every which way and finally get it in, but it's very uncomfortable and makes my cramps worse. The girls tell me I must not have it in the right way. One of them says, "She never had her cherry popped. That's why she can't get it all the way." Now everybody is talking about my period and sex life, of which I have none. I go back into the bathroom until I finally get it in the right way. By then, I need to change it and start all over again. Tomorrow I'm stopping at the 7 Eleven first chance I get and buying some pads.

I try to be okay because it is Sue's birthday and I don't want to spoil her party. Everyone wants to know my story. They think it is brave of me to be a runaway. All I can think is how lucky they are to have a home and family.

The next day I take a shower, and my underwear is stained so badly with blood that I throw them away. The girls are up early so they can go into the restaurant with their mom. I go with them and rush into the bathroom to buy a few pads. I buy myself some breakfast and waste as much time as I can before calling Jane to see if it's okay if I come over right away.

∞ ∞ ∞

The 7 Eleven stores is across the street from Betty's Restaurant. The aisle where the pads are is easy enough to find. You have to look for the brown paper-covered boxes. They do that so that no one knows what you're buying, but everyone knows what's hidden behind the brown paper wrapping. I don't think I'm the only girl in the world who hates buying her pads. Maybe they'll think I'm buying them for my mom; I tell myself so that I have the nerve to put them on the counter. To make matters worse, the cashier is a man, so I walk around the store a few minutes longer, trying to get the nerve to step up to him.

"It's all part of growing up and being on your own," I hear God say.

"Oh, why'd you have to go and make us girls' lives so miserable, anyway?" I ask.

"My mom needs a pack of Winston, too," I say to the man as I place the box on the counter.

He rings everything up, stuffs it in a paper bag, takes my money, and hands me the change without ever looking up at me. I can't get out of there fast enough.

The walk to Jane's house is long, but it gives me time to think about what I'll do next. I wasn't expecting to get my period, and it makes things more complicated. At least if I end up back at Stenton, I won't have to go to a gynecologist doctor now.

It's nice to have a place to hang out for the day. We watch old movies and eat popcorn with lots of butter. But I can't stay overnight. Her dad asks too many questions about me, and she's afraid he'll find out I'm a runaway.

"Can I use your phone," I ask her.

"Sure," she says.

I call Mary Faith. She can't pick me up tonight but will come tomorrow morning. "I've been talking with this guy named Ernie about your situation," Mary Faith says. "He's the pool manager at my apartment complex here. He says he knows a few ladies who need a live-in babysitter if you're interested."

"Do you trust him?" I ask.

"Oh, he's a great guy," she assures me. "Besides, I'd never do anything to put you in harm's way."

"It sounds too good to be true. I'll do just about anything right now, not to have to go back to Stenton. Thanks, Mary Faith," I say.

"So, do you have any ideas of a good place I can go for the night?" I ask Jane.

"Sometimes I like sitting on the hill looking out over the graveyard on a nice night. I have a nice quiet spot there that I go to," she says.

"The graveyard!" I say.

"Come, I'll show you," she says. We sit up against a tree, looking out over all the graves. The sky is clear, and as the sun goes down, the moon glows brightly. It's one of those hot nights, and to be honest, it feels good to be in the outside air. Jane sits with me until it gets to be her curfew time. At first, being alone feels creepy. The katydids suddenly sound louder. Every once in a while, I hear a stick snap, or something falls from the tree. It feels like a tap on the head or shoulders, giving me the willies down my back. I imagine that it's the ghosts of the graveyard wanting to know what I'm doing here. But of all the things I could imagine happening in a cemetery at night, it turns out to be peaceful. After a while, I curl up on the blanket that Jane gave me and fall asleep.

It is the sound of the katydids that I fall asleep to and the sound of the birds chirping that wake me up as the sun begins to rise. All the different songs of the birds grow louder as if every bird in the neighborhood is saying good morning to each other. But it doesn't end there. They go on and on as if they are telling each other what they did yesterday and what they are going to do today. The squirrels run about chasing each other, and brown bunnies munch on the grass. They all know how to live their lives and survive without much thought. I wonder why we humans, who are supposed to be the smartest of all God's creation, make life so complicated.

I love being surrounded by nature. I could live like a hermit in the wilderness, except I like the convenience of a bathroom too much.

∞ ∞ ∞

Mary Faith picks me up in her dad's big red Impala. It's as long as a boat and glides across the road like it's on water.

"Remember that first winter, I came here, and we used to sit in your Dad's car to get warm?" I asked.

"Yeah, I'd turn the radio on we'd sit in it singing till we had to go in," she says.

"I sure miss those days. Don't you?"

"That was a fun winter," she says.

"Things sure have changed for both of us," I say.

"Sure have," she says.

"So, what's the plan with this guy Ernie?" I ask.

"He had one lady lined up for you, but she chickened out once she realized you were a runaway. He's working on someone else, and he'll let us know as soon as we meet with him this afternoon at the pool," she says.

"Cool," I say.

"Does your mom know I'm coming over?"

"No, I thought it was better if I didn't tell her. I'll have to hide you out in the laundry room down the hall from our apartment," she says. "It will only be for a little bit. I'll do a load of laundry, so it seems like you're doing it in case someone comes and wonders why you're just sitting there."

"Okay," I say.

I'm starving by the time we get to the pool and have to go to the bathroom. Thankfully there's both snack machines and a bathroom. Ernie does seem nice. He looks Italian and works at the pool during the day and the casino at night. He tells me he knows a woman named Maggie, who has three young boys. She works at Caesars Palace as a cocktail waitress and needs someone to stay with the boys overnight while she works.

"That sounds perfect," I say. "Do you know Maggie well?" I ask him.

"Well enough," he says — "Maggie kind of looks like you. I bet you could pass for sisters," he says. "She's excited to meet you. I told her I'd bring you over to meet her here today."

I can't believe I'm doing this, God, but I'm trusting that since I'm so desperate and this is all falling together that you're a big part of making this happen.

We drive across the Bucks County line, and I think maybe I'll be safe since I'm no longer in Philadelphia. In my imagination, it's kind of like crossing into another state or country. We pull up to a Burger King, and a lady gets out of her Grand Prix and comes up to us.

"This is Maggie," Ernie introduces us.

She has fair skin, light freckles, and green eyes like mine. Her hair is as red as an Irish Setter's, swiped up into a ponytail at the crown of her head, and hanging down past her shoulders. She's about five feet, eight inches tall, not thin and not heavy, but solid. She looks tired and worn but carries herself with determination. She smiles when she meets me, but a serious face comes back into play quickly. I like her right away. Maybe it's because she doesn't ask me too many questions. It seems like there's an unspoken understanding that we need each other right now, and that's all that matters for the time being.

"I have to go so I can make it to my next job. Here's a card with my name and number. Call me if things don't work out, and I'll come to get you," Ernie says.

"Are you hungry?" she asks me.

"Starved," I say.

"Do you mind eating on the way to my house? I have to get back and get ready for work," she asks.

"Sure," I say.

"I thought we'd give this a trial run tonight and see how it goes. Then we can both decide if it's going to work," Maggie says.

"Okay," I say with a mouth full of burger. It's the first time I've eaten a Whopper, and it tastes so good; I'm enjoying every bite.

∞ ∞ ∞

As we walk into Maggie's house, her boys are running back and forth. A girl about my age is trying to get them to settle down.

"They haven't stopped since you left, Maggie," the girl says.

"Connie, this is Cris. She lives around the corner. I think you both might be the same age. How old are you?" Maggie asks me.

"I'm fifteen, going into tenth grade this year," I say.

"Me, too," Cris says. "Are you going to Neshaminy High School since you'll be living here? That's where I go."

"We'll have to wait and see if she lasts that long," Maggie says.

Cris looks at me, rolling her eyes. I'm not sure what that's about, but I think it might have to do with how out of control the boys seem to be when we walked in.

Maggie pays Cris. As she's walking out the door, she says to me, "Maybe we can hang out tomorrow before Maggie goes to work."

"That sounds great."

"I'll come over, and we can walk back to my house," she says.

"Okay."

Maggie brings the boys out of their room to meet me. Gregory is ten, Sam nine, and Gus is eight years old. The two younger boys run through the living room and into the kitchen, going around and around nonstop. Gregory sits with Maggie and me. He is looking at me studying every move I make. It's annoying.

"Should I call you Greg?" I ask him.

"No, my name is Gregory. You kind of look like my mom, but not as pretty," he says.

"She doesn't look like anything like Mom, she's ugly," Sam says.

"Sam, that's not nice. Now say you're sorry," Maggie says, grabbing his arm.

"Yeah, she's a poopie face," Gus adds his two cents.

Maggie gets up, grabbing his arm too. "Now both of you apologize," she demands as she squeezes them a little harder.

"Sorry!" they both say together.

"Now, all of you go to your room while I discuss things with Connie," Maggie says.

As we continue talking, all three of the boys are looking out from their bedroom doorway. Gregory on top, Sam in the middle, and Gus at the bottom. Gregory continues his annoying study of me while Sam and Gus are making faces. Maggie can't see them from where she sits. Oh boy, this is going to be a challenge, but I'm going to do everything I can to get them to like me.

"Come on," she says. "I'll show you around."

It's a small house with two bedrooms, one bathroom, a kitchen, and a living room. The boys sleep in the same room with bunk beds and a single bed for Gregory.

"We'll have to share my bed," she tells me, "but I don't get home until about 3:00 in the morning, so you will hardly hear me coming in."

Ew! That creeps me out, but I tell myself I can do this. I slept with Kathy most of my life and learned how to stay on my side of the bed. If this is one of the sacrifices I have to make for now, then I'll make it work.

She asks me a little bit about my parents, and I tell her that my mom is crazy, and my dad drinks too much. She tells me she doesn't get along with her parents either. She's glad they live in Florida.

"I get along fine with my dad," I tell her. "Just so you know, if I ever find him, I'll want to go live with him."

"I understand," she says, "but for now, I think we're going to get along just fine."

"Me, too," I say.

"What happened to your husband?" I ask her.

"We don't talk about him around here. The boys barely know their father anymore, and I'd rather you don't bring him up to them as well."

"Okay," I say. I wonder what that's all about.

I sit with Maggie while she gets ready for work. She's a barmaid at Caesars Palace and tells me she makes great tips there.

"It takes about 45 minutes for me to get there from here with all the traffic at 5:00. When I leave for home, there's hardly anyone on the road at 3:00 am."

She twists her hair up in a towel. Then smooths foundation all over her face. Adding a little blush, she blends it all with a makeup brush to a beautiful polish. She applies dark eyeliner above her eyelid, bringing it to a sharp point, then another defining line below her eyes. She finishes by gluing on long fake eyelashes. Her green eyes pop, looking like two sparkling emeralds. Combing her long hair out, she brings it high up on top of her head, using a ponytail ring to secure it; she then wraps a black ribbon around it.

"Why don't you wear it down," I say. "It looks so pretty down."

"I have to wear it pulled back, so my hair doesn't get in anyone's drinks."

Taking her robe off, she's wearing a white turtle neck and black underwear. She slips on a pair of black pantyhose, then a black leather mini skirt and white go-go boots.

"Now, I get why you were wearing the robe over your turtle neck. You didn't want to mess your hair up, putting it on over your head," I say.

"Not just that, I'd get my makeup all over it, too. What do you think?" Maggie asks, smiling.

"You look cool, Maggie," I say, I don't have the heart to tell her what I think. She looks hard and kind of slutty.

"Thanks, I don't feel cool, but it's nice to hear at my age."

"Your age! You look so young to me. I can't believe you have three kids."

"That's just it; nobody wants a thirty-year-old divorcee with three kids. It's all downhill for me, kiddo."

When Maggie leaves for work, the two little devils come out. One of them is dressed like an Indian, the other a cowboy, and they are both determined to take me captive. I play along with them at first. We're having fun until they start getting mean. Sam kicks me in the shin, and Gus bites my arm. I make them go to their room. Gregory is in Maggie's room. He's sitting in front of her magnified makeup mirror with the lights shining bright. When he looks up at me, he has green eyeshadow on and is holding the mascara wand in his hand.

"What the heck are you doing?" I ask.

"I always play with Mom's makeup," he says.

"Does she let you do that?"

"Yes," he says.

"We'll see about that when I ask her," I say. "Until then, stay out of her stuff, and go clean that off your face." What the heck is a boy doing putting girls' makeup on?

I tell the boys they can stay up if they sit down and watch TV quietly. I walk through the house, this time on my own. The hallway walls have dirty handprints all over them. The boy's room smells like pee and poop. The towel Maggie had wrapped around her head is on the floor beside the bed, along with a few other clothes strewn around. The bed is the only thing that looks made.

I'm not sure if Maggie is just a slob or a mother doing her best, who doesn't have the time to take care of things the way she should. So, I decide I'm going to do what I can to help her and show my appreciation.

"Gregory, where's the cleaning stuff?" I ask.

"Why?" he asks.

"Because I'm going to do some cleaning to help your mom out," I say.

I start with the walls in the hallway, but I'm soon discouraged by how hard it is to scrub the rough texture of the sharp stucco walls. The harder I scrub, the more it shreds the cloth I'm using. I look for a scrub brush, and that does the trick. It makes me think of Miss Betsey and all the times she made us girls scrub things when we got in trouble.

The boys fall asleep watching TV, so I help them to bed. It smells so bad in there that it makes me gag.

"Why does it smell so bad in here?" I whisper to Gregory.

"You should talk," he says to me, "You're the one who smells."

I guess I do smell pretty bad. The only clothes I have to wear are the ones I ran away in. I find Maggie's robe balled up on the floor and take it into the bathroom. Locking the door, I turn the shower on and stand for a long time, letting the hot water run over me before washing up. Gathering my dirty clothes, I put them in the washer, so I have something clean to wear in the morning. I find a big tee shirt to wear to bed. I hope Maggie doesn't mind me borrowing it. I'm so beat that the moment my head meets the pillow, I'm out. I don't even hear Maggie when she comes in.

∞ ∞ ∞

I feel a tickle around my nose. Rubbing it away, I turn on my side. Now I feel it around my eye, my nose, and mouth until I reach up and grab a long feather out of Sam's hand. The boys go running out of the room, giggling. It's 8:00 am, and all I want to do is sleep in a little longer. Maggie is still sleeping, so I guess I need to get up and feed the boys. Walking into the kitchen, I can't step anywhere without feeling the crunch of cereal beneath my feet. I stand frozen in place for a minute as I look around. It's as if a hurricane came blowing through here. Cereal and milk lay spilled on the table and floor. I reach down to pick up an empty Captain Crunch cereal box.

"Boys," I call to them, but they're already standing in the doorway behind me, giggling. "You're going to help me clean this up, or they'll be no TV tonight." They start to come in to help, but I have to stop them, or they'll carry crumbs on their feet throughout the house.

"Gregory, get me the broom out of the closet first, please."

"Only if you promise not to tell my mom about the makeup," he whispers in my ear.

"Okay," I say as I look at him for a moment. "We'll talk about this later, you and I."

I sweep a pathway to the washer so I can put the clothes I washed the night before in the dryer. The boys have disappeared and settled down in front of the TV. It's just as well that I clean it up myself, realizing it's easier if they're not in the way.

By the time Maggie wakes up around 2:00 pm, I've cleaned the boys' room, washed their sheets, made their beds, cleaned the kitchen, and cleaned myself up. Maggie doesn't notice anything until I tell her what I did.

"I even pulled their beds out and cleaned behind them and under them. I found dried up poop under the bed," I say.

"Oh, they're boys," she says. "If you hang around long enough, you won't even wonder anymore why they do the things they do," she says.

"So, what do you think after your first night? Do you want to try to make this work between you and me?" she asks.

"I think it's the perfect answer for both of us right now," I say. "But I am going to need a few things."

"Okay, shoot," she says.

"I only have one pair of underwear, and I'm probably going to need a few more things to wear, especially for when I start school," I say.

"I can buy you the underwear," she says. "Let's go out before I get you all something to eat and see what else we can get at the secondhand store."

Rummaging through the clothes at the secondhand store was something I'd gotten good at in Stenton. Only there, I was fighting for the best stuff against the other girls. We had a bag full of stuff that cost Maggie only a few bucks. I'd have enough to get me through the rest of the summer, and Maggie said we'd come back for school clothes later. We stopped at Burger King again to eat, then headed home.

Home! That word sounded nice. I'd finally found a place I could call "home."

∞　∞　∞

Cris comes to visit a few days later, and when Maggie finally wakes up, I ask her if I can go over to Cris's house for a while.

"As long as you're back by 5:00 this evening, she says.

"My mom can't wait to meet you," Cris says.

"Me! Why me?" I ask. "You didn't tell her about me, did you?"

"Well, yeah, she's my mom. I tell her everything. Don't worry; she's not going to do anything," she says.

Her mom gives me a big hug when I meet her. I don't even know her, and she hugs me like she genuinely cares. Cris and I sit around her table, eating cookies and milk, but her mother doesn't say a word. She hangs out in the kitchen, preparing something for dinner.

Cris gets a phone call and pulls the phone from the hallway into the kitchen. I hear her talking with a friend about going to the Boulevard dance tonight.

"I wish you could go with us tonight, but you have to watch the boys," she says.

"I wish I could go, too. It sounds like a lot of fun," I say.

"With the way Maggie works, I wonder if you're ever going to be able to go out and have fun," she says.

We go into Cris's room, and she gets another phone call. This time she pulls the phone into her bedroom, lying back on her bed, curling her finger around the phone cord, looking all googly eye while she talks with some guy. She has a big smile with perfect white teeth. Her hair is almost as red as Maggie's. She has freckles like me, but she's lucky enough to be blemish-free. She's maybe about five feet four inches and has a cute little figure. I envy her in so many ways and wonder if she knows how lucky she is.

"That was Jason," she says. "He's so dreamy. He wanted to know if I was going to the dance tonight. I can't believe he called me. You have to help me pick out the perfect outfit to wear tonight." She starts pulling one thing after the other out of her closet.

"Look at all your clothes," I say. "You could wear any one of these outfits and look great."

Cris tries on a pair of white bell-bottoms and a wild psychedelic halter top.

"Now that looks great," I say, "but you're going to roast in those long pants," I say.

"Yeah, especially once I start dancing," she says.

She trades off the bell-bottoms for a white mini-skirt.

"Come on," she says to me. "I want you to meet someone before you have to leave."

We walk across the street, and Cris introduces me to a lady named Diane.

"I wanted to take you in," she says to me.

It took a moment for me to realize she was the Diane that Ernie first told me who needed a live-in babysitter.

"I was afraid of what could happen to me if the law found out I was harboring a runaway. I'm not willing to take the kind of chances Maggie does. She's fearless. How's it working out so far for you?" she asks. "I know those boys of hers can be pretty wild."

"That's putting it mildly," Cris says.

"I'm doing pretty good so far," I say. "At this point, I'm just glad to have someplace to stay."

"How do you know, Maggie?" I ask her.

"We worked at a few nightclubs together. I'm a piano singer, so sometimes I move around to different places."

I like Diane. She seems like a very caring person, but I'm glad I'm with Maggie because I feel as if I'm more on my own with her. She doesn't ask any questions or make me feel like a kid.

Cris walks me back to Maggie's and tells me again that she wishes I could go to the dance with her.

"Maybe some other time in the future, we can work things out with Maggie so I could go," I say.

"You'd have to get someone else to come in to watch the boys, and then Maggie would have to pay them. She's pretty stingy about having to pay babysitters," Cris says.

"I don't know if she's stingy," I say. "I think she's just trying to get by the best she can."

"You're too kind about her. Lord knows what she does after work," she says.

"That's pretty harsh," I say.

"I'm not the only one who wonders about her. At any rate, I'm glad you're here, and I hope you get to stay. We can ride the bus to school together and hang out."

"Me too, Cris. I had fun today. You'll have to let me know all about the dance tomorrow. I'll want to hear every detail," I tell her.

∞ ∞ ∞

"Maggie, a man came to the door last night. I didn't open it, but when I looked behind the curtain, he showed me his badge. He said he was a detective. Maggie, did you hear me?" I feel like I'm going stir crazy. All she does is sleep and work. She's so tired all the time, and I know the boys miss being with her.

"Maggie, do you think he's after me?

"Don't worry, kid. It's probably something to do with my ex-husband. They've been around before," she says, finally getting up. "Hey, what's the matter?" she asks.

"I don't know. I guess I'm feeling a little nervous about school coming up. What are we going to do? I mean, how are we going to get me in without them asking too many questions.

Won't the Department of Child Welfare find me that way?" I ask her.

"You worry about things too much," she says. "The way I look at things is there's no sense in worrying about what hasn't happened yet, and if you want something bad enough, you have to be willing to take some chances. You do want to go to school, don't you?" she asks.

"Of course, I do," I say.

"Then trust me. Get yourself cleaned up, and we can go to that secondhand store to pick up some school clothes. I'll take you to school on Monday and get you registered. Well, pretend we're sisters, and you're staying with me to help me out. How's that sound?" she asks.

"Okay," I say. "But I'll warn you; I'm not very good at lying. Most people can see it in my face when I'm not telling the truth," I say.

I'll take care of everything," she says. "It will be easier than you think."

I'm hanging my new outfits up in the closet when I hear a loud bang at the door. Maggie comes running back to the room and tells me to hide in the closet.

"There are two men at the door. I think they might be detectives. Don't come out unless I tell you to," she says.

I step in, pushing all the shoes aside, and hide between the hanging clothes. I'm shaking from head to toe. My face feels red hot, my underarms, and the palms of my hands are wet. *Please don't let them take me away, God.*

Maggie opens the door taking my hand to help me out.

"I'm sorry, Connie, but you're going to have to go back with these two detectives," Maggie says.

"But, are they going to take me to jail?" I ask.

"No. The detectives are taking you back to Stenton," she says.

I start crying, and Maggie pulls me toward her. Now, listen," she says, whispering in my ear. "You come back anytime you want, and we'll figure things out," she says.

∞ ∞ ∞

Windows. It's weird how there's always a window to lean my head against as I ride along the different roads of my life. The ride I'm taking now doesn't feel as free as it does when I take a bus someplace. It's more like being a captured prisoner in an unmarked cop car. I'm behind the driver. I feel his eyes looking at me. The thought of it gives me a shiver down my back. Why do I keep finding myself right back in the same place? I thought this time was different. I thought I'd made it, found the perfect place to live. I wonder how they found me? Maybe it was that detective that came to the door. Maggie said it was probably about her husband. He did ask my name, and I was stupid enough to give it to him.

Stopping at a red light, I watch a young couple walking hand in hand, talking, laughing. He kisses her.

"That's what I want, God. To love and be loved the way they seem to care for each other. That's what You promised me I'd have someday. I don't understand why You keep letting this happen to me; why I keep going around in circles. Why can't you help me find my way out?"

"Would you listen to me if I asked you to stay?"

"How will I ever find what I'm looking for if I stay and do nothing?" I ask.

"Trust."

"The only thing I trust about You God is that You're always there, but You never actually do anything to help me out," I say.

"But I'm a good listener."

"Yes, you are, but it's like talking to a wall sometimes."

"I give you hope."

"That's true, too. I don't know where I'd be if I didn't believe that someday I'd have happiness the way, You promised I would. How will I ever find it by doing nothing?" I ask.

"Whether you stay or not, let that belief be your guide. The only one who can stand in the way of what you want is you."

"I'll try to stay this time, God, but I can't promise I will."

∞ ∞ ∞

"Well, well, look who's back," Miss Betsey says. "Wasn't specting ta ever sees ya again."

"Where do you want me to start scrubbing this time?" I ask her.

"Ain't no sense. Nothing gonna teach you to stop running. Sides being back here be punishment enough for ya'."

"It was so perfect, Miss Betsey, this place I found to live. This lady Maggie needed me as much as I needed her."

"Watcha mean she be needing ya'? What grownup be needing a kid to helps them out?"

"She's a single mom trying to raise three little boys. She has to work, so I was a live-in babysitter for her."

"How you spose ta watch her kids when you be going to school?"

"She works at night."

"Where she be working at night?"

"In a nightclub."

"Oh girly, you should be learning by now nots to trust anyone."

"I don't trust anyone, but she's a chance to get out of here."

"You thinking 'bout going back?"

"All I'm going to say is I'll give it a try here one more time."

"Just so you know, since you been gone, they already sends ya sister Mary ta that there, St. Joseph's of Gonzaga home for girls."

"Oh! Well, then, my running away was a good thing for her."

"I agree with ya there. They ain't no way yous two was gonna gets in that place at the same time. Beds don't open up two at a time in a place like that so easy. Maybe it won't be long till ya' get in there too now."

"I don't want to go there, but I don't know what's worse, going to Germantown High School or Catholic School and being put back a grade."

"Well, you be starting school in two days, so ya' can see how it goes. Maybe it not be so bad," Miss Betsey says.

Chapter 10 – September 1968

I follow Diane to school. She looks back to make sure I'm not falling too far behind her, but she won't walk with me. As I get on the city bus that takes us to school, I feel like a green olive packed into a jar of black ones.

All incoming sophomores are supposed to go to the gym for a welcome introduction. I get inside the school and have no idea where to go.

"You look lost. Can I help you find where you're going?" a black boy asks. As he's pointing me toward the gym, a girl comes up, grabbing his arm away from me.

"Don't you be talking to that white trash," she says to him. She gives me a dirty look and walks away with her arm linked through his.

I sit on the bleacher and get pushed into the middle of the row. I've never seen so many colored kids in one place. So far, I haven't seen another white kid. Most of my friends from Leeds Junior High are going to a Catholic school rather than come here.

After our welcoming speech, they hand out maps of the school, telling us how to get from here to there. I sit until I feel safe enough to move without bumping into anyone.

It's hard to find where you're going when you're looking down at your feet the whole time you're walking. This is not a place I feel I can stand strong. One wrong move and I feel as if I'll be eaten alive.

∞ ∞ ∞

"What's going on with ya, girly?" Miss Betsey asks me. "You been going around here with a long face for the past two weeks."

"I can't sleep, Miss Betsey." I keep having this awful dream about school."

"What kind of dream?"

117

"I have nightmares of black girls all dressed in black with their mini leather skirts, turtle necks, and black go-go boots. They crowd themselves around me until their Afros touch, forming a cloud of bouncy puffy hair. All I see is their big eyes and bright white fanged teeth, like vampires moving in for the bite. I escape through their legs, running as fast as I can, running to where I don't know. Then suddenly, it's as if I'm running in slow motion. My mind is telling me to move faster, but it feels as if I have nothing more to give. I'm running on empty. I can't move, and the cloud of Afros pens me in again. Each girl wants first dibs as they yank me back and forth between them. That's when I wake up screaming and sweating and shaking all over. I can't take it anymore, Miss Betsey."

"Girly, you got some wild imagination that be fur sure. If it ain't for ya being so serious, I'd be laughing bouts now. What I don't gets is why you be feeling so stressed out. I ain't ever seen anything you can't handle on ya' own."

"Are you kidding? I can't defend myself in a school surrounded by black kids who hate white ones."

"What color you be, girly?

"White."

"What color I be then?"

"I guess if I'm white, you'd be black."

"So, what be making me any different than ya'?"

"The color of your skin."

"And black people, they has all the same things white people has if you takes our skin away."

"I don't have a problem with black people. I try to be friends, kind and nice, but they hate me. Even Diane said to me that black and white people can't be friends. There's too much between us. I don't hate the kids at school. I'm scared to death of them because I feel like they want me to pay for all the wrong that's been done to their people."

"Let me tells you something. What you be talking 'bouts is what we black people been dealing with all our life. It ain't never been easy for us living in this here white world. We was born into it and lives it every day of our life, everywhere we goes. Now you is living in our world, feeling what it be like for us. What they should be doing is treating you the way they wish your people be treating them, but the hurt and anger it go too deep. My people, they been oppressed way too long."

"I don't want to live in your world any more than you want to live in mine. I just want to find a way to live together and get along."

"I think that what my people want, too. But it gone take a long time for that to happen, and that be what my people fighting for right now."

"Miss Betsey, I got enough of my own troubles to deal with right now. I feel like I'm in the middle of something I don't belong in. I have to get out."

"I know you gonna do what you gots to do. It ain't gonna make no difference what any of us has ta say round here. I can't be telling ya what ta do child. But I pray whatever it be, you is smart, careful, and safe."

Miss Betsey digs down between her breast again, pulling out that little change purse she keeps buried in there for safekeeping. She rakes her long fingers through the change and hands me four quarters."

"What's this for?" I ask her.

"It be for whatever you need it to be. I don't want ta know whatcha be doing with it. You is a good girl. I know that from the start. Just remembers Miss Betsey be one black person who always like you for who you is."

"I love you, Miss Betsey," I say as I give her a big hug, "and thank you for always being there for me."

"*I tried God.*"

"**I know you did.**"

"*Why'd You ask me to stay this time?*"

"**I never asked you to stay.**"

"*Yes, You did!*"

"**The statement was, would you stay if I asked you?**"

"*You remind me of this guy on Star Trek show that played God. He was a grown man in outer space who was still like a child in his mind. He had the whole world in his hands, but he played with it like it was a toy. He'd play games with people's lives, pitting them against one another, putting them in dangerous situations, even sacrificing them for the sake of himself.*"

"**Is that the kind of God you think I am?**"

"*Sometimes, because when I go to church, all I see are sad faces, sacrifice, and lots of guilt. And I don't understand why You let bad things happen to kids who have no control over what happens in their lives.*"

"**When you lean your head against the windows of your life like now, what do you see on the other side of the glass?**"

"*Everything I want is out there. That's why I get so excited when I run away. I feel free to go out there and find what I'm looking for.*"

"Yet, you are still on the bus looking outside yourself, and I am always here within where you feel safe."

"That's what I love about You, God. You never leave me, and as long as I know You are with me, I feel kind of safe."

"Kind of safe?"

"Well, You have let some pretty awful things happen to me already."

I pull the string on the bus to get off in front of Betty's Restaurant. I call Maggie from the payphone outside. "I'll be there in ten minutes," she says.

"Please let this work this time, God. I'll try to be good and listen to You all the time."

Part 2 -

Living with Maggie

The Promise

Chapter 11 – September 26, 1968

aggie takes me to Neshaminy High School to register for school. It's beautiful with lots of green grass and trees around it. It's clean and bright inside too. The secretary at the reception desk asks Maggie if she's a relative of mine and as we planned, she tells them she's my sister. She asks me what school I last attended was, I tell her Germantown. She shakes her head, saying what a rough school that is, and that's it. I'm signed up and ready to attend the next day, once they get my roster of classes set up. I can come in tomorrow.

"Now that you're registered, I don't think they'll come and pull you out of school," Maggie says. I don't know how she knows that. I want to believe her because I'm super excited yet scared at the same time. Whenever things are too good to be true, something always happens to pull the rug out from under me. I'm going to try to think a little more positive, like Maggie, and try not to worry about anything until it happens. I don't want anything to spoil how happy I'm feeling right now.

I'm so glad I met Cris the first time I came to live with Maggie. We don't have any classes together, but she meets me after school so we can take the bus home together.

"You need your eyebrows plucked," she tells me. "Come to my house after school, and I'll do them for you," she says.

Maggie lets me go over Cris's house for a little while before she has to leave for work. Cris's mom gives me another big hug and tells me how glad she is to see me. Her dad is funny and kind, too.

"You're lucky to have parents who love you so much," I tell her.

"So, tell me about your family," she says.

"I'd rather not if you don't mind. Maybe some other time."

"What's it like to be a runaway? I can't imagine what that's like being out there all alone."

"It's scary and exciting at the same time as if taking your life in your own hands. Knowing what you want, but having no idea how you're going to get it. I want it so bad I keep going after it."

"What are you looking for, you know, going after?"

"I don't know for sure how to put it into words. I want to matter to someone. I want to be loved for who I am. I want to fall in love, and I want to find my dad."

"Well, who doesn't want all those things. I have a good life and still want all those things, except the dad part. I already have him."

She has no idea what it's like to be all alone.

"But you are loved and cared for."

"Yeah, but I still have to do what my parents say. You can do whatever you like, and there's no one to tell you what to do."

"As much as I want to be on my own, sometimes it's good to have someone to keep you from going too far."

"Yeah, like with boys and that stuff, right? It sure is hard to fight that feeling of wanting to be close to them. We're going to have fun together, and I have a lot of friends that want to meet you."

"You told people about me?"

"Yeah, and they think you're cool. I thought I'd bring some of my friends over on Friday after Maggie goes to work."

Everything feels like it's moving too fast all of a sudden. I want to slow down and take a breath, but it all sounds so exciting after being cooped up for so long, from having fun.

Chapter 12 - December 1968

I call St. Joseph's girls home to see how Mary is. Maggie is right; sometimes, when you want to do something badly enough, you have to take a chance. I figure I don't have to tell anyone who I really am when I call.

Mary is so excited to hear from me and know I'm okay. She asks me to visit her, but I say I don't think that is a good idea. The nuns might take me back to Stenton, but she said that they told her I could visit her anytime I want.

Sitting on the bus this time, heading back in the direction of Stenton doesn't feel quite as liberating as leaving there did. But taking that unknown chance is exciting enough to get me going. I don't feel much like doing anything. I've been so tired lately, but it's almost Christmas, and I want to give Mary a little something.

The sun is shining through the window of the bus. It feels warm and cozy, making me sleepier. I have to fight dozing off, or I'll miss my stop. When I get on the next bus, I notice that my throat feels sore. I hope I'm not getting sick. My mouth feels dry; maybe I just need a drink.

When I come to my final stop, Mary is there waiting for me. I haven't seen her for four months. For some reason, she seems more grown-up. We give each other a big hug, and she tells me again how much she's missed me. I never thought I'd feel this close to her. We never got along, but she is my little sister. I realize for the first time that I do love her.

"Come on, Con, I'll show you around the home," she says, taking my hand. Sister Mary Philip meets us at the door. She asks me how I'm doing but doesn't interrogate me the way I thought she might.

"The nuns are pretty cool," Mary says. "They let us cook with them. They teach us to sew, and they do all kinds of fun crafts with us. They also help us with our homework.

It looks remodeled inside, almost too modern for how old the building is. Mary shares a room with another girl. She shows me her clothes.

"They're all mine, and I don't have to share them with anyone else as we did at Stenton," she says. "We do our own laundry, help with the dishes, and keep our rooms cleaned up. They want us to feel like one big happy family here."

"So, you're happy here?" I ask.

"It's not so bad. Of course, I'd rather be with Mom, and it's much better than being in Stenton, that's for sure."

"Do you see Mom much?"

"Sometimes. Mom's going to nursing school now to be an LPN. So that takes up a lot of her time. She says once she graduates, she'll be able to get a decent job, at least one that pays better than the sewing factory. Then she'll be able to take me home with her."

"How long will she have to go to school for this?" I ask.

"Two years."

"So, you'll be about thirteen or fourteen by the time she finishes."

"I try not to think about it so much anymore," she says.

"Does she ever talk about me?" I ask.

"I told her we talked a few times. She wanted to know if I know where you are. I told her I don't know because you never gave me your address or phone number."

"It's best if we keep it that way. I'll call you like I've been doing."

"You want to play a board game with me?" she asks.

" I'm not feeling so good. If you don't mind, I think I'm going to head back."

"You do look pale," she says.

She walks with me back to the bus stop. I give her a goodbye hug.

"You're burning up," she says. "I bet you have a fever."

"My throat is killing me, and I'm so tired. I'm sorry to ruin our visit, Mary."

"I'm just glad to get to see you finally. Next time you visit, we can do more. At least you know now what it's like here, and that it's not so bad," Mary says.

I get off the bus at Betty's Restaurant and call Maggie from the payphone.

"Could you come and get me at Betty's? I feel like I have a fever and I'm shivering all over," I say.

"Well, I have to go to work tonight, so you're just going to have to do your best to take care of the boys," she says.

The moment I get in the car, her hand goes to my forehead.

"Ooh Wee! You're as hot as a bed of coals," she says.

"I don't feel hot. I feel freezing," I say.

I climb into bed with all my clothes on, not even taking my coat off. Maggie takes my temperature, and it's 103. She brings in some aspirin with water, but I can barely swallow my saliva.

"You have to take this. It will help break the fever and ease the pain," she says.

She helps me get undressed and puts a sweatshirt and pants on me.

"Can I have another blanket?" I ask.

"I'll let you sleep for now," she says as she lays another blanket over me, "But when I leave for work, you'll have to lie out on the couch so you can keep an eye on the boys."

I'm asleep before I even have a chance to answer her. The next thing I remember is Maggie trying to get me up.

"Where we going?" I ask. I don't want to go anywhere. "Leave me alone. I just want to sleep," I say.

"Come on, Connie. I need to get you to a doctor. It's been three days, and you still have a fever. You're not eating or drinking."

"But they might ask questions. I can't go to the doctor," I say.

She puts my coat on me, wraps a blanket around my shoulders, and leads me to the car.

It doesn't matter what the doctor asks me once we get there. I can't think straight enough to answer anything anyway. He says I have mononucleosis. There's not much he can give me for it except some pain medication for the throat.

"I know it hurts, but you need to try to drink water and eat," the doctor tells me. "The pain pills will help. You're going to be in bed for a few weeks yet, and rest is the best thing for you. It usually takes up to four weeks before you start feeling better. Then you still have to work your strength back up."

On the way home, Maggie starts complaining about me being so sick, saying, "This is all I need. Now I have a babysitter who can't even babysit."

"I'm sorry, Maggie. It's not like I tried to get sick," I say.

"You know mononucleosis is what they call the kissing disease. I know you have boys over all the time, Gregory tells you're always kissing boys."

"You sound just like my mom, always insinuating that I'm doing something dirty and nasty when I'm not," I say. "You want me to leave; I will."

"No, I don't want you to leave. I'm sorry. I'm just frustrated about what I'm going to do for the next few weeks while you get better."

"I can lie on the couch at night and watch them. Maybe you could talk with the boys and explain how sick I am so they don't give me such a hard time," I say.

"I can do that, but you know how out of control they can get," she says.

She must have still been talking to me when I fell asleep on the way home. I don't even remember getting out of the car. Next thing I know, Maggie is getting me up again and helping me out to the couch. I lie there, half-awake, and the boys won't leave me alone. They want this and that. They are fighting and running through the house. I pull the covers over my head. I don't care what they do. I'm not cleaning up after them anymore.

Chapter 13 – January 1969

"You still look like crap," Cris says as we head back to school the first Monday after New Year's.

"I still feel like crap. I don't know how I'm going to get through the day without falling asleep, but I can't miss school anymore, or they might come after me."

"Who's going to come after you?"

"The Department of Child Welfare. I think the only reason they haven't come yet is that I'm attending school. At least that's what Maggie's been telling me. She keeps pushing me to go back to school. It's not like I'm trying to be sick. I'm afraid she's going to send me back because she's tired of me not taking care of the kids for her."

"Yeah, she had Dawn and me come over a few times, long enough for the boys to go to sleep. "Don't you remember us being there?"

"All I remember is that I could hardly swallow, and Maggie yelling at me to wake up. I don't even remember Christmas coming and going."

"You look skinnier, too," she says.

"I guess so. I haven't eaten anything for two weeks."

∞ ∞ ∞

Even by the end of January, I'm dragging, but it's my sixteenth birthday, and Maggie is trying to make up for how badly she treated me when I was sick. She's taking me to the Latin Casino Theater Restaurant for dinner and a show.

"Guess who's playing?" she asks. "Tom Jones!"

I don't even like Tom Jones.

"You don't have to do that, Maggie; I still feel so tired all I want to do is stay home and sleep. Besides, I don't even have anything nice to wear to a place like that."

"You are such an ungrateful brat. All I wanted to do was something nice for your sixteenth birthday. You're going because I already got the tickets for you and a friend. I thought you might like to take Cris with you. Plus, I got you that cute dress for Christmas you can wear."

"To be honest, Maggie, I don't remember anything about that day."

She goes back into our room and gets the dress out of our closet. "Here it is," she says. "Why don't you try it on?"

It looks like one of the jackets the Beatles are wearing on the front cover of "Sargent Pepper's Lonely-Hearts Club Band" album. It's a red A-line dress, with a high neck collar open about an inch in the throat area. It's outlined with gold braid, which also runs around the wrist of the sleeves. Gold buttons run down over the bust line and on the wrist bands as well. With my new tiny figure, it looks cute. As I look myself over, I smile for the first time in I don't know how long.

I've never been to a live show before. We each pick the steak dinner, and before the show starts, a few waiters bring a small cake out singing Happy Birthday to me. The show doesn't start until 9:00 pm. Tom Jones doesn't come on until 10:00. I can't stand his voice. I think he ruins a perfectly good song when he sings, "Yesterday," by the Beatles.

"Isn't he just dreamy?" Maggie says.

I smile back at her, taking a quick sip of my soda. I sure wish we could go soon, but I don't want to spoil her fun.

Chapter 14-May 1989

"What are you reading?" Cris asks as she sits next to me on the bus.

"The Valley of The Dolls."

"Isn't that some slutty dirty book?"

No, it's about growing up, making difficult choices like with sex and drugs. Mr. Jennings wanted our English class to learn how to enjoy reading, so he brought in a bunch of books for us to read. It's so good I can't put it down. Even though it's about going out on your own after graduation, I feel like I'm already facing some of the same decisions."

"Lucky you," she says. "We're reading about mythology in English class now."

"Oh, I love that. We read it at the beginning of the year."

"What's in the bag? Is that the jumpsuit you're making in Home-Economics?" Cris asks as she pulls it out. "I love the bright green, red, and yellow colors running through it. What is this design called?"

"Paisley. I always loved this design."

"Well, it's really in now, too," she says.

"I got a D+ because I wouldn't model it for the class. It turned out dumb."

"Do you think Maggie will still let you go to the Boulevard dance this Friday since you got such bad grades?" She asks.

"Cris, she doesn't care about my grades. She won't let me go anyway. All she cares about is that I'm there to babysit the boys. That's all I've done since I've been here through sickness and health, Summer, Fall, and Winter. It's been seven months, and I feel like I'm going stir-crazy. Now, it's not only watching the boys; she expects me to clean the house and feed them. I feel like I've become their mother. Worst of all, they never listen to me and fight all the time. Every time I turn around, Gregory is watching me. It creeps me out."

"I don't think he's looking at you the way most boys look at girls. I think he might be a homo, or he's going to grow up to be a crossdresser. It seems like he watches how we move, dress, and put makeup on, don't you think?"

"I don't know much about that kind of stuff, but maybe you're right."

"Wow, you mean I know something about life that you don't?" she says sarcastically.

"I don't know everything there is to know, and most of what I know, I wish I didn't have to know at my age. All I want to be is a teenager, doing teenage things like you. All your talk about how you wish you had the freedom I do, and all I wish is that I had someone who cared about me the way your parents do you."

"You know what? Sometimes being around you is nothing but depressing. I'm glad I have a place to go to get away from you sometimes."

"Thanks a lot, Cris," I say as we get off the bus. She goes her way, and I go mine.

I guess I can be pretty depressing to be around. I don't want to be. I wish things were as happy as they were in the beginning when I came here to live. Why does everything good have to turn bad for me? Maybe it is just me. Maybe I bring it on myself.

∞　∞　∞

Hi, Mary Faith! It's Connie."

"Was just thinking about you," she says.

"Isn't it always that way with us. We have that ESP thing going on when it comes to each other," I say.

"So, how are things going between you and Maggie? Last time we talked you were going stir crazy," she says.

"I finally told Maggie I was going to leave if she didn't start letting me go out once in a while. She got nice and said, "Oh, don't do that. We'll work it out." She let me go to the Boulevard dance twice, but then after that, complained about having to pay a babysitter for a few hours, I was away. Now summer is coming, and I don't think I could stand being here all day and night with these kids."

"Is she still coming home later in the morning?"

"Yeah, and she sleeps all day. She doesn't even make us dinner or buy anything for me to make. We go to Burger King to eat just about every other day."

"Yeah, those Whoppers and fries are pretty good, but I don't think I'd want to eat them that much," she says.

"I think she might have a boyfriend. Maybe that's why she's coming home so late."

"I was wondering the same thing," she said.

"Her parents came to visit for Easter time. They didn't stay here, but they were over every day. Her mother would follow me around, watching how I cleaned and made beds. They ran a hotel in Florida and said if I wanted to go back with them, she'd give me a job in a minute as one of their cleaning girls. I thought about it, but don't want to move that far away. My dad will never be able to find me if I move that far away."

"Connie, it's been how long since he left you?" she asks.

"Four years. I know what you're thinking, but just like we have this strange connection, I have the same thing with my dad. I know he's out there somewhere looking for me. I can feel it."

"So, what are you thinking of doing?" she asks.

"I don't know yet, but if things get any worse, I'm going to run away again. One of my boyfriends was talking about running away to the beach. He said it's easy for kids our age to find jobs there for the summer."

"I hope you're not thinking seriously about doing that. It doesn't sound very safe. Besides, who is this guy?" she asks.

"Nobody I want to run away with anyway. He just put the idea in my head. It sounds kind of fun but scary at the same time. I'm not afraid. I mean, I've already done a lot of running away and being on my own. But this would take me to an unknown territory and a whole new level of being a runaway. If I did it, I'd want to go with someone else until I knew what I was getting myself into. Honestly, this guy Brian, there is no way I'd want to run away with him. All he wants to do is get inside my pants like all the other guys. It's unbelievable. I have one boyfriend after the other. They all think I'm easy. It seems like they are all trying to see which one is going to get the runaway girl to go to bed with him. They don't even care about me, just how far they can get," I say.

"Maybe it's not you who they think is easy, but the circumstances you put them in that makes their chances easier," she says.

"What do you mean?" I ask.

"I don't mean like it's your fault or anything. Maggie doesn't let you go out, but she lets you have anyone you want over. When the boys go to bed, and you're all alone with a guy necking for hours, things are going to happen," she says.

"I know. I did go a little too far with Billy one night. He's not as bad as the others. I mean, we enjoy talking with each other and all. He wants our relationship to be more than just good friends. Sometimes, the way a guy makes you feel when he wants you is like you're the most important person in the world. I want to matter to someone for who I am, not because they want my body. I mean, how do you know the difference between when they like you for who you are, or they want to have sex?"

"Let's back up here," she says. "What do you mean you went a little too far?"

"He thought he went all the way, but honestly, it didn't feel like he did."

"How could you not know that?"

"I don't know. I never did it before; neither had Billy. It just didn't feel like he did, and it scared me enough that I won't ever let it happen again."

"I hope not, Connie. What would you do if you got pregnant? It's hard enough right now taking care of yourself," she says.

"I know; you don't have to remind me. It's not like I want this kind of thing to happen. That's what's wrong. I don't get to go out to movies, dances, or parties. I sit here in this house, and the only fun I have is when I have friends over here," I say.

"I know you're doing your best. I don't mean to sound like a parent. I worry about you," she says.

"You're the only real person in this world I can trust and lean on. I know you care, that's why I know I can tell you anything, and you'll tell me honestly what you think. I don't know what I'd do if I didn't have you," I say.

"Well, summer will be here soon. I've been studying like crazy, with this being my senior year. I haven't had much time for anyone. I need to have good enough grades to get into college and get my nursing degree," she says.

"Oh, you'll do fine. You always get A's and B's. You're smart and determined. I admire and envy that. You know what you want to do with your life. I have no idea."

"How could you? All you've been able to think about is how to survive from one day to the next. Don't sell yourself so short, though. You have a lot of determination, too, and someday you'll find what you're looking for; I know you will," she says.

"I knew I'd feel better after talking to you. Thanks for being there for me," I say.

"Keep in touch and call me if you need me any time," she says.

"I will bye, and thanks again, Mary Faith."

∞ ∞ ∞

"Hey-you," Cris says, jumping into the seat next to me on the bus. "How was your weekend?" she asked.

"Could it be anything else but boring?" I asked. "I thought you were mad at me?"

"Oh, that. I couldn't stay mad at you for long," Cris says. "I was just in a bad mood, and I needed some time to myself."

"Lucky you, even being able to make that choice. I wish I could have some alone time," I say. "But, you know, if I didn't have you, then I wouldn't have anywhere to go to get out of the house."

"Well, then, I have just the thing that will make your day. We can hang out at my place after school today and catch some warm rays around my pool. Wear that new baby doll bathing suit, Maggie's parents bought you."

"Oh, that. I think Maggie's mom was trying to bribe me into going back to Florida with her," I say.

"Why is it so hard for you to believe that maybe someone might want to do something nice just because they like you?"

"Because in my life it's never been about me. It's always about what other people want."

"Ah, come on, don't be raining on my parade today. The sun is out, it's Friday, we only have a few weeks of school left before the summer break, and tonight we're gonna party hardy at your place," she says.

"Did I hear the word party? Danny says from behind us. Someone else on the bus hears the word party and says, "Yeah, I heard you have some pretty wild parties at your pad, Connie."

"Oh, my God! No, I don't. Where'd you hear that?" I ask.

"Word gets around," he says.

"Hey, you idiot stick! Nobody said you're invited," Cris stands up and yells back to him. "But you can come," she turns around, looking at Danny, all dreamy-eyed.

"Cris!"

It's only one more person," she whispers in my ear.

When we get off the bus, I run inside the house, grab my bathing suit, and tell Maggie I'm going swimming at Cris's. I'll be home by 5:00.

"It better be no later," she says as I'm walking out the door.

"You know by the time I get my bathing suit on, I'm gonna have to turn around and go right back," I say to Cris.

"Then I guess you better stop poking around and get moving. I figure you'll have a good hour to soak up some rays. We'll lather on some baby oil, too. That'll give us a quick tan, so we look good for tonight," she says.

I don't care about looking so great tonight. No one I want to impress is going to be there anyway.

I stand in front of her mirror and think about how cute my bathing suit is. I love that it goes down below the panty line.

"Ah, you look like you have baby doll pajamas on with all those tiny little blue flowers running through your bathing suit. It's cute, but it sure doesn't show off your little figure. And white! Yikes! You know you can see right through white when it gets wet?" she says.

"But it has a thick lining where it's needed," I say.

"There's no better time than now to check it out while it's just you and me around," she says.

Cris jumps in the pool, and I tiptoe down the steps. It's freezing, but I eventually work my way under the water. My bathing suit passes the test; nothing shows through.

"I can't wait for tonight," Cris says, "I'm starting to enjoy the parties at your place more than going to the dances on the weekend."

"It's not my place. It's Maggie's, and things are starting to get out of hand. She doesn't mind me having a few people over, but kids are showing up that I don't even know. Then there's the beer and some of them smoking pot. I've had to tell half of them to leave. It's hard to keep things quiet when too many people are in the house. I'd rather be going to the dances any day," I say.

"So, are you looking forward to seeing Billy again?" she asks.

"No! We're just friends. That's all."

"I don't think that's the way he sees it. He's like a dog in heat, following you all over the place," she says.

"I know. I see Billy following me around in his daddy's batwing tail Chevy. He looks so small in that big car."

"Well, he is only a few inches taller than you," she says. "You guys look cute together."

"Knock it off, Cris. We're just friends." I wish I could go back and start all over again as if nothing happened between Billy and me. I can't let myself get in that kind of situation again.

The boys are finally asleep, and people keep coming to the door. I don't even know half of them. I go out front to tell them they have to leave, but one guy catches my attention. He's wearing one of those loose-fitting leather jackets that go down to his thighs. His hair is dark brown and shaggy looking. I notice he has sad, dark brown, puppy dog eyes when he comes up to me.

"Well, hello beautiful," he says, and I turn around to see who he's referring to.

"I'm talking to you," he says.

"Me!" I say. "You really must be high."

"Got nothing to do with it," he says. "So, what's this story I hear about you being a runaway?" he asks.

"I don't talk about that," I say.

"Well, I think it takes a lot of guts to go off on your own and do what you got to do to survive. I think you're pretty brave and cool besides being beautiful," he says.

"Who are you, and where did you come from?" I ask him.

"My name is Ray, and I'm a senior at Bensalem High School," he says.

"Why do you look so sad?" I ask.

"Oh, that's because I got drafted. I've joined the Marines, and I'm leaving for boot camp at the end of the summer," he says.

"That stinks," I say.

"To make matters worse, the girl I've been going with for the past four years broke up with me," he says.

"No wonder you look so sad," I say.

"Yeah, but now I met you," he says.

"Well, if that's such a good thing, why do you still look so sad?" I ask.

"Maybe I just need to smoke another joint," he says as he pulls out his bag of weed.

"Oh, no. If you want to smoke that stuff, you're going to have to go someplace else to do it."

"Aren't you going to come with me?" he asks.

"No, I don't do that stuff, and neither should you. It will mess your life up."

"Ah, a little bit of pot ain't going to hurt anyone," he says.

"Sorry, the answer is still no," I say.

"How about drinking a beer with me?" he says.

"I don't drink beer, either," I say. "Three little boys are sleeping in the back room. I'm responsible for them."

"Okay, I can respect that," he says. "Can I at least drink inside the house?

"Sure, everyone else is," I say.

"How about some music? Don't you have any albums around?" Ray asks.

"I got a few for Christmas," I say. I'm kind of embarrassed because I don't know much about them. I was sick over Christmas and don't remember much about that day, let alone what I got."

"I can't imagine not remembering what you got for Christmas. Then this will be like Christmas all over again. Let's see what you got; the Monkees, they're too ape for me," he says, cracking up.

"You look so handsome when you smile; you should smile more," I say.

He looks up at me, meeting my eyes, and steals a quick kiss. Then another one, only this time longer. He gives me that butterfly feeling like they are fluttering around inside me. I've never been kissed like that before, slow and thoughtful. Most of the guys who kiss me make me feel as if they want to gobble me up.

"I thought we were checking out the albums," I stop him.

He pulls another one out, and his face lights up. "Oh my god, you have the Doors, and you never even took the cellophane off the cover yet. You're going to dig them," he says.

He's right. I do dig the Doors. They seem to express all the anger and frustration we both feel inside for our own reasons. I'm not only digging the music but Ray too. He's different, maybe because he's hurting and as unsure about his future as I am. I don't know if it's the music or him that makes me want to shut everything else out, live in the now, at this very moment.

We've been talking so much I don't even notice that the party has wound down until Ray gets up to get another beer. He comes back with two, handing me one. I take it reluctantly but think what the heck. One won't hurt me. I don't usually drink, so it doesn't take much to make me feel a little warm and fuzzy. We put the Doors on the record player again and sit on the floor. Ray pulls me close to him until we are lying down, making out. It starts to get hot and heavy, so I sit up.

"I can't do this, Ray. You don't have anything to lose, but I could get pregnant, and I can barely take care of myself," I tell him. "Plus, I hardly know you."

"But you like me, don't you?" he asks. "I know I like you and want to get to know you better," he says.

He kisses me again, laying me down gently. I keep trying to stop him even though everything inside me wants to say yes. I can feel my protective guard breaking away. I no longer hear that parental voice inside telling me what I can and can't do. Like a pent-up animal, I'm set free, and nothing else matters because the desires of my body tied together with my longing to be loved have met. I never knew how wonderful it could be until it's over, and suddenly the reality of what just happened sinks in. I feel guilt creeping into me. I've lost a part of who I was, and there's no turning back. I've become a tramp like my mother said I would.

"I have to go," Ray says. He stands at the door with me, kissing me goodbye. "Hey," Ray takes my lowered chin in his hand. "Who looks sad now?" he asks.

"Just go," I say with tears in my eyes.

"Don't cry. I'll call you tomorrow," Ray says.

"Please, just go, Ray," I say as I open the door.

I lean my head against the shut door, crying softly, so the boys don't hear me. When I turn around, Gregory is standing there.

"Why are you crying? He asks me.

"No reason," I say as I start cleaning things up.

"Did that boy make you sad?" he asks.

"No, I just miss my dad," I say.

"I miss my dad too, but I don't know him very well," he says.

It's okay, Gregory. You go back to bed," I say.

"I can help you clean up," he says.

"You are a sweet kid, Gregory, and I'm sorry, we woke you up. I know things are getting out of hand. I didn't mean for things to get like this. Someday you'll understand when you get a little older. I won't let it happen again, I promise. Please don't tell your mom," I say.

"I won't tell if you let me play with my mom's makeup," he says.

"Okay, I can do that," I say, "but you have to promise me you won't mess your mom's stuff up."

"I won't," he says and wraps his arms around me.

"Now go on and get to bed," I say.

"Sorry, God. I know I let you down, but it's myself I have to live with now, and I feel bad enough. There's not much more you could do to make me feel any worse than I already do. I wish I could die. I just wanted to feel loved, and you know what? I did feel loved for a brief moment. I'm confused. How can something that feels so good be wrong? I never knew how hard it would be to hold these feelings back. I don't understand God. Why'd you go and make everything we do so tricky? It seems like the older I get, the harder the choices are. I know I'm not ready for this or for what the consequences could be, like getting pregnant. It's hard enough being a parent to myself. I can't begin to imagine what it would be like to take care of a baby, too. I don't know how much longer I can keep going like this. Please help me find my dad, God."

I wait to hear God answer me, but I can't seem to reconnect with Him the way I used to. It's as if the line that connects us has been unplugged. He said He'd never leave me. Then I remember the story of the Footprints in the sand; this must be one of those times when He's carrying me.

Chapter 15 - June 1969

"Hi, Mary Faith, how's your summer going?"

"I've been chilling out around the pool most days," she says.

"I can't imagine what it feels like to finally graduate from high school," I say.

"After all that hard studying I did so I could get into nursing school, it feels good to be doing nothing but enjoying my summer. I met a guy I like a lot," she says. "We went out a few times. But I can't get serious about anyone right now. I want to get through nursing school first."

"You still have to have some fun in your life. Anyway, how are you gonna meet the right guy if all you do is study?" I ask.

"I know, but you know as well as I do how hard it is not to get too involved with a guy you like," she says to me.

"How are things going with you and Ray?" she asks.

"Not so good. It's been awful," I say.

"What the heck happened? I thought things were going great between the two of you," she says.

"He told me he couldn't see me anymore because he went back with his old girlfriend. He said he never stopped loving her, Mary. Can you believe it? I'm so brokenhearted; I want to die. I think if Maggie had any pills around here, I would have taken them. All she has is vitamins, so I took a bunch of them. All it did was make me sick in my stomach," I say, bursting out laughing through my tears. "I can't even kill myself right."

"Look, Connie, there's no guy worth throwing your life away over. You've come too far and overcome so much. In a few years you'll be old enough to make your life the way you want it," she says.

"I know, but it hurts so bad. Anyway, I went to the park on the same day and met up with some friends during the afternoon. They were all sitting around in a circle, passing a joint around. When someone thought they saw a cop, they all scattered, and one of them gave me a sandwich bag half full of diet pills. I ran off and hid in the middle of a bunch of bushes. I sat there for a while, looking at the bag of pills, thinking about how I could take a handful, and that would do the trick. But I don't want to die. I just want the pain to go away."

"I know what you're feeling. Remember what I went through with Jimmy? This Ray guy, he isn't worth it. You'll meet the right guy someday. Don't be in such a hurry," she says. "And next time call me when things get so bad. I don't want anything to happen to you. What would I do without all the crazy excitement you bring into my life?" she laughs.

"You're just saying that. I know I'm a pain in the ass, but honestly, I don't know what I'd have done if I didn't have you to turn to."

"I have to go, but keep in touch now," she tells me.

"I will! And thanks again for listening to me."

∞　∞　∞

"Mary Faith, it's me again. I'm sorry to call you back so soon, but you're never going to believe what happened today. I thought I was going to die for sure," I say.

"Calm down, Connie. I can't understand a word you're saying. What happened?" she asked.

"Two men showed up at Maggie's this afternoon. Gregory opened the door, and the next thing I hear is him saying, "Daddy." They came busting into the house, shouting, "Where's your mother?" He told them she was at the store and would be home soon. Then he wanted to know who I was. Gregory told him I was their live-in babysitter. He starts shouting, "Where're your brothers?" and Gregory tells him he thinks they're hiding and that he'll go get them. His Dad tells him to sit his ass down. He has a deep, loud low voice, and yells for Samuel and Augustus to get their asses out here and say hi to their father. The boys walk out shyly. I never saw them act so scared of anyone. He asks them, "What's the matter with you boys, don't you even know your daddy when you see him?"

Gregory says, "I don't think they remember you because they were so young when you left." The dad told poor Gregory to shut his mouth, that he doesn't know anything about anything, that he never left anybody. The police took him away because their mother got him in trouble. Poor Gregory started to cry. His dad told him to stop crying like a girl. Little Gus climbed on my lap, and Sam stood beside me, holding tightly onto my arm. Their dad started talking about what it's like when they put you in jail. He tells his friend to help him move the couch. Then he tells us all to line up against the wall to put our hands up and spread our legs apart. "See, they frisk you to see if you're carrying any drugs or weapons. Like this," he says as he slams me against the wall. He holds my hands tightly up above my head with one of his strong hands. He kicks my legs apart, and he whispers in my ear, "Carrying any weapons or drugs on you, sweetheart?" I can still feel his hot, smelly breath on me. He felt me up and down with the other hand slipping it inside my bra. Just as he was about to move his hand down my pants, Maggie came walking in.

She screams, "What the hell are you doing here?" The boys break away and run to her.

"I'm back is what, and you're going to pay for getting me to put in jail," he says.

"Whatever you have to do is between you and me. Leave the kids out of it," she says.

"Maybe I will, and maybe I won't. For now, I want you all to get into my friend's car. He's taking us for a little ride down by the boatyard."

I'm telling you, Mary Faith, all five of us piled in the back seat tighter than a can of sardines. My heart was pounding a mile a minute, and I'm saying to God, *I don't want to die yet.*

The dad pulled Maggie out of the car and beat her good. The boys were crying, and the other guy kept turning around telling them if they didn't shut the hell up, he was going to tie them up and put them in the trunk. I thought they were going to kill us and throw us in the lake. But Maggie's husband opened the car door and threw Maggie back in the back seat with us. Blood was running from her nose. She's trying to calm the boys down, telling them she was okay. They drove us back home. He pulled Maggie out of the car again, grabbed her by the chin, looked her straight in the eyes, and told her, "I'll be watching you, bitch." Then he turned and winked at me.

I'm' scared to death, Mary Faith. I have to get out of here."

"Can you wait it out until tomorrow? I can get you in the morning when I leave for Mass about 10:30," she says.

"I'll meet you at Cris's house. That way, Maggie won't know you came for me."

After spending a few nights with Mary Faith, her parents are getting uncomfortable with me being here. I'm feeling depressed, and all I want to do is sleep all the time, living inside my dreams, being in that world instead of this one.

"Maybe you should try calling your sister, Kathy," Mary Faith suggests.

"Yeah, maybe since she's married now, I could go live with her in Ohio. Do you think your parents will let me make a long-distance call to her?" I ask.

"I'll ask," she says.

"My mom thinks that's a great idea for you to call your sister for help, but don't stay on too long."

We haven't heard each other's voice in two years, making us both tear up after saying our hellos. When I tell Kathy how desperate I am, she wishes she could help, but they can barely make ends meet for themselves with money right now. She tells me that mom got a letter from dad. He's been drunk for four years and got so bad he ended up in rehab. Now that he's getting some help, he wants to see us kids. He's been living in Lancaster all this time. It's somewhere in Pennsylvania.

"I have his address and phone number," Kathy tells me. "Maybe if you call him, he could come and get you,"

When I hang up the phone, I feel like I can hardly breathe. Mary Faith tells me to sit down and put my head between my legs. I start to cry.

"What happened?" she asks me.

"I found him," I say.

"Who? What are you talking about?" she asks.

"My dad," I say. "Kathy just gave me his address and phone number. He lives in Lancaster. Do you know where that is?"

"Oh my God, Connie, that's about sixty miles from here. It's not far at all," she says.

"Do you think your mom will let me make another long-distance call?"

Mary Faith goes into her parents' bedroom, and I can hear them talking. Her mom is not happy. She says they've been putting up with my running away all these years. "Your daddy's a lawyer, and he can't be a part of this. I'm going to have to call the Department of Child Welfare and do things the right way. I don't know her father. He left them. I can't just let her go with him," Mrs. Matthews says.

When she comes out to talk to me, I ask her, "Please, let me call him. I've been praying for this day to come for four years. My dad is a good man. He just got mixed up in too much drinking, and now he's sober. Can I call him, please?" I ask again with tears in my eyes.

"You can call him, but I'm still calling the Department of Child Welfare to get things straightened out and done right," she says.

I dial the number Kathy gave me and man answers. "Could I speak to John Miller?" I ask him.

"This is him," he says.

"It's Connie, Dad. I knew I'd find you one day."

"Oh, my god, Connie, you sound so grown up," he says.

"Well, it's been four years since I saw you last," I say.

"I know, and I'm so sorry about what I put you and the rest of the family through. Where are you all? I wrote to your Aunt Tee so that she could give my letter to your mom. I never heard from anyone. I was hoping I could visit you and the rest of the family. I know I can't make up for what I did, but I'd like to be as much a part of your life as I can now that I'm sober."

"That's why I'm calling, Dad. I'm all alone. I have nowhere to go, and if you don't come to get me, my friends' mom is calling the Department of Child Welfare, and they'll take me away again. Please come and get me, Dad. I have so much to tell you and explain, but I don't have enough time to be on the phone with you."

"Give me the number, and I'll call you right back," he says.

When he calls back, I tell him that Mom gave Mary and me up to the Child Welfare two years ago, then I ran away from Stenton Child Care Center and was living with Maggie for the past year. My friend Mary Faith was always helping me out, but her parents can't keep taking me in.

Dad said, "I'll get you in a few days as soon as I can find someone to drive me to Philadelphia."

"Mrs. Matthew wants to talk with you," I say and hand him the phone.

She tells my dad that she is still calling the Department of Child Welfare. When I get back on the phone with him, he tells me not to worry about it. He's coming to get me.

"In the meantime, I'll write you a letter, Dad, and tell you all about everything," I say. "But, please come for me as soon as you can. I can't wait to see you."

July 7, 1969

Dear Dad,

I hope this letter finds you well and doing fine.

I don't know how to start. I mean, I have so much to talk to you about.

Well, I'll tell you what happened today. Mrs. Matthews called my social worker, Miss Dolly, but she wasn't in. She waited for her to call back, but Miss Dolly never did. So, Mrs. Matthews called and asked to talk to a supervisor. They tried to give her a story that the supervisor wasn't in either. Mrs. Matthews got mad and said, "Well, I'll sit here on the phone until someone does come in." About three minutes later, the supervisor got on. She told Mrs. Matthews that they did know where I was this past school year. Mrs. Matthews asked, "Did they investigate?" They said that the Catholic Social Services people did, which isn't true. Mrs. Matthews got angry and said she was going to call the commissioner to report the people there. She did, and now he's going to see what he can do. I don't know what's going to happen, and now I am getting scared. I'm afraid this is all going to go to court.

Mary Faith, my girlfriend, tells me not to worry, but at the rate, things are going, I don't know. I mean, the Department of Child Welfare doesn't seem to care what happens to me, so I don't see why I can't come out with you when you get another apartment. I wouldn't be any trouble for you. I'm old enough to work now, so I could help pay rent and buy whatever I need. You could help me with school work, and in bettering myself. Dad, I need you more than anything else in this world right now. I don't even know what it's like to be loved anymore. Johnny was the only one who ever seemed to care about me, but then he left when he was sixteen. He couldn't stand being around Mom. Since then, I've been all alone in this world, looking for one thing, and that's just for someone to care about me. That's why I always run. You know my main goal was to try and find you. I still can't believe I've talked to you.

You know, it's very hard to express yourself in a letter, that's why this letter might be a little difficult to understand. Letters can make a person look completely opposite than the kind of person they are, but then they can also bring the true person out. That's one reason why I like to watch how I write a letter. It's especially hard for me to write a person if I have a lot to say. I go from one thing to another.

It is 3:15 am. Mary Faith and I watched a movie which was over at 12:30, and from that time on, we have been talking. We do this almost every night. I think a lot better at night, real late. I can never sleep anymore at night. I get to sleep around 5:00 am and wake up around 2:00 pm. I sit up in bed, making plans for what I want and how I'll get those things. It's like I'm living through my dreams since I can't really have these things. I know it sounds crazy, but it helps me keep my sanity. Do you know what I mean?

You know, Dad, I'm nothing at all like Kathy, Johnny, or Mary; I'm the wild one. I'm living in my own world, my way. I don't like being like everyone else. I like being like myself, and want others to like me for who I am. The only reason I'm saying this is so you can get to know what I'm like now.

It's Tuesday, now. Mr. Feldman, the supervisor, called, but I was asleep. He is calling back later. Now it's a whole different story, he's telling us. He told Mrs. Matthews; he doesn't know what to do. Some supervisors he is! He doesn't even know how to do his job. I might have a better chance of coming with you now, I hope.

Well, I'm going to go, for now, so you can get this letter faster. I'll let you know what's up, and you do the same.

Love and miss you,

Connie

Part 3 -

Living with Dad

Chapter 16 - July 1969

Lancaster, Pennsylvania

*D*éjà vu is what I've heard it called. It's not the beautiful Lancaster County farmland I'm looking at that seems familiar. It's the place I'm looking at it from; there's always a window and a stranger driving the car. I'm like a fish in a bowl looking out at the world. It's different this time. I'm no longer worrying about where I'm going or where I wish I could be. Dad is in the passenger seat up front, and his friend Paul is driving the car. What I see on the other side of the window is my wish, come true. I no longer have to settle for looking out at it. This time I have the freedom to roll down the window and let it become a part of me. The blast of fresh air hits my face. Like a dog hanging its head out the window, the wind blows through my hair. Just like sleeping beauty, I've awakened from my long dream. While I'm taking it all in, enjoying the sweet smell of the farmland, it suddenly turns foul.

"Pew!" what's that awful smell?" I ask.

"Welcome to Lancaster County," Dad says. "That's chicken shit, you're smelling. I think it's the worst smelling manure, but it sure does make the land rich around these parts."

"I don't know how anyone could eat anything grown in that shit," I say.

"It's a great metaphor for life," Dad says, "it's the shitty things in life that help us to grow the strongest."

Hmm, I think, as I continue to let the air blow through my hair. If that's true, then I've been just as richly fertilized as the farmland.

"So, what's Lan-caster got beside farmland?" I asked.

"It's pronounced Lanc-aster," he says. "Everyone who comes here pronounces it wrong at first. But to answer your question, it has a town and city, but it's much smaller than Philadelphia."

"Is that where you live in the city?"

"Yes, it's where I work, where I went to college, where I met your mother, and where we got married," he tells me.

"That was the biggest mistake of your life," I say.

"No, it wasn't. If I hadn't married your Mother than you kids would have never been born," he says.

"Maybe we would have been better off," I said.

"Maybe you would have," he says as he turns away from me.

"I'm sorry, Dad. I shouldn't have said that. Sometimes things come out of my mouth before I have time to think of what I'm saying."

"Nothing can make up for what I did. You don't have to apologize to me. I'll go to my grave with the pain I caused," he says.

"I don't blame you for leaving. Mom drove us all away, and I hate her for it."

"Don't hate your Mother. It's not her fault. There's a lot you don't understand about her," he says.

There isn't anything he could say that would make me hate her less.

"It doesn't matter," I say. "I'm here with you now, and every thing's going to be better."

"Now, the apartment is not quite ready for you to come live with me yet. Everything happened so fast I haven't had time to get you a bed and dresser. Paul and his wife have offered to let you stay with them for a few days. That's the only way I could come get you so fast," Dad tells me.

I can hear the slow, squeaky leak of air seeping out from my pumped-up excitement. It drowns out the words I don't want to hear. The reality of the situation sets in. I should have known. Nothing good happens to me without a hitch or hiccup.

Paul pulls up to a tall rowhome, and Dad starts to get out of the car.

"Come on, Connie, I'll show you the apartment."

"Thanks, Paul. We appreciate all you're doing for us," Dad says to him.

"Glad to help, John. Don't forget dinner's at 6:00," Paul says.

"Here we are," Dad says as we stand in front of the house where his apartment is. It has a lovely big porch to sit on, but only one rocking chair. I memorize the house number on the door, 545. Dad points to the last set of windows at the top of the house.

"That's our apartment," he says.

I like the sound of that, our apartment.

As we walk into the vestibule, a little old lady sticks her head out the door. "Hello, Mr. Miller," she says.

"Hello, Mrs. Musser, this is my daughter Connie I was telling you about," he says.

"Oh, she looks just like you," she says. "You'll have to come down and visit with me during the day when your daddy goes to work. I'll give you a nice cold glass of iced tea and some cookies. It gets pretty hot up there on the third floor in the summer."

"I'd like that," I tell her.

We walk up the first long, narrow flight of steps to a small landing. Another apartment door is to the right of us.

"It smells like someone is cooking spaghetti sauce in there," I say to Dad.

"That's not spaghetti sauce, your smelling." Dad whispers, "It's marijuana."

"Oh!" I say. I don't remember it ever smelling like that.

"But the guy that lives there is nice," he says.

The second landing winds around so that you're going up the next flight of steps right above the first flight. As soon as we step onto the next landing, Dad's apartment door is to the right. The door across from us opens, "Hi, John, this must be Connie," the man says.

"This is Lou Moore. He's my sponsor from Alcoholics Anonymous. He's been a great help to me during my recovery," Dad says.

"Hi, Mr. Moore, it's nice to meet you," I say.

"You can call me Lou," he says. "Come on out here, Barb," he says to the woman peeking her head around the doorway. "This is my fiancée, Barb."

"If you need anything, you let us know," she says with a quiet voice that sounds foreign to me.

"I noticed you have an accent. Are you from another country?" I ask Barb.

"Oh no," she says. I'm from Lebanon County," she says.

"Where's that," I ask.

"About two to three miles from Lancaster," Dad says as they all laugh at me.

"In Lebanon County, the people talk similar to the Amish around here. It's called Pennsylvania Dutch," Barb tells me.

As we enter the apartment to the left of us is the bathroom. It has an old deep clawfoot bathtub, the kind I love to soak in. The toilet is next to it, and a small sink is in the corner. Across from the sink, there is a water heater in the opposite corner. There's a big dresser next to that with a mirror above it.

To the right of the bathroom is a short hallway. The first doorway to the left leads to the living room, and the second doorway straight ahead leads into a large bedroom with old green ivy wallpaper. The two long windows we saw from the outside lookout to the front of the buildings. Another door from the bedroom leads into the living room. It's small and only has one studio couch and a small TV on a stand in the corner. Through the living room, you walk into a small kitchen. There's a door that leads out to a small balcony that Dad opens. It helps bring some air through the apartment. A cute little table with two chairs sits below a window next to the door.

The small stove sits by itself against the back wall. A big walk-in pantry opens at the corner of the next wall. Next to that and across from the table is a little refrigerator. Dad opens it up to show me how small the freezer is. Next to the fridge is a sink attached to the wall, with the pipes exposed below it. A long cabinet going up to the ceiling is on the wall beside the sink, and at the end of the wall hangs a phone with a long curly cord. The old tile floor finish has no design left in it, only scratched marks of yellow and blue remain.

"Look at this," Dad says. He takes me into the pantry, and there's another doorway that leads down two steps into another empty room. "I thought I could insulate the walls and make this your room."

"It's perfect," I say.

"But until then, we're going to have to share the big front room. I could put a bed for you at the other end and get a screen to separate us. How do you feel about that?"

It feels a little creepy to think about, even though he's never given me any reason not to trust him. I can never get out of my mind the friend I had who slept in the same bed with her dad. I found out later that he was doing more than sleeping with her, and even tried to molest me. I don't trust most men, but I do trust my dad.

"If I can sleep in the graveyard, I can share a room with you, Dad."

"You slept in a graveyard?"

"Yeah, I had nowhere else to go. I slept out under a tree in the graveyard overlooking the graves. It was spooky at first, but then after I got used to sitting there, it felt kind of peaceful. I was lucky it was a hot night, and the moon was out so I could see everything pretty good."

He gets tears in his eyes and lowers his head, "I'm so sorry. I guess I can't begin to imagine what you've been through."

I hug him and say, "It doesn't matter anymore. I'm here now, and that's all that matters."

∞ ∞ ∞

Dad and I walk two blocks on Pine Street then turn left onto Chestnut. I love this street with all its shady trees, corner stores, churches, schools, and bars. Most of the houses are attached, but each has its style. Some have big porches, and others open right out to the sidewalk. As we walk farther up the road, the houses become big stately single homes.

"This must be where the rich people live," I say to Dad. "Does Paul live in one of these houses?"

"No, he lives up further on the 200 block where the houses turn back to row homes again. It's nice though because he's so close to the middle of town," he says.

"It's hard for me to imagine living in the city. I guess because when I used to ride the train into Philadelphia, it looked like slums, all dirty and run down," I say.

"Philly is no different than any other city. There're good neighborhoods, and then there are the ones full of poverty. We have our share here, too, but you won't see much of it on our end of town. I go into a lot of those neighborhoods with my job working for the Department of Welfare. I interview families and check out their living conditions to see if they're eligible for temporary welfare income and food stamps."

"That's what I want to do someday, help people who are in need like we were in Philadelphia. Maybe I could help make it better for them. Then they wouldn't have to have their children taken away, like Mary and I were. I want to be a counselor. I help my friends all the time with their problems," I say.

"It's not easy to do what I do. You see a lot of things that you can't change. Things that break your heart, and you have to be able to leave it at work when you go home each day."

"I know about that stuff. I lived it. We were on food stamps for a while. It was embarrassing to go to the store and use them. Everyone would look at us like we were the scum of the earth. It wasn't like we weren't trying. Mom didn't make enough money at the sewing factory, so Kathy and John had to work, too."

"I know," he says, putting his arm around me. "I'm sorry you had to go through that, but there are people who take advantage of the system, which makes it harder on those who need it."

"Oh, wow!" I say as I look at the mansion on the corner of Chestnut and Charlotte street. It's called Lancaster Business School. That's what my major in school is, business training. I wouldn't mind being a secretary, too, but I want to help people."

"Then you should go to college and get your degree so that you can do that," he says.

"I don't think I have good enough grades to get into college. I can barely make it through high school."

"Well, now that you're with me, maybe I can help you with that," he says.

"What's the public high school like here?" I ask.

"It's called McCaskey High School. It's where your mother graduated from," he says. "I'm not sure I want you to go there, though. They've had a lot of racial problems going on this past year. I thought you could go to Lancaster Catholic High School."

"What!" I say, stopping in my tracks. "Catholic school? I can't believe this keeps coming back to haunt me."

"I'm confused," Dad says.

"One of the main reasons I kept running away was to avoid going to Catholic school," I said.

"Why?" he asked.

"Because they'll hold me back a grade."

"Who told you that?"

"Mrs. Becker, my caseworker at Stenton, and Mom. They said my grades were so bad that I'd probably get held back."

"I don't think they'll hold you back in your junior year. Why don't we see what the school has to say, and we'll take it from there?"

"I guess it won't hurt to hear what they have to say. I don't want to go to McCaskey after my experience at Germantown High School."

"You went to Germantown? That's a pretty rough school, I've heard. McCaskey's not that bad. I think you've been through enough. Going to Catholic High might be a little harder academically, but you won't have all the racial tension there. As I said, I can help you with your schoolwork now."

∞ ∞ ∞

"Paul and his family are kind to take me in, God, but I don't want to be here. I'm tired of feeling as if I don't know where I belong. I'm afraid to fall asleep for fear that when I wake up, my day with Dad will turn out to of only been a dream. I know one thing for sure. If it's not a dream, first thing in the morning, I'm going to find my way back to Dad's apartment. I waited too long to be with him. I don't care if he doesn't have a bed for me yet. I'll sleep on the floor if I have to."

God doesn't say anything, but I feel him all around me, and that's all I need to know.

I retrace the same steps that Dad and I took to get to Paul's, only I'm going in the opposite direction. I look at all the houses, churches, stores, and bars as landmarks. When I reach the corner of Pine and West Lemon Street, where Smithgall's Pharmacy is, I know I'm at the right place. Dad's apartment is across the street.

Opening the vestibule door, I quickly press the doorbell. It makes a loud buzzing sound. I don't wait for him to ask who it is. I dash up the steps, hoping to meet him when he opens the door. I'm surprised when I see a woman standing in the doorway.

"Oh, you must be Connie," she says.

"Is my dad here?" I ask.

"Sure, come on in," she says.

She takes me through the living room into the kitchen, where Dad sits reading his newspaper. He jumps up from his chair when he sees me.

"What are you doing here? I told you I'd come and get you later today," he says.

I look at him, and then I look at her. I'm not stupid! "I'm sorry; I didn't know I'd be interrupting anything."

"Would you like some coffee?" she asks me as she fills the coffee pot up with water.

"No, thanks," I say, as I watch how familiar she is with everything.

"This is my friend, Elaine," Dad says. "We met at Eagleville during our recoveries. She stands close to my Dad and holds his hand.

"Your dad's is being shy. We knew each other before that, too," she says.

Dad pulls his hand away from Elaine's and says to her, "I think it's time for you to go."

"But I don't want to leave, John. I thought we were going to talk to Connie together," she says.

"I never said that, Elaine. That's what you wanted to do. I can't take care of you anymore. You've got to start figuring your own life out, the same as I've had to do. Now I have a responsibility to my daughter. I've let her down enough," he says, looking at me.

"But we can take care of her together," she says, "You and I need each other, remember?"

"That was all drunk talk, Elaine. It's time for both of us to go our separate ways. I'm not the person that can give you the help you need. That's your sponsor's job."

Elaine grabs her stuff and storms out the door, slamming it shut so hard it shakes the walls. A few minutes later, we hear a knock at the door.

"What the hell's going on, John?" Lou says.

Dad gives him the lowdown, and Lou invites us both in for some coffee.

Lou and Barb's apartment is tiny but cozy. We sit in their living room, and Barb offers us a coffee. They have a little air conditioner in the window. It's much cooler than Dad's place. I sure don't understand why anyone would want to drink coffee when it's so hot.

"John, I've told you time and again that Elaine is bad news for you. She's only going to pull you down with her. You've come too far for that. Now you have a chance to make something right in your life by taking care of Connie. That's what the twelve-step program is all about."

"Dad, I can't go back to Paul's house," I tell him. "I've waited so long to find you. Now that I'm here, I'm afraid if I don't hold tight onto you that someone's going to snatch me away from you. I can sleep on your couch or the floor until we get a bed, but please don't send me back there."

"There's a house around the corner on Pine St that's having a garage sale today," Barb says. "I read in the morning paper that they have a bed and dresser for sale."

"Here, John," Lou says as he pulls his wallet out and hands him $25.00. "It's all I have to spare right now, but maybe it will help."

"Thanks, Lou," Dad says, "I'll pay you back as soon as I can."

"Let's go now, Dad, before it's gone," I say.

"Thank you," I say to Barb and Lou as I hug them. "You're like two angels sent from God."

"Oh, I'm no angel. I've had my share of wrongdoing, but helping others is good for the soul, that's for sure," Lou says.

We go around the corner, and there's a single bed leaning up against the porch pillar. The man says it's a bunk bed set, and he wanted to sell them together. Dad tells him we don't need them both and would pay him half price for the one. The guy says no.

"Please, Mister," I say. "I just came to live with my dad after not seeing him for a long time. The Department of Child Welfare is going to take me away from him if I don't have a bed of my own to sleep in."

"Jay," a woman calls out from behind the screen door, "give that poor girl that bed for $25.00, and the dresser that goes with it. Where do you live, honey?" she asks, coming out to help.

"Right around the corner," I say.

"Boys, come on out here and help carry this stuff for these people. These are our two sons, Jake and Willy," she introduces them. They look about twelve and fourteen years old but strong enough to help us. "Is there anything else you'll be needing, honey? I have a few clothes here that you can look through. Take whatever you need. What doesn't sell is going to Goodwill anyway."

"Thank you so much," I say. "All I have are the clothes I'm wearing," I say.

"You poor thing. I won't ask where you been, but it looks like you've come home again."

I look through the clothes and find a few summer dresses that are small enough to fit me. That gives me three different outfits to wear off and on for the week. I can wash them by hand if I have to and hang them out on the balcony. I brought a few pairs of underwear with me when I left Maggie's. Now I can keep ahead of them, too, until we go to the laundromat.

"Here's a pair of sheets that go with the bed and a blanket too," the lady says as she hands them to me.

Dad gives me one of his tee-shirts to wear to bed and his robe to cover myself as I go from the bathroom to bed. A fan blows cool air into our room, and I lay there looking up at the ceiling with a sheet covering me.

"Thank You, God. You kept Your promise, just like you said You would. I'm finally here, living with Dad. It's the beginning of my second half of life, almost anyway. It'd be nice to be a regular teenager for a while before I dive back into the adult world. Like the lady around the corner said, I've come home again."

∞ ∞ ∞

Dad kisses my forehead before he leaves for work. It triggers the last memory I have before he left four years ago. I'm as sleepy as I was that day, where I'm between my dreams and real life, but fear awakens me before he goes out the door, and I call out to him,

"Don't leave me, Dad."

He comes back and sits on the side of my bed.

"I'm only going to work," he says as he holds my hand. "I'll be home after 5:00, and we'll go to the Italian Villa for dinner. Then to Pantry Pride for some groceries."

I hold onto him tightly, "Promise?" I say

"I promise. I have to go now before my ride leaves. Get some rest. You've been through a lot."

I fall back to sleep and wake up around 11:00 am. My body aches all over, so I decide to soak in the tub, filling it up as high as it will go. Lying back, I relax until my toes begin to turn white and wrinkly, a sure sign it's time to get out. As I pull the plug, the sound of the water going down the drain reminds me of the bath Nurse Jones gave me the first day I went to Stenton Child Care Center. I begin to shake all over as I stand watching the dirty water swirl around the mouth of the drain. The lower the water gets, the louder the gulps become until all the fragments of my old life go down the throat of the pipe, and there is nothing left but the sound of silence.

Wrapped in my towel, I sit on the edge of the tub, my hair dripping, the same as it did that day. It's the faint sound of birds outside the window that brings me back to where I am.

"You are all right, now, Connie. All that was is in the past, and this is your new beginning," God says.

"Yeah, you're right, God," I say with new excitement. "I just wish I didn't feel so afraid that I'll get taken away from Dad."

"Trust!"

I slip on my new pink, sleeveless shift dress. The one I got from the lady at the garage sale. It fits perfectly, but I can only see in the mirror from my shoulders up. So, I put the toilet seat down and stand on top of it. Now I can see from my shoulders down below my knees. It looks nice, but too long. I can fix that with a needle and thread.

I rummage through my purse for my comb. It's the same one I got that first day at Stenton. It was the only thing that I felt was mine after that day. As I start to comb my hair, it doesn't feel like straw the way it did then. It is in pretty bad shape, though, from all the hair dye I've used in the past year.

I look around the apartment, checking in drawers for a needle and thread. I see some cigarette butts in the ashtray. Dad's a chain smoker, lighting up one cigarette after the other. I find a butt that looks half-smoked. I've been so desperate for a cigarette ever since I've been here. I straighten it out and light it up, coughing after taking a drag. I don't know how he can stand these unfiltered Pall Malls. I need to tell Dad I smoke. I don't want to sneak around. I want everything to be upfront and honest between us. I'll tell him at dinner this evening. My list of things I need at the store is getting bigger, needles, thread, toothbrush, deodorant, and cigarettes.

As it gets closer to 5:00, I go downstairs and sit on the steps to wait for Dad. Isn't it funny? I think to myself; I used to do the same thing when we lived in California. I spent most of my time outside away from Mom and her crazy moods. Sometimes I'd play with the roly-poly bugs, letting them roll around in my hand. They are one of the few bugs I will touch. Sometimes I'd sit on the edge of the garden, smelling the alyssum flowers. I thought they looked like tiny fairy bouquets. Or I'd sit on the curb by the road watching the ants going one way and coming back with their load of treasures on their back. There's nothing but sidewalk and streets to see. It doesn't take long, though, before I get into people watching. They go in and out of Smithgall's Pharmacy. Some come out licking ice cream cones. I could go for an ice cream cone on this hot day myself. What am I thinking? I could go for ice cream in any weather. I even get into watching the cars go by, but what I take the most interest in is the house across the street where there are a lot of cute guys coming and going. A few characters sit out on the porch laughing and having a good time.

A car pulls up in front of our house, and Dad gets out.

"This is my friend Sandy from work," he tells me.

"Hi, Connie, I heard all about you. I can't wait to get to know you better. We'll have dinner sometime. Goodbye, now," she waves, driving off.

"Are you ready?" he asks me.

"I'm starving," I tell him.

We turn left at the corner of West Lemon onto Pine Street, walking one block to James. We pause for a moment as Dad points to the left, "See those buildings down there. That's Franklin & Marshall College."

"Is that the one you went to?" I ask.

"Yes, I'll show you around on another day. My fraternity is down that way too. Phi Kappa Psi," he says as we turn to the right and continue walking.

"Wow! I didn't realize the college was that close. That must be the reason I saw a bunch of guys coming and going from the house across the street," I say.

"They call that place the Zoo. They have some pretty wild parties there. We used to have some, too, at my fraternity, but we had rules to follow. Those guys do whatever they like."

We walk about five blocks until we come to the corner of James & Mulberry Streets, where we walk into the Italian Villa Restaurant.

"Ya' know, Dad, nothing seems that far away when we're walking and talking together." I get my favorite meal, spaghetti with meatballs.

"What do you think?" Dad asks me.

"It was okay, but I still like the way my Mom makes it the best."

"That's the first time I've heard you say something nice about your mother."

"I still hate her."

"I wish you wouldn't say that. Your mother can't help the way she is."

"You keep saying that, but I don't understand how a grown-up can't help the way they act. I thought when you grew up; you became more responsible. Being my age, I can't help the way I act because I'm still learning how to grow up."

"Grownups are supposed to be more responsible, but the process of learning that doesn't simply stop because you become an adult. I should have known better and been more responsible, but your mother has mental health issues that you don't understand."

"Then help me understand why she calls me a slut, beats me when I walk in the house, accuses me of doing things I've never done. She hates me, and I don't know why, except that I remind her of you. Or is it because of what happened to her after I was born? Is that why she hates me so much?"

"So, you know about her breakdown back then?"

"No, I know that something happened, but I don't know what."

"You were three months old; Kathy was four and Johnny three. I'd come home from work and find my clothes folded neatly in my drawers, but they'd be soaking wet. Another day the whole back of her dress was burned as if she'd leaned against the stove. Finally, one day, I came home and found her in a catatonic state."

"What's that?" I asked.

"You know how Johnny used to play with his robot? He could turn it on and off; well, that's what it was like. It was as if something had turned her off, and all she did was sit and stare into space. She was non-responsive to my voice and movements. I had to call the ambulance and sign papers to have her committed to a mental hospital. It was one of the hardest things I'd ever had to do, but she needed help. She had to have shock treatments by someone as a child. The doctors concluded from the way your mother talked, that someone molested her as a child. That's why I think she is so paranoid about what you're doing and why she accuses you of doing slutty things. They diagnosed her as a paranoid schizophrenic and said the shock treatments would help her forget. Eventually, it would all come back, and she'd need the treatment repeated. I could never get her to go back and see another doctor about her mental state."

"Yeah, and us kids suffered for it. If she had gotten help, maybe things would've been different. Maybe you wouldn't have drunk so bad and left us. Maybe Mary and I would have never gone to Stenton. You know we were put in there because she supposedly had a nervous breakdown, but she never got any help. She just went on with her life, as you did."

"I can't make excuses for myself, but there are things that happen to us sometimes that are out of our control. When the alcohol gets hold of me, I feel like I can't get away from its grip. It's the same with your mother's mental illness. When you don't think you need help, there's no reason to seek it. You keep living in your distortion."

"How did you find your way out?"

"I ended up in the hospital. I was killing myself with alcohol. When I got through the worst of my detox, it was as if I'd awakened the day after I left all of you. The pain I caused you kids, and your mother was so unbearable all I wanted was to drink to forget. I didn't care if I drank myself to death. Now, every day, I have to say no to one more drink."

"Would you like any dessert?" the waitress asks us.

Dad looks at me, and I shake my head, no. "I'll take a little more coffee," he says. As I watch him light another one of his Pall Malls, I ask if I can have one, too.

He pauses for a moment, then pulls one out. I put it between my lips, and he strikes a match, holding it up for me. I take a drag and cough a little. "How can you stand these unfiltered cigarettes?" I ask.

"It's what I've always smoked. I like unfiltered cigarettes, the same as I like my coffee black."

"I like my cigarettes with filters, and my coffee with lots of milk and sugar."

"So, when did you start smoking?"

"About the same time, you left us. The smell of smoke always made me feel somehow closer to you."

"I'll have to get you a pack of your own when we go to the store," he says.

"That's good. It was one of the things I had on my list."

Our walk back to the apartment was quiet. After shopping, Dad carried two double-lined paper bags with handles, one in each hand, full to the top with all we need until he gets paid again on Friday.

I don't' know about him, but that dinner gave me more to digest than just-food. One thing I learned for sure, being grown-up doesn't mean you stop having problems. It seems like everyone's still trying to find their way the same as I've been doing these past few years.

"Ya' know, Dad, I thought when you grew up, life would be easier."

"Life is what you make it, but it always takes work. Sometimes the work is harder than other times, but if you keep your eyes set on what you want, you can make anything happen."

"That's what I believe. That's what got me this far. I kept believing that someday you'd find me, and here we are."

"How did you learn how to have so much faith?"

"I talk to God all the time. No matter how mad I'd get at God for all the things that happened, I still held on tight to Him, because I was afraid if I let go of God, I'd lose myself as well."

Dad puts the bags down for a moment, pulls his hankie out, wipes his eyes, and blows his nose.

"Are you okay, Dad?" I ask.

"I'm fine," he says, as he picks the bags back up. "I got a little something in my eye."

∞ ∞ ∞

We open the door to the vestibule, and Mrs. Musser comes out, telling us there was a lot of commotion upstairs while we were out.

"Then I saw that woman that used to visit you come running out," she goes on.

"Elaine," Dad says.

When we get to the second set of steps, my dresser, bed frame, and mattress are lying at the bottom.

"How the hell did she climb over all this?"

"Never mind that. How the hell did she pick it all up and throw it down here?" I ask.

"She's drinking and mad. When you put the two together, a person can get pretty crazy," Dad says.

"What the hell happened here?" Lou asks as he and Barb come walking up behind us.

"Elaine!" Dad says.

"I told you that woman's bad news," Lou says.

"Are you going to help me here, or keep rubbing that fact in?" Dad asks him.

"Don't you worry," Barb says, as she puts her arm around me. "Lou and your daddy will put everything back together. They won't let that woman hurt you."

"She better not come around here again," I say.

"Maybe you should call the police, John," Barb says.

"I think you should, too," Lou says.

"I'm not calling the police on her," Dad says.

"I don't want the police involved, either; they might take me away from dad, saying it's not safe for me here," I say.

"Then I'm taking you out to buy a new lock for the door, so she doesn't come back when you're not here and bother Connie," Lou says.

"I know where she is," Dad says.

"Where? The "Town Tavern" down the street? Now is not a good time to be going in that place, John," Lou says.

"Sometimes, you're in my business too much, Lou."

"That's what a sponsor is supposed to do, John. Besides, you have Connie to take care of now. I'll go with you," Lou says.

"No, stay here, so I know Connie's safe until I get back," Dad says.

Lou looks at Dad for a few minutes and shakes his head like he gives up. Soon after they put everything back in our apartment, Dad leaves.

"Let me know if you need anything, Connie. We'll be right across the hall," Lou says.

I put everything away, then sit down for a smoke, thinking about what happened. I wonder what it is between Dad and Lou that there's no trust. I'm too restless to watch TV, so I start taking the hem out of the other summer dress I got from the garage sale. It's so hot that I turn the overhead light on in the bedroom and sit on the tile floor in front of the fan while I sew the hem. Dad's been gone for an hour now. I hope he's okay. He has to be tired after working all day and doing all we did afterward.

It's almost midnight when I go to bed. Dad is still not home, and I can't go to sleep until I know he's back. Lying in bed, I think about our conversation at dinner about Mom's illness, trying to understand how a person can't control their thoughts and actions. Then I think about what Dad said about his drinking problems. How it only takes one drink for the alcohol to get a hold of him, and he can't break loose once it does.

I hear the front door open and close below, the tap of footsteps getting closer, the key in the lock, the door opening and closing slowly. Dad goes right into the bathroom. I can hear him washing up, brushing his teeth. He walks lightly into the room. I pretend to be asleep. I hear the springs of his mattress squeak as he sits on the side of his bed, taking his shoes off, the jingle of his belt as he slips his slacks off, and then more squeaks and scrunches as he gets situated in bed. In no time, he's snoring. Now I can go to sleep, too.

"So, what did you do with your day?" Dad asks, sitting beside me on the step.

"There's not much to do. I don't know anyone. It's too hot to be upstairs, but I don't mind sitting down here on the steps. Mrs. Musser came out with some of her sweet ice tea. I told her it was the best I ever had. She told me it was her husband's favorite, too. When I said to her, "You must miss him a lot," her eyes teared up. I didn't mean to make her sad, but when she started talking about him, her face lit up. She said he was the love of her life, and he treated her like she was the most precious woman in the world."

"That's the kind of love I want to find someday, Dad. I've watched a lot of movies about love stories, and all the fairy tales come true. To hear a true-life story gives me hope that maybe I can find it someday, too."

"I have a book you might like to read called *As A Man Thinketh* by James Allen, He says, and I quote,

"Dreams are the seedlings of realities."

"It's not easy to keep those dreams alive when you feel like you're living in a nightmare," I say.

"But somehow you kept finding your way back to the hope, dreams, and desires of your heart."

"I couldn't have done it without God and his promise to me."

"What is this promise you keep talking about?"

"It seems like I was always talking to God in one way or another. One day when I came home from school, Mom was in one of her moods. I was so sick of feeling scared all the time. I was outside like I'd been most days, waiting for you to come home from work. It was one of those California days when the air felt cool, but the sun felt warm. The cement porch was too cool to sit on. So I walked over to the old Dodge sitting in the driveway, figuring I could get inside and warm up. But I saw the sun reflected off its black color and sat on the back fender instead, slowly adjusting to the heat as I leaned against the sloped back."

"Wow, you remember every detail," Dad says.

"Have you ever experienced a miracle, Dad? Something so unexplainable that after a while, you wonder if it's true? Yet you know it has to be true because there's a part of it that never goes away. God showed me what my life was going to be like in the days to come. I didn't remember any of the details, only that it was going to get worse. He promised me that if I stayed strong and held in there, that I could make my life the way I wanted it to be. All I had to do was hang on to His promise. Even though I know God isn't a person, His presence was always with me. He was the only one who didn't leave me, even when I was angry with Him. He'd remind me over and again that someday I could make my life the way I dreamed it could be."

"That's what James Allen says in his book,

"Dream lofty dreams, and as you dream, so shall you become."

"I don't normally like to read books, but that sounds interesting."

"Reading will help you to do better in school. We'll have to go to the library and find some other books for you to read to get you through the rest of the summer," he says.

"Could I have some writing paper and envelopes, too? I wanted to write to my friends but couldn't find anything to use."

"Let's go upstairs. I'll fry us up hamburgers for dinner. Then, after the news, we can walk around the college. We can go to the campus store there and pick up some writing paper and envelopes for you."

∞ ∞ ∞

Two blocks up West Lemon Street, we cross over College Avenue. Dad points out the North Museum and tells me they have a neat planetarium where you can sit back and look up at the stars. We proceed up College Avenue toward the grand entrance to Franklin and Marshall College.

Wow! Never mind the cool old buildings. Look at all these cute college guys everywhere. Wait till I tell Mary Faith and all my other friends. They'll want to visit me for sure now.

"Where are all the girls?" I ask Dad.

"It's a male college, but they're talking about making it co-ed starting this coming semester," he says.

"It's not very big," I say to him.

"That's what makes it nice. There's more opportunity for everyone to participate. I loved debating and the various subjects we were learning. You'd never be able to do that in a large class," he says.

As we continue through the campus, Dad points out the place where married couples lived. "Your mother and I lived here for my last year of college. I had some pictures of us living here," he said. "They were in the old album I used to have."

"Wally kept them for us when we left California," I told him. "He eventually sent them to Mom. I guess she still has them. I used to love looking at your old albums. You always looked like you were having a good time like you were happy back then."

"It was an exciting time in my life," he says.

We go into the college store, and I get my paper, envelopes, and some stamps for my letter writing.

"Let's walk down James Street, and I'll show you the fraternity where I lived before your mother, and I got married." We stand in front of a big old house at the corner of Pine and James Street with a sign above the porch that reads, "Phi Kappa Psi."

"What do the words mean?" I asked him.

"It stands for a brotherhood of honorable men who pledge to live up to a standard for the good of all. I'm afraid I failed in my commitment when I was a drunk, but in my sobriety, it is a pledge I aspire to live by in heart."

"I always admire how smart you are, Dad, but when you drink, it's like you become a clown, and all your smartness becomes a joke."

"You are very perceptive for your age, Connie, but I guess you've had to grow up faster than most kids," he says.

"The only smarts I have, Dad, are the ones I've learned about how to survive."

"That makes you a hands-on learner rather than one who learns better from books. That's okay. Everyone learns in their way."

"Yeah, but we're all expected to pass the same test and are graded by that outcome."

"Good point," he says. "However, I still think if you could enjoy reading, you'd be surprised what you'll begin to retain and comprehend."

"Well, I sure have plenty of time to give it a try the rest of this summer with nothing much else to do, "I say.

∞ ∞ ∞

Dad says the more I read, the better I'll do at school

He has a box of books I can look through in the unfinished room off the kitchen. I get distracted from my mission and start looking around the room, thinking, I can't wait for Dad to fix it up for me. I imagine exactly where I'll put my bed and dresser. I bet it would be cooler back here, too, since the big maple tree in the backyard lies over the roof. I could even have a chair in the corner with a lamp or maybe a desk to do my homework. Maybe I could just put posters all over the walls and cover the insulation. Then Dad wouldn't have to worry about putting a bunch of drywall up. I open the back door, and It pulls the stuffy hot air out of the room, creating a gentle breeze from the front windows of the apartment. The doorway leads out onto the roof of the deck below us out. I sit up against the wall that leads up to the main roof. The branches of the tree form a canopy of shade, and I feel as if I'm sitting in a treehouse. It is so peaceful and quiet, compared to being out front where all the action happens.

I go through the books, pulling out one at a time, *Great Expectations* by Dickens, *The Odyssey* by Homer, *In Tune with The Infinite* by Trine, *Testimony of Two Men* by Caldwell. Hmm, that might be good. At the bottom of the box, I find the book I'm looking for *As A Man Thinketh* by James Allen. I love it just because it's a little bigger than my hand and only 72 pages. I flip through it, reading a few lines as I sit out on the roof. Dad says when you read a book, every detail is essential from cover to cover. So I look at each page, flipping through reading this verse and that until one touches the depth of my soul, that puts the meaning of God's promise into word, on page 60:

"Cherish your vision; cherish your ideals; cherish the music that stirs in your heart, the beauty that forms in your mind, the loveliness that drapes your purest thoughts, for out of them will grow all delightful conditions, all heavenly environment; of these if you but remain true to them, your world will, at last, be built."

"Dreams are the seedlings of realities."

All this time, I held onto God's Promise even though it never seemed possible, I kept it alive in my dreams and thoughts. It's all about remaining true to God's promise for me, and most of all, believing in the actual possibility.

Wow! I never knew I could understand anything as deep as this. Maybe Dad is right; reading can help me to learn better.

The Promise

Chapter 17 - August 1969

"What are you doing up already?" Dad asks me.

"I'm excited to go shopping in town today and couldn't sleep," I tell him.

Dad flips the calendar over and says, "Today's August 1st.

"I've only been here for three weeks, but it seems like so much longer," I say.

"Yeah, it does," he says as he jots a few appointments on the calendar. "We have a few things coming up this month," he shows me. Monday the 4th, we go to Sacred Heart Church to talk with Father Taylor about registering you for Lancaster Catholic High School. Thursday the 7th, your caseworker from Philadelphia is coming to meet with us so she can close your case."

"That makes me nervous," I say. "I don't want anything more to do with those people. Why can't they do it over the phone."

"They just want to make sure you're all right," Dad says.

"They didn't care all that time I was away living with Maggie. Why should they care now?"

"When the Department of Child Welfare takes a kid away from their parents, they don't make it easy to get you back," he says.

"But that's what scares me. What if Miss Dolly says our living arrangements aren't good enough?" I ask.

"After all you told me about Mrs. Matthews' conversation with them, I think they want nothing more than to put your case to rest. Don't worry; it will be fine.

"I would be so happy if I never had to worry about them taking me away again. So, if the Department of Child Welfare does close my case, we'll have to celebrate my freedom," I say with a smile.

"I have to get going," Dad says. "You know the stores don't open until around 9:00 am?"

"I know, but I couldn't sleep thinking about my new adventure in town."

"How about if I meet you for lunch at Greens? It's on the corner of Queen and Orange Streets."

"Isn't that a store?" I ask.

"Yes, but they have a restaurant in there too, and they make the best meatloaf and mashed potatoes."

"Groovy," I say. "I'll see you there at noon."

I leave at 8:00 and start walking up West Lemon Street toward town. I'm glad I'm going early in the morning while it's still cool. The walking is making me sweat already. Nothing is open yet, so I walk around looking in the windows of J.C. Penney's, Garvin's, Sears, Watt & Shand, Hager's, Woolworth's, and various little shops in between. For a small town, they sure do have lots of places to shop. I go into Watt & Shand, but I want to get the most for my money, and they seem expensive. I walk across the street to a little shop called Logan's. An older lady comes up, asking if I need any help.

"I'm just looking right now," I tell her.

"Well, my name is Mary Rife. If you need anything, let me know," she says.

I don't even know what size I am. I never actually shopped in a real clothing store without Mom. I find this striped tunic and matching skirt I like. I look around some more but keep coming back to the tunic outfit. Mrs. Rife brings over a white short-sleeved shirt and says, "This would go perfectly with that, but that size might be too big for you."

There isn't anything smaller, so she pulls out a bright green skirt and says, "Now this would look nice on you with your green eyes. Why don't you try it on?"

I look at the tunic outfit. My heart sets on getting it, so I take both in to try on with the blouse. The skirt is cute and short the way I like it, but it's not what I'm looking to buy. I love the tunic outfit. It is big on me, but I can get away with it because it's supposed to be loose fitting anyway.

"How's it going in there," Mrs. Rife asks.

I come out smiling and tell her I'll take the tunic outfit and blouse.

I watch as she rings it up. She is so well put together in her navy-blue dress and matching heels, yet so grandma likes with her white bun on top of her head. She wears red lipstick and matching nail polish. There's something comfortable about being in her presence. She isn't pushy and knows how to treat customers. I'll be back here for sure.

As I am walking out the door, I ask her what time it is? "10:00 am," she says.

I pause to think about what I'm going to do for two hours.

"Can you tell me where the library is?" I ask her.

"You go straight down King Street here until you come to Duke. Right at that corner is the courthouse. Turn left. You'll see the library on the other side of the road. You can't miss it," she says.

"You're not from these parts?" she asks.

"No, I just moved here from Philadelphia to live with my dad three weeks ago. I'm learning my way around. I'm supposed to meet him at Green's for a hot lunch."

"The library will be a good place to go then to kill some time and find a good book to read," she says. "I hope you'll come back and visit us again."

"Oh, I will, Mrs. Rife, you've been very helpful. By now," I say. I mosey down the road, still looking in the windows of the shops I pass. Garvin's has their fall display out already. Looking at wearing warmer clothes in the hottest month of summer somehow doesn't appeal to me, but I guess it's a good way of reminding people of the upcoming season. I don't even have a winter coat or boots for snow. I should think about getting a job so I can help Dad out and get the things I need.

What a neat old library! I have no idea where to look or what I want to read. I ask the lady at the desk where I can find the books that Dad mentioned to me, and how many I can take out. She asks me if I have a library card.

"No, I don't," I say.

She gives me an index card to fill out, and that's all there is to it.

"Congratulations," the librarian says to me. "You are now the proud owner of your very first library card."

I feel as if I've gotten the very first important card I'll ever own. I can take out four books at a time and return them in four weeks. I have no trouble browsing around all the different sections of books. I have to carry whatever I take out all the way home, so I only get two paperback books.

"You amaze me," Dad says. "I'm proud of how you took the initiative to get your very own library card.

"I've been doing things like this on my own for a long time, Dad. I may not always know how to do things, but I'm not afraid to try or to ask for help."

"What books did you get?" He asks.

"I got the ones you mentioned to me, *I Never Promised You a Rose Garden,* by Hannah Green, and *A Man's Search for Meaning,* by Viktor Frankl.

"Great choices," he says.

Dad was right. The meatloaf, mashed potatoes, and dark gravy are so tasty; I want more.

∞ ∞ ∞

Waiting to cross the street at the corner of Nevin and Walnut Street, Dad and I stand beside the Sacred Heart Convent; I look up at a gray stately Catholic church in front of me. The words "Church of the Sacred Heart of Jesus" are carved deeply into the ornate doorway. It's not a not very big, more like a smaller version of a grand church.

"Is that the Catholic school I'll be attending? I point to the one across Nevin Street.

"No. That's Reynolds Junior High School. Your mother went to that school before attending McCaskey High," he tells me.

"Where is the Catholic High School?"

"You'll have to take a bus to get to it, but Father Taylor will fill in all the details for us. Come on," Dad says, "I want to show you something," and I follow him as we walk behind the church. "See this building here," he points up to a red brick building, this used to be the old Sacred Heart Church. It's where your mother and I got married. I used to have pictures of your mother and I standing at the top of the steps after our wedding."

"I remember those pictures," I say. I wish I had those pictures to look at now. You and Mom have quite a history here."

"This is where it all started for us," he said.

"You look happy when you talk about it. You must have loved each other back then," I said.

"We were very much in love," he said.

"Do you think there's a chance that you would ever get back together?"

"No. That candle blew out for us a long time ago. Too much between us now. Too many issues of our own to deal with," Dad said.

Dad looks at his watch, saying, "We still have some time kill. Why don't we go inside the church where it's cooler until it's time for our appointment?"

We open the tall doors and step into the vestibule. It's not as traditional as most old churches are. The lights are dim, giving the shiny cobblestone aisle the effect of a tunnel becoming brighter as it leads toward the altar. A ray of light shining brightly through the stained-glass windows illuminates the gold pillars and the tabernacle in the middle of the altar. We dip our fingers in the holy water fonts out of habit and bless ourselves with the sign of the cross. We genuflect toward the Eucharist locked inside the gold skirted tabernacle, blessing ourselves again before slipping into the last pew. I look at the murals that stand out around the tapestry. There is no happy face one would expect to see in the presence of God. We sit in the cool quietness, taking it all in. The smell of incense lingers in the air as if it's seeped into the walls of the church. Candles flicker in front of the statues of the holy family. I wonder why Mary and Joseph look so sad holding the baby Jesus.

"I remember watching Grandma and Aunt Honey kneeling in front of the statue of blessed Mary after lighting a few candles. Their rosaries dangled from their hands and their mouths moved a mile a minute as they looked up at Mary with such devotion. I knew that I wanted the kind of faith they had; at that moment, they looked so beautiful," I whisper to Dad.

"But you do have it. I hear and feel it in you when you express your relationship with God. My mother and sister are two of the most faith-filled people I know. They are honest, true, and live what they believe in every part of their lives. We all have different ways of finding God. Some people find it in the church; some find it in everything around them. That's what you have. Don't ever doubt the faith you have," he says.

"Why'd you stop going to church, Dad?"

"I don't know. At some point, I started to question what I believed. I feel like I'm still looking for answers. The one thing I do believe for sure is that there is a God, a creator of all things, and we're a part of it."

I look over at another statue where the candles flicker beside it. It's Mary holding her son Jesus, lying dead across her lap.

"I always feel an overwhelming sadness inside the church," I say.

"Yes, something is alluring and beautiful about the Catholic church that pulls you within. However, at the same time, you feel the heaviness and darkness that conger up fear," he says.

"That's exactly how I feel, but what if we're wrong? What if we are supposed to fear God? I can't imagine believing in a God like that. Isn't that more the way humans think, that God is so angry with us that he demands we be and do as he says, or else? If that's true, then God would have said good riddance to me a long ago," I said.

"Me too," Dad says. "I think there's something much greater about a God who created the heavens and earth than we give him credit for," he says. "I think we spend our lifetime searching for the answers. That's why we're here in this world."

A priest comes in from the side doorway and walks over to us. "Are you the Millers? he asks. "I'm Father Taylor."

Dad looks at his watch, apologizing for overlooking the time. Father Taylor says, "No problem. Let's go into my office." We follow him back through the side door from where he came through. It leads right into the rectory.

Dad tells Father Taylor a short version of our story and how I've come to live with him.

"Connie's been through so much and hasn't done well in school because of it. I was hoping with my help and a healthy school atmosphere that we could make her last two years of school her best."

"I think I can work with that, but I have a few conditions," Father Taylor says. "Mr. Miller, you have to continue going to your AA meetings. I think Connie should go to some counseling. I could get her in to see a counselor over at Janet Avenue, right next to Catholic High. She could go right after school. And you both must attend Sunday mass."

"What do you think?" Dad asks me.

"I'd be willing if you are, Dad."

"Then it's a done deal," Dad shakes Father Taylor's hand.

He hands me some papers to read all about the school.

"School starts September 2, the day after Labor Day. You'll be needing to get a uniform to wear. We have some used ones you can get at the school. I'll be keeping an eye on you; I'm the principal there, you know. Anytime you need to talk, come to my office," he says.

∞ ∞ ∞

"I see you have your books here. Can't you decide which one to read first?" Dad asks as he sits beside me on the front porch steps.

"I feel so distracted like my mind is going a mile a minute," I say.

"What are you thinking about?"

"Lots of things. Sometimes I sit and think about all I've been through, the things I did. Where I got the nerve to run away, live with a stranger, stand up for myself, and not fall apart in the middle of it all. Then I start thinking about the feelings I had in church the other day, wondering if I've been creating a God for myself that isn't real. Maybe I should have feared Him all along. The thing is when my life was at its worst, and I was angry at God, He never left me, even though I pushed him away. He kept on loving me, believing in me, and giving me hope. Then I suddenly understood what God is."

"What's that?" Dad asks.

"Love! It's beyond anything we can understand, but you know what? God teaches us in a way we each can understand if we're open to it. That got me thinking if we can love with our limited human abilities, how much greater Gods' love must be for us in all His perfection. But then I hear a voice in my head saying, what if you're wrong? How can I know something to be so true in my heart, and turn around and question it? See, I think that's why we humans should stop trying to figure out God and concentrate more on who He created us to be."

"As I said in church the other day, those are the questions I believe we are here on this earth to find answers for," Dad says. "You know, for someone who finds the book "As a Man Thinketh" deep, you are pretty deep yourself."

"I don't want to wait a lifetime to find the answers, though. I want to figure them out now. Maybe there's more to learn at church than I'm giving it a chance to teach me. I'm not even sure if I want to be Catholic, but maybe since I've never given it a chance, it's a place to start. I haven't made my mind up yet, but I'm giving it some serious thought," I say.

"You know, life is full of lessons. It seems as if as soon as we learn one thing, we find ourselves on another path, learning something new and different each time. There are many journeys we go on through life," he says.

"Talk about lessons! I had an interesting one today, talking with Mrs. Musser that was pretty educational," I say as I chuckle.

"Oh, this should be good," he says, laughing.

"Don't look over there right away, but you know that place across the street?"

"You mean the Zoo?" Dad asks.

"Yeah. Every time I come out here to sit, the same guy is sitting out there, too. He's usually messing around with the other guys, but he's been checking me out lately. So, he came over and asked if I wanted to go for a walk with him. We walked over to F&M's football stadium and sat on the bleachers. He turned to me and asked if I wanted to have sex with him."

"Did he touch you? Which one is it? I'll show him a thing or two messing with my little girl."

"Calm down, Dad! Let me finish," I say.

"I told him he was nothing but a small-minded little boy and that I thought college guys would be more mature than the ones in high school."

He says to me, "The difference between a boy and man is we don't waste time, we get right to the point of things."

"I said, you're no man. You're nothing but a stupid jerk, and I walked away, leaving him standing there with his tail between his legs. I got the feeling he was not used to girls saying no to him. He was pretty good looking."

"Oh, my God, Connie, the things that come out of your mouth," he says, laughing.

"What comes out of my mouth! You should hear what Mrs. Musser said to me. When I got back here and sat down, she came out with her ice tea. It was perfect timing. I was hot and thirsty.

"How's your day going, dearie?" she asked me. "You look deep in thought today."

"Mrs. Musser, I don't understand why boys treat us girls like we're a dog in heat?" I asked her.

"My mommy told me once that men need to try each woman on for size, like buying a pair of shoes and trying to find the perfect fit," she says.

I burst out laughing so hard it brought tears to my eyes, and she was laughing just as hard right along with me.

"Well now, you learned something new, and that's one I never heard before," he says, laughing.

∞ ∞ ∞

How'd your visit with Miss Dolly go?" Dad asked me.

"She told me that Mom knows I'm living with you now. She wants to bring Mary to visit you."

"Yes, Miss Dolly asked me when I saw her if it was all right. I need to do this with each of you. It's what I requested in the letter I sent to your mother. It's the most painful part of my recovery, facing each of you, even your mother. The very thought of it makes me want to drink. That's why I need to get on the other side of this. It's the only real way, I believe, I can have a clean start. I know it will be hard for you to see your mother after all this time, but in a way, it's like taking your first step toward forgiveness and recovery from all that's happened to you," he says.

"I guess it's time, but I'm still uncomfortable with the idea. I'm not sure I want a relationship with Mom," I say.

Dad opens his wallet and takes a little card out, "This is the serenity prayer we say at AA."

> God Grant me the serenity
> To accept the things I cannot change,

The courage to change the things I can,

And the wisdom to know the difference.

By Reinhold Niebuhr

"Keep it," he says as he hands it to me. "I know it by heart. It's a simple prayer that helps us put things into perspective," he says to me.

"I asked Miss Dolly if Mom was planning on getting back together with you. She said that you and Mom have two challenging conditions of your own to **work** through, that if you got back together, you'd both most likely drag each other down,"

"At Eagleville, I learned that becoming sober and staying that way means you have to make changes in your life. Your mother didn't drive me to drink, and I didn't cause her mental illness. Once our diseases came out in full swing, it was as if we kept each other infected by them. It was easier to blame each other for our conditions than to admit that we each had our problems. That's the first step in the twelve-step program, to admit we are powerless over our addiction, that our lives have become unmanageable as a result of that. In my case, every day, I have to make a choice not to take that first drink. But in your mother's case with mental illness, she can't choose to be mentally sane. It's easier for her to blame everyone else for the way she acts. If she could admit that she's powerless over her condition, it would be the first step toward recovery for her, too. But you can't change what you can't see," he says.

"I don't think she'll ever admit she needs help. She's too afraid of what would happen to her if she did," I say.

"I think you're right about that. Plus, mental illness has such a stigma to it that many people don't get the help they need because they don't want to have the label of mental illness."

"Don't you feel the same way about being labeled an alcoholic?" I ask him.

"It's a huge struggle with me. The many times I've tried to get sober in the past, I'd convince myself I could stop when I wanted to. I still feel that way now. I don't like labels and people telling me what I can and can't do. I feel powerless when I'm drinking, it's true, but I don't believe that God is going to make everything better for me. I believe that it's a partnership. He points the way, but He doesn't make everything better for me without my participation. Otherwise, we'd be nothing but puppets on a string. Humans make puppets. God makes humans with a brain of our own to think. If anything, I am nothing without God. I am an empty shell walking upon the earth. But with him, I feel as if I'm the person He created me to be."

"We are not human beings having a spiritual experience; we are spiritual beings having a human experience."- Pierre Teilhard de Chardin

"We are spiritual beings having a human experience. Wow! So that must be what our soul is, the spirit riding along inside the body experiencing everything we do along the way."

"Yes, and that's what I mean by a partnership. There's the mind, body, and soul, all three, working together as one," he says.

"That reminds me of the Holy Trinity, Father, Son, and Holy Spirit," I say.

"Yeah, that's a pretty good analogy," he says.

All this deep stuff makes my head spin. I miss my friends hanging out and not thinking so much about life, but living it, meeting boys, singing songs, dancing, doing goofy things.

"So, when are Mom and Mary coming to visit?" I asked.

"I was thinking Saturday, August 23," he said. "I thought I'd call your mother from the office tomorrow to set it up."

"By the way, one of the ladies from Al-Anon has two daughters who go to Catholic High. One of the girls is in the same class as you are. Her name is Pat. She said she'd pick you up and take you into school so you can rummage through some of the used uniforms for school. We'll send it to the cleaners and get it all freshened up like new for you. I'll give my friend a call tomorrow and get that setup. Schools only a few weeks away," he says.

"It's going to be strange, wearing a uniform, but then I won't have to worry every morning what I'm going to wear. I was thinking when I went shopping that maybe I could get a part-time job. I noticed some signs in the windows of the shops where they needed help, but I don't know how to go about it. If I could get a job, I could buy some of the things I need and help you out, too," I said.

"You don't have to help me out, but if you got a job, you would have some extra money to get the things you want. The first thing you have to do is get your working papers," Dad says as he jots another thing down in his little marble notebook. "I'll check that out for you to tomorrow." He says.

"What's this Al-Anon meeting I hear you and Lou mention sometimes?" I ask.

"It's a support group for people whose lives are affected by someone else's drinking," he says. They meet at the same time as the AA meetings but in another room. You're welcome to attend someday if you like," he says.

"You're not drinking, so I don't see any reason why I'd need to go," I say.

"I feel the same way about going to my AA meetings. I'm not drinking, so I don't see why I have to go, but Lou is always on my case to go. I'm glad he isn't living across the hall from us now. Don't get me wrong, I like Lou, but he takes this sponsor thing above and beyond the call of duty," he says.

"Oh, that's just because he cares about you. Maybe helping you stay sober also helps him stay sober as well," I say.

"I'm sure it does. But I can take care of myself. I need to know that I'm doing this of my own accord, not because someone else wants me to," Dad says. "Don't tell Lou I said this, though. It's between you and me."

Chapter 18 - September 1969

September 10, 1969

Dear Mary Faith,

You're never going to believe it, but after all these years of fighting the idea of going to a Catholic school, that's where I'm going to spend my last two years. I met a nice girl named Pat, who's in my class. She picked me up and took me to school so that I could pick out a used uniform. They're pretty cool, for a uniform. It's a plaid gray and navy-blue pleated skirt, a white Peter Pan collar blouse, and to top it off, a navy-blue blazer. I had to hem the skirt, as usual. You know the protocol: nothing above the knees, but most of us girls roll them up all the time. We have to watch out for Sister Mary Raymond. She's the disciplinary nun and often stands around the corner, waiting to catch us off guard. If we get caught enough times, you get detention. I call her the "Skirt Gestapo."

So much has happened in the past month since I've been here. My mom and Mary came to visit twice. It hasn't been good. She continues to make me feel like I'm doing nasty things with my Dad. I try to remember she isn't right in the head, that she doesn't mean it, but it does hurt. I can't help feeling that she hates me. The first time she came, my dad's old girlfriend walked right in the apartment without knocking. She opened the front window saying she needed to let the stink of my mother out. Then she picked up Mom's and Mary's suitcases and threw them out the front third-floor window. She got in my mom's face, but I stepped in-between, telling her to get the hell out before I picked her up and threw her out the window. I guess I got that same crazy look in my eyes the same as I did when I stood up to Billy Joe at Stenton Child Care Center. It was enough to stop her. We stood there, waiting to see who would make the next move. Dad guided her toward the door and told her she'd done enough damage to go and never come back. You can't trust her when she drinks.

You know my coming here has brought a lot of change into my Dad's life. It wouldn't have been so bad if it was just me. Now with Mom and Mary showing up and his unpredictable girlfriend coming by, it's more than he can take. I know he's drinking. He tries to hide it from me, but I can smell it on him. I miss his sponsor Lou. He used to live across the hall from us and kept a good eye on Dad. I get so scared that if the Department of Child Welfare finds out, they'll come and take me away.

At least I got a job. It was Lou who helped me get it. His landlord has a pizza place called Joe's Pizza, and he needed some help. It's pretty cool. It reminds me a little of Betty's Restaurant where we used to hang out. I met a guy named Dave there. We went out a few times. I knew he was a little older than me. I thought he was about twenty, but he told me he's was twenty-four. He is the sweetest guy I've met. He knows how to treat a girl, but he's already serious about me. I don't know how I feel about him being older. I mean, it's not like he's thirty, but he is eight years older than me.

Dad was saying October 24-26th is F&M's homecoming weekend and that his fraternity is having a party. All the alumni are welcome and their families. I thought it would be fun if you wanted to come for a visit. Then we could go together and check out all the cute guys. The Greyhound bus is only $5.20 round trip. I can meet you at the station when you come. Let me know.
Love always
Connie

∞ ∞ ∞

I like my job. I'm finally getting to know some people. I take orders and sometimes help by making subs. People want to talk. I'm a friendly person, so I listen, join in the conversation, and answer their questions. Joe doesn't like it. He says to focus on the job at hand, move people in and out, because that's what he believes they want, fast service. He doesn't like it when the young people come in and sit at the booths hanging out. He says I take too long getting their orders. I can't help the way I am. I'm not going to ignore people when they talk to me.

"Come with me," Joe says.

I follow him down the basement steps, and he takes me to a metal kitchen prep table. There are supplies on shelves along the wall. He pulls a big bag of onions over to the counter. It comes up past my waist. "I need you to slice onion for subs," he says to me. "I'll show you how." He holds the onion in his big hand and peels away the outer skin quickly. He proceeds to slice it, nice and thin, all the while still holding it in his hand. "Now you do it," he says. He stands over me, watching to see if I do it right.

"No, like this," he says as he shows me how to hold the knife.

I try again but can't hold the onion and the knife in my hands the way he does. His hands are twice my size. He's like a drill sergeant, going over and over it. "You're still not holding knife right. You cut too thick," then starts to shout in Italian, throwing up his hands.

"Can't I lay them on the counter and slice them like this?" I show him.

"No! You do like I show you," he says. He takes two big cafeteria pans off the shelf and says, "You fill pans."

Every day I work now, he puts me down in the onion dungeon where it smells as if I'm wrapped inside a sub. He always complains I don't cut them right because I can't hold the knife the way he wants me to. I can barely see what I'm doing as my eyes water from the moment I cut into the first onion to the last one. I try because this is my first job and think I have to earn my way and prove to him that I can do what he asks of me. My hands are stained green, and no matter how hard I scrub them, I can't get the stain off. I smell like an onion, not only when I leave here, but everywhere I go. I can't get rid of the smell. It's like having a bad underarm odor. I'm embarrassed at school, but no one says anything. I know if I can smell it on me, everyone can.

Finally, the knife slips in my grip, and I puncture my hand right below the thumb. The blood drips all over the pan of onions. I run cold water over the cut, trying to get it to stop bleeding, but it won't stop. It begins to throb with pain as I go upstairs to tell Joe. He doesn't look at my cut. He runs downstairs to check his precious onions and starts complaining because I got blood all over them. He throws the dirty towel he keeps tucked into his belt at me. "Keep it wrapped tightly, stupid girl," he says. I can feel the anger building up. It takes all I have to hold the words, F---you, stupid man, from flying out of my mouth.

I go upstairs to call my dad.

"Can you come to get me? I cut my hand badly, and I think I need stitches."

"Where's Joe? Put him on the phone," Dad says.

"Joe, my dad wants to talk to you," I say.

"I can't come to the phone. Can't you see I too busy?" Joe says.

"He won't come, all he cares about are his precious onions," I say.

"Do you have it wrapped tightly?"

"Yes, with the dirty rag he gave me," I say.

"That son-of-a-bitch," Dad says. "Listen, I don't have a way to pick you up. Do you think you can walk to St. Joseph's Hospital? It's right across the street, two blocks down on College Avenue. If we both leave now, we should meet up there about the same time."

"I'm leaving now." I say, "And Dad, I'm telling Joe I quit."

The nurse in the emergency room tries to clean my hand so the doctor can sew it back together. She tells me it's deep, but it looks like one stitch will pull the skin back together. After the doctor stitches me up, the nurse wraps my hand with gauze. "You know there's a trick I learned from my grandmother on how to get rid of the onion smell on your hands. Take a stainless-steel spoon, rub your fingers with it under cold water, and the smell will be gone. It works, but it might take a few tries for you since your fingers are stained so bad. It's worth a try."

"I guess I'll be looking for a new job," I said.

"I don't want you to go back there anyway," Dad says.

Chapter 19 - December 1969

I have lots of new friends now that I've been in school for the past few months. I've also met a few at the new job I got at the F & M College cafeteria. It's more money and more hours than I was getting working at Joe's Pizza Place. Plus, the guys are cute. I can't believe it's already December, the last month of 1969.

I get on the city bus that takes me from school to the courthouse in town. I walk up the ally to the back entrance of Woolworth's and out the front doors to catch the connecting bus home.

"Hey," Eddie calls out as he catches up with me. "You want some company today?" he asks.

"I can't. I have to work at 4:00," I say.

"Aren't you going with us to the dance tonight?" Eddie asks.

"Yeah, Jimmy's picking me around 8:00 tonight."

"Jerry and John are going with us too," he tells me.

"How's your dad doing?" Eddie asks as we wait for the bus.

"He's growing those long Sergeant Pepper sideburns now and listens to the Beatles album all the time."

"Man, your dad's so cool and funny, especially when he's had a few too many."

"He stops at the "Town Tavern" down the street almost every day now. I'm really worried about him," I say.

"Ah, he's just having a little fun after a hard day's work," Eddie says.

"You don't understand Eddie. He's an alcoholic. He can't control it, and to top things off; he's spending all his paycheck on booze. I had to take money out of his wallet the other day and hide it inside a flower pot so I could pay the rent. If we get evicted, I could be taken away from my dad the same as I was from my mom."

"Man, I didn't know it was that bad," Eddie says. "My parents smoke pot all the time. We even have a plant growing in the kitchen window," he says.

"Man, nothing shocks me anymore, Eddie, but that one takes the cake," I say.

"Yeah, life sure isn't like the "Father Knows Best" shows we grew up watching," he says.

"Everyone is screwed up in some way or other these days," he says.

"You know, the one thing I've concluded about our parents is that they are no different from us. Just because they are grown-up doesn't mean they have all the right answers. They still have the same kind of problems we do, but more pressure to make the right decision. I think that's what life's about figuring how to live right. My dad gave me a book to read called, *As a Man Thinketh*. It talks about how we create our own reality," I tell him.

"How does a kid do that when we don't have control over our own life yet?" he asks.

"I wondered the same thing until I read more and realized I'd been doing it all along. See, even though I was in an awful situation, it's how I choose to let it affect me. I could have given up and done nothing, but I wanted something more. I wanted to find my dad and had no idea where he was or how I was going to make it happen. But I kept picturing what it would be like and believing it was going to happen someday, and here I am," I say.

"Man, that's cool, but I hope you have bigger dreams that go beyond being with your dad because it doesn't seem like this one is working out so good for you," Eddie says.

"Oh, I do. Being with my dad is only a short portion of my dream, but the fact that it came true makes me more hopeful that what I dream about will come true," I say.

"Come on, spill it out, what's your big dream?" he teases me.

"I know it sounds all fairy-tale-like, but I'm going to fall in love and live happily ever after."

"Wake up, girl. Look around; this is the real world in which we live. I mean, who do we know that is really happy?" he asks.

"I believe in it because God promised me I could have it. Believing in that is the only thing that's kept me from falling apart. Always, when things, were at their worst, and I thought I couldn't face another thing, I'd hear a voice inside, encouraging me over and again to hang in there, reminding me that the day will come when I can make my life the way I've always dreamed it could be. One thing I've learned for sure, Eddie, is that God leads the way, but the work is up to us. Being with my dad isn't as perfect as I'd liked it to be, but I'm still glad to be with him."

"I don't get how you could have any trust in God after what you've been through," Eddie says.

"I know God's not a person, and I don't feel right referring to God as an, "It." I've concluded that the only possible thing God could be is pure love. Isn't love the one thing we all want most of all. It's like a craving we have inside."

"Yeah, I have that craving all the time. I'll give you some loving if you want it," Eddie says.

"I'm serious, Eddie, I'm not talking about sexual feelings. I'm talking about what it means to love and be loved."

"I know what you mean; I'm just kidding around. I think the sex part is just the bonus that comes with it," Eddie says.

"Here's my bus, Eddie. I have to go. I'll see you tonight," I say.

∞ ∞ ∞

"I hate dances," Jerry says as he scrunches up his paper bag around his mouth and breaths the fumes of glue.

"Man, you're going to mess your brain up doing that," John says, as he takes a swig of cough syrup.

"Shut up, man," Jerry says. "You're messing with my high."

"You're both crazy," Jimmy says as he drives the car.

"Why do you hate dances so much?" I ask.

"Cause the only way to pick a girl up is to dance with her, and I don't like dancing," Jerry says.

"See, that's why I like smoking pot. The high lasts longer and makes you feel happy," Eddie says.

"No, drinking lasts the longest," Jimmy says.

"You haven't been drinking have you, Jimmy," I ask.

"Not yet, sweetheart, but when we get to the dance, I'll take a few swigs of the Southern Comfort I have stashed away in the trunk. You're welcome to join me if you like," he says, touching my hand.

"If I knew you guys were going to be doing all this stuff, I'd have never come with you. I'll find another way home," I tell them.

"Ah, come on, Connie. What's your problem, man, you sound like a parent," John says.

"Maybe that's because that's what I feel like I am," I say. "I have to deal with my dad drinking all the time, wondering when he's coming home or if we have any money left to pay our bills or have food in the fridge. Now I have to put up with you clowns. I just want to go dancing and have a little fun, feel like a teenager again.

Now I have to worry about being around you guys and if we'll get stopped by the cops."

"I don't have to drink," Jimmy says. "You don't have to find another way home. I'll get you back there safe if you promise me a slow dance tonight."

"Thanks, Jimmy. Of course, I'll dance with you," I say.

We meet up with some of the girls I work with at F&M. They all go to McCaskey, but I run into a few girls I know from my school, too. We mostly hang out talking, although we can hardly hear each other over the music. I love getting in the groove, swaying to the music, moving to the beat. It makes me forget everything. Jimmy grabs me to dance when the music slows down. I don't like it when a guy pushes himself on me and moves too fast. He holds me tightly against me, and I don't even know if I like him that way. It's turning me off.

When we head home, we have one less guy as John picked up a girl and left with her.

"Hey, why don't we go hang out at my place?" Jimmy asks.

"No, I'd rather go home, but you're welcome to hang out with me for a while if you all like," I say.

When we get into the apartment, Eddie looks around and asks me where my Christmas tree is?

"Maybe they're one of those families that wait till the night before Christmas to put theirs up, Jimmy says.

"I don't think we're going to have any extra money for Christmas this year," I say.

"That sucks," Jerry says.

"We can't let Connie go through Christmas without a tree," Eddie says to the guys.

"Come on, let's all go find you a tree," Jimmy says.

"We pile back in Jimmy's car, but none of the tree stands are open. "It's okay, guys. I don't have to have one. Besides, what would I put it in?" I say.

"We can steal one from one of those Christmas trees stand. No one will see us," Jerry says.

"No stealing, guys. Remember, I can't be a part of anything like that," I say.

"We can cut a tree down from the woods in back of my house," Jimmy says.

"We can figure out how to hold it up with something, Connie," Eddie says.

Jimmy gets a saw out of his garage, and the guys take off into the wooded area behind his house. They come back laughing with a short fat tree that has a thick trunk. They pile back in the car, but I say, "Wait, what about the tree stand?" Jimmy runs into the house and comes out a few minutes later with one.

Back at the apartment, the guys carry the tree up. They try to put it in Jimmy's tree stand, but the trunk is too fat. So, we put it in a pot of water and lean it up against the corner wall. I don't have anything to put on it, but I remember the chain of pop-off beer can tabs I've been collecting, and drape that around it.

Dad comes in soon after we have it all set up. He's drunk as a skunk and goes around giving all the guys a big hug, telling them that there's nothing wrong with men showing each other a little affection. He likes the tree and tells me we'll buy some decorations for it tomorrow. I won't hold my breath. I know we don't have the money for that kind of stuff.

"Hey kids, you have fun now, and I'll see you later," he says as he heads off to the bathroom. I hear the water filling the bathtub.

Eddie puts my Sergeant Pepper album on the stereo. "Sergeant Pepper's lonely, Sergeant Pepper's lonely, Sergeant Pepper's Lonely-Hearts Club Band," we hear dad singing from the bathroom. Being in the tub makes him sound like he's singing through a microphone.

Jimmy breaks up, sounding like a laughing rooster, which only makes the rest of us laugh harder. In the silent moment that comes between laughter, Dad's voice slips through the quiet, unaccompanied by the Beatles. He begins another rendition of the song, "Sergeant Pepper's lonely, Sergeant Pepper's lonely, Sergeant Pepper's Lonely-Hearts Club Band."

The laughing rooster starts up all over again, and we're all rolling over with laughter.

"Man, I'm gonna bust a gut," Jerry says, and another burst of laughter comes out.

"Stop, Jimmy," I say, "You're going to make me pee my pants," and another burst comes from the laughing rooster.

We finally settle down, and I say, "Man, I haven't laughed that hard in a long time. That felt good."

We all lay on the floor in silence, enjoying the high that laughter brings with it. Then I suddenly realize that Dad's still in the tub, and it's too quiet in there.

"Dad!" I knock on the door. "Are you all right in there?" I don't hear anything and run back out to the guys.

"He's not answering me. What if he fell asleep and slipped under the water? Would one of you open the door and check on him for me?"

They look at one other laughing, saying, "I'm not going to do it."

"Why can't you do it? He's your dad?" Jimmy asks.

"Because he is my dad. I don't want to see him naked!" I say. "Come on, guys, you all have the same thing. I thought guys didn't care about that stuff."

"Yeah, but it's your dad," Eddie says. "We don't want to see him naked either."
They all burst out laughing.

"It's not funny! What if he's drowned himself," I say, almost crying?

"I'll do it if you make out with me afterword," Jimmy says.

"Oh, forget it. I'll do it myself," I say, going toward the hallway.

Eddie stops me and says, "I'll take a look." He opens the door and says, "He's okay. All the water's gone out of the tub. He'll wake up as soon as he gets cold enough."

I give Eddie a big hug. "You're a good friend, Eddie. Thanks for doing that for me."

"Come on, guys," Eddie says. "Time to hit the road." They each hug me as they leave.

I knock a few more times on the door. Finally, Dad wakes up.

He sits on the side of his bed and starts crying. "I'm sorry, Connie. I wish I could be the kind of dad you deserve," he says.

"I love you, Dad, and I don't want any dad other than you. It's just the dad you want to be, and the one you choose to be are two different things. When you're sober, I love being around you; the conversations we have, the things you teach me. That's my real dad. I know you're still inside there. It just hurts me to see you become less than you are," I say.

He cries harder, "I promise I'll be better."

"Why don't you call Lou tomorrow and maybe go to a meeting with him?"

"Okay, Connie," he says as he lays down, falling fast asleep.

I cover him up like a mother would her child and kiss him on the forehead. I've learned too many times now not to get my hopes up. After all the broken promises, maybe this time will be different.

The next morning when I get up, the tree is standing straight in the tree stand. Dad is sipping his coffee at the kitchen table, reading the paper.

"How did you get the tree to fit in the stand?" I asked.

"I chopped it with my little ax until I could get it in. I didn't forget my promise. I'll call Lou today and see what we can do to make this a nice Christmas for you.

∞ ∞ ∞

Sitting in the backseat of Lou's car, I listen to the conversation that goes back and forth between Dad and Lou about Alcoholics Anonymous. Lou tells Dad he's willing to do whatever it takes to help keep him sober, "But you have to follow the twelve-steps, admitting every day that alone you are powerless over alcohol."

"I get that. What I can't get beyond is this idea that God is going to make everything better for me if I give it all over to Him. I believe in God, and I believe He wants the best for all of us. But I also believe that he gave us the ability to make things right for ourselves," Dad says.

"That's that intellectual mind of yours getting in the way of the simplicity of the program," Lou says. "When you realize and accept how powerless you are without God, it frees you up to do the work you have to do," he goes on.

"I don't think it's my way or God's way, I think it's supposed to be a partnership where we work together," Dad says.

"This is what you do, John. You make what is planned out for you more difficult to follow because you think too much into it. Just follow the program for now so that you can get a handle on your drinking. Then when you've been sober long enough to think straight, you can make more informed decisions about your life," Lou says.

Dad doesn't say anything else. I can feel the tension between them. It's thick enough to cut with a knife. They are two very different, bullheaded men.

"What did you think of the Al-Anon meeting?" Lou, ask me.

"It was okay," I said.

"Just okay?" Lou asked.

"It felt kind of weird being the only teenager there. I couldn't relate to the alcoholic's spouse, and they didn't understand what it was like to be a teenager of an alcoholic."

"I can't believe that," Lou said. "Maybe you weren't listening to them right."

He sounds just like the Al-Anon people. When I said it was different for a kid than an adult to live with an alcoholic, they said it doesn't matter if you're a spouse, child, or friend. The alcoholic has to want to quit for himself before they can be successful. "Why isn't love enough reason?" I asked. All they could say was that my dad was powerless when it comes to alcohol, that I can't make him better, that none of them can make their loved ones better, that only God can do that, and only God can help us through it, as well. I know that part already. If not for God, I don't know where I'd be right now. It would just be nice to have a little more human understanding.

"I know what's going through your mind, Connie," Lou says. "You're trying to figure out how you can get your dad to stop drinking."

"Don't talk about me as if I'm not here," Dad says. "You make me feel like a child."

That's what you become when you drink, a child, and I feel like the parent. I wish I could scream it out loud, but I won't. I stuff it inside with all the other crap I've stuffed for so long. I can't even tell Miss Janet, my counselor, about Dad's drinking. I'm afraid if she knew how bad it is, she might contact the Child Welfare Department, and they'd take me away from Dad.

∞ ∞ ∞

Christmas morning, I get the little package out of my drawer and take it out to Dad. He looks up from his newspaper, and asks, "What's this?"

"Just a little something I got you. Open it," I say.

"A new tie," he says. "I like it.

"You wear the same suit all the time and a white shirt. I thought a new tie would change things up a little for you."

"It's perfect," he says. "I have something for you, too. He pulls out a white envelope from his pocket.

"I was going to get you a pair of winter boots, but thought you might like to pick them out yourself."

"Wow! Dad, $25.00. That's a lot of money," I said.

"I put a little aside for you each week. I keep it locked in my drawer at work, so I wouldn't have it in my wallet to drink away."

"I won't sit here and make any promises; I've broken too many already. I do love you enough to want to quit. That's the only thing right now that makes me want to try. I know, though, that until I start to love and care about myself enough first, nothing else that I try is going to stick. Seeing anything lovable about myself is pretty hard after all I've done over the years. It's too big for me to do alone. I know that. I can let God carry me for a while, but what do I do when He puts me down to carry on my own life. I have to love myself enough to do the work I need to do to stay sober. You or God can't do that for me. So, for now, all I can do is take one step at a time, one day, one minute or hour at a time."

"Just the effort is the best Christmas present you could give me, Dad. Having the sober you back to talk with today makes it even better. I've missed our talks."

Chapter 20 – January 1970

*H*appy Birthday," Dad says to me before he leaves for work.

"Thank you. I didn't think you'd remember," I said.

"That's one birth I couldn't forget. It was pouring rain, and I thought you were going to be delivered in the taxi before we made it to the hospital. I no sooner poured my coffee and started to sit down when the nurse came in to say, "Mr. Miller, Congratulations. You have a healthy baby girl, and your wife is doing fine."

"Whatever made you pick the name, Constance?" I asked.

"I liked the way it sounded, smart and sophisticated," he said.

"Boy, you had me pegged all wrong. I'm neither sophisticated or smart. No, Connie fits me much better, it's a little sweeter and softer around the edges," I say.

"Maybe so, but I think you're smarter than you think, sophisticated the way you get things done, strong when you need to be yet always soft at heart. They don't come any sweeter than you do," he says.

"Ah, you're just saying that because you're my dad."

"You know you have great manners, always saying thank you for this and that, but when it comes to compliments, you always look for a reason to devalue them."

"I don't mean to be ungrateful. I guess I've thought of myself as being so unlovable that it's hard to know how to react when someone does say something nice about me," I say.

"You don't have to say anything, but thank you, and accept it for the gift that it is," Dad says.

"Well, thank you!" I couldn't ask for a more beautiful gift on my birthday," I say.

"How old are you now?"

"Seventeen."

"One more year and you'll be old enough to go off on your own," he says.

"I know, and I won't ever have to worry about the Child Welfare taking me away again."

"Do you still worry about that?"

"All the time, especially now that you've started drinking again," I say.

"I have it under control," he says. "You don't have to worry anymore. How about if I take you to Lombardo's for dinner after work to celebrate your birthday?"

"Oh, I love that place. They have the best meatballs and lasagna. I'll be thinking all day about which one I want to eat," I say.

But by the evening, he doesn't come home, so I walk down to the "Town Tavern." There he is laughing and carrying on with his friends. He's already drunk when he announces to everyone in the bar that it's my birthday. The bartender hands me the coke and says it's on the house. The guy sitting next to me starts hitting on me. He's cute but probably about ten years older than me. Dad tells him to leave me alone.

"I guess we're not going to Lombardo's today?" I say

"I'm sorry, Connie," he says.

"You hungry, darling?" the guy next to me asks.

Before I have time to say anything else, he's ordering me a hamburger and fries. He flirts with me, saying how cute I am. Dad keeps telling him to lay off, but the guy ignores him, and I don't care what Dad thinks. It's my birthday, and I'm not going to cry even though I want to.

Chapter 21-May 1970

I usually get up at 6:00 and dash out the door to get the bus at 6:30 across the street. I set the coffee up the night before, so all I have to do is plug it in first thing in the morning. While it's perking, I brush my teeth, wash my face, and put my make-up on. It's been so much faster having a uniform to put on each day. I get my coffee, adding lots of milk and sugar, head back to the bathroom to pull my curlers out. My hair is finally starting to grow again after getting it cut short at the beginning of the school year. After all the dye damage, I had to do something. Now I can brush my curls into a flip or a bob at my chin line. I was worried about what my hair would look like when I got my senior pictures taken this summer.

Senior, boy, does that sound good. The race to the end begins in one more month when I finish up this junior year. I am passing, which is much better than I thought I'd do.

School doesn't start until 8:00 am, but the 6:30 bus is the only one that gets me into town on time for the exchange bus that takes me to school. I get there with plenty of time to spare, wishing I could still be sleeping, but it gives me a chance to meet up with my friends for a few smokes before school starts. We all stand across the street where we are off school property. In the back of us is the Juliet building, where I go for my counseling sessions with Miss Janet. I have to dash over there to see her after I check into my homeroom today.

Miss Janet is a nice older woman who looks like she should be in some kitchen baking cookies. She holds a notebook and always asks me the same thing, "How are things going at home?"

"Fine," I always say. I only tell Miss Janet what a great relationship Dad and I have. But I never tell her the truth, that he's back to drinking more than ever. Or that I have to go into the Town Tavern to bring him home each night after I work.

She studies my face for a while before talking. I've never been good at lying. It shows all over my face.

"You know I can't help you if you don't tell me the truth," she says. I wonder if she knows something more about what's going on than I give her credit. Dad's been missing some work off and on, too. Maybe she checks on him, or perhaps she's talked to Father Taylor about how much I've been missing school.

"My mom is doing good. She got a nursing job at a convalescence home," I said to change the subject.

"Do you see her much anymore?" she asks.

"No, but that's okay, I'd rather not see her anyway," I say.

"Why is that?" she asks.

"I don't know. I don't like the way I feel when I'm around her."

"How do you feel when you're around her?" she asks.

"I don't know. I guess I still feel angry at Mom. It's still hard to understand why she is the way she is," I say.

"You mean her mental illness?" she asks.

"Yeah, she still says and does these off the wall things that are hurtful," I say.

"Like what kind of things?" she asks.

"Scary eyes," I say. They get big, wide open, and they don't ever seem to blink the way they should. When those eyes land on me, they feel penetrating. That's when the snarling accusations come flying out of her mouth."

"What kind of accusations?" Miss Janet asks.

"She tells me I'm nothing but a whore, that she knows what's going on between my dad and me."

"You mean of a sexual nature?" she asks.

"Yes, but nothing is going on. My dad has never done anything like that to me. He loves me like a daughter and would never think of touching me. If he did, I'd have left a long time ago." We sit there, quiet for a few minutes as she studies my face again. I hate it when she does that.

"What's your biggest fear about your mother?" she asks.

"It's not so much about her as it is me. I'm afraid of becoming as crazy as she is someday," I say.

"First of all, we don't use the word crazy anymore. Your mother has a mental illness. Most people who are mentally ill have no idea they are. You are not your mother.

"Then why am I here?" I ask.

"I suspect because Father Taylor could see you've been through a lot. It would be normal for a kid to feel depressed after all you've experienced. Talking it out, we hope to lessen some of the effects it will have on you. That's what will keep your mind healthy, getting it all out."

"But I worry about it being in our family's blood," I say.

"Well, genetically, some mental illnesses are passed down, but it sounds like your mother's illness was brought on by a traumatic incident in her childhood. Most people with schizophrenia are very confused and don't have any idea that they are ill. The very fact that you ask the question is an indication that you're not mentally ill. You might be depressed at times because of what you've been through and have some anxiety, but that's why you're here talking to me. It would be normal for anyone who's been through what you have to be depressed," she tells me.

With the school year coming to an end, she tells me our sessions will end for the summer. "We can start up again as the new school year begins in September. That is if you'd like to continue our sessions." She says. "Just let Father Taylor know, and we'll set things up again."

I thank Miss Janet for her help and tell her I'll think about it. Getting through this last year is what I want to focus on. One more year to go, and my life will be my own. No one will ever be able to take it away again.

Part 4 -

Tommy

The Promise

Chapter 22 - May 30, 1970

"Love your top," Sally says as I approach her house.

"Isn't it great? It's made of polyester, but feels like satin," I tell her.

"The emerald color makes your green eyes stand out. It's a perfect color for you," she says. "I have boring dark brown eyes."

"Nothing is boring about your big dark eyes, Sally. With your fair skin and dark auburn hair, I think you're beautiful," I say to her.

We both look down the street at the same time as we hear the familiar jingle-jangle of Zoe's bracelets getting closer. She's wearing one of those mod suede leather floppy hats over her long, auburn hair. She's as unique as they come, with her half hippie and half girly-girl look.

"Man, who's holding down the fort at the college cafeteria if the best servers are all here?" she says.

"Being the last weekend in May, most of the college kids have left for the summer break," I say.

"I know," Sally says, "and that means we have one more week of school at McCaskey left before summer officially starts for us, too. Right, Zoe?"

"Digging' it!" Zoe says. "Like when is your last day of school?" She asks me.

"Friday, June 5th," I say, "and we're all going to be seniors finally."

"Woohoo!"

"I'm digging this weather," Zoe says as she takes a drag of her cigarette. She has a deep raspy voice with a slow drawl kind of like John Wayne or someone high on drugs. "But I'm digging that Camaro even more," she says as Bill pulls up in front of Sally's house.

Ham gets out of the front seat. He reminds me of Jackie Gleason from the comedy show "The Honeymooners." Gordy comes out from the back seat. He looks like one of the guys from the Monkees band.

Another car pulls up behind them, and two guys get out. The driver is Dick. He looks so much older than he is, like a college guy. He's kind of cute. I've never seen the other guy before.

"Who's that?" I ask Sally.

"Oh, that's some guy named Tommy. They call him The Scuzz. I don't know much about him. Bill says he's been away at college and just came home for the summer break."

"He's cute," I say. "I wonder why they call him Scuzz? That's not nice. If anybody's a Scuzzy, it's Bill."

"I don't care if Bill is Scuzzy," Zoe says, "He has a nice car." She smiles.

Tommy stands with his hands in his pocket, checking Zoe and Sally out. When he looks at me, our eyes lock for a moment, and I smile at him. He has thick dark wavy hair, a little too long. Like most guys today, he could use a haircut. He has a kind of ivy league look with a blue oxford shirt, navy blue khaki pants, and dark brown wingtips. He's a bit out of style for these days, but it's nice to meet a guy who cares about his appearance, compared to most of them who look so sloppy today.

"Let's head over to Buchanan Park," Bill says.

"Where in the heck are we going to fit everyone in the cars?" Ham asks.

"Zoe and Sally can go with us, and Connie can go with Dick, Tommy, and Gordy," Bill says.

"I'll walk," Tommy says. "It's just up the street.

"I can walk, too," I say. "That is if you'd like some company?" I ask,

"Sure," he says with a big smile. "What's your name?" he asks me.

"Connie."

"I'm Tommy."

"I know," I say. "Why does everybody call you Scuzz? I think that's mean."

"I don't know, that's just what they call me. We all have nicknames," Tommy says.

"Hey, how'd you get so tan this time of year?" I ask.

"From lying out on the college grounds," he says. "Man, with those warm rays, we've been getting these past few weeks at college, no one wanted to do anything but lie in the sunshine. Plus, I tan pretty easy."

"You look like a hot dog perfectly cooked all around," I say.

"What college do you go to?" I ask.

"Bloomsburg," he says.

"I have no idea where that is," I say.

"It's about 100 miles from here, up in the mountains area. It was my first year," he says.

"What's your major?" I ask.

"Math," he says.

"What school do you go to?" he asks.

"Lancaster Catholic High," I say.

"That's where I went. "Class of 69'.""

"You graduated the year before I started. I never went to Catholic school until my junior year. It was kind of weird at first with all the nuns and strict rules. But it's not as bad as I thought it would be. I kind of like it. As far as being Catholic, I don't know much about it, even though I've been one all my life."

"Oh, we eat, breathe, and live it in my family. Put that with going to Catholic school all my life, and it just becomes a part of who you are," he says.

"So, what are you doing for your summer break?" I ask.

"Working mostly. I need to pay for college. I have a job lined up at Armstrong, where my dad works. It's pretty good money," he says.

"What will you do there?" I ask.

"I'll work on one of the lines," he says.

"I have no idea what working on a line means," I say.

"It's Armstrong floor plant, where they make tile floors. It's the biggest factory in Lancaster. Haven't you ever heard of Armstrong?"

"No, I'm not from around here," I say.

"Where you from?" he asks.

"I was born in California and lived there until I was twelve. Then we moved to Philadelphia. I lived there for four years, and here I am."

"Did you like living in California?" he asks.

"Yeah, I liked it a lot, especially the weather. You know it doesn't get humid there as it does here. It just gets hot. I do like the changing seasons here, though. I love the snow. When I first came to Pennsylvania, there was something about the rolling hills and farmland that felt good to me, like I was coming home even though I'd never lived here before."

As we approach the park, we can see the gang hanging out around their cars.

"Hey, Scuzz," Bill yells out as we catch up with them. "Looks like you two are getting along pretty good."

"Don't call him Scuzz," I say.

"How about lover boy?" Bill says, teasing.

"Did anybody ever tell you that you look like Howdy Doody when you smile, Bill?" I tease him back.

"It's Howdy-Doody-time," Gordy sings.

"All right, that's enough from the peanut gallery," Bill says, giving us his big wide Howdy smile. He opens his trunk, looks around, then discreetly starts handing cans of beer out. Zoe puts a few in her purse, and others hide them in their pockets.

"Don't you guys want any?" Bill asks us.

"No, thanks, I can't get caught drinking," I say.

"Come on, no one's going to catch us," Howdy says.

"She said no, Bill," Tommy says.

"Man, you two are party-poopers," he says to us.

"I have to go," I say to Tommy, "I honestly can't afford to be a part of this," I tell him.

"Let's go up and sit on the hill by ourselves then," he says.

"Yeah, I'd like that," I say.

We walk up to sit under the trees, finding a soft patch of grass looking out over the park. Even though the sun was starting to go down, we could see the vibrant colors of the rose garden blooms. The statues look like shadowy figures.

"You're awful quiet suddenly," Tommy says. "Would you rather go home?" he asks me.

"No. Sitting up here on the cool ground, looking out at everything like this reminds me of another time in my life. Only I was by myself," I say.

"Tell me about it," he says.

"I don't know where to start," I say.

"Start with what it reminds you of," he says.

"It reminds me of a time when I slept in a graveyard."

"Why'd you do that?" he asks.

"I ran away and didn't have anywhere else to go," I say.

"How old were you?"

"Fifteen."

"So that was what, only a few years ago when you lived in Philly, and where were your parents?" he asks.

"I told you it's a long story."

"Well, we have all night," he says.

"What are you doing here with me? I mean, why don't you want to be with Zoe or Sally?" I ask him.

"Bill and the guys were talking about how great the two of them were, but then when we got there, I saw you, I thought, wow! Anyway, why are you with me instead of someone else?" he asks.

"I guess I had the same reaction when I saw you," I say.

"So, go on, tell me why you ran away?" he asks.

I began the story when my dad left us, trying to give him a quick version of how I got from there to here, but he keeps stopping me to ask questions.

"So, is this why you're so careful about the things you do and why you are afraid of getting caught?" he asks.

"I'm scared all the time that the Child Welfare is going to take me away again. I only have one more year of school left to get through, and then no one can touch me ever again," I say.

"That makes a lot more sense to me now," he says.

"You look so cold, you're shaking," he says.

"I get this way when I start talking about it. I can't tell half the time if I'm cold or just nervous.".

"Come over here," he says as he pulls me in closer, wrapping his arms around me.

"Wow! God. Being with Tommy feels the same as it did when I had that experience with You. Like I was being covered in the warmth of your comfort, God. You promised me that one day that love would come and I could make my life the way I'd always dreamed it could be. Tommy sure is nice, and something feels special about him, but I'm afraid of getting hurt. How does anyone ever know for sure who is the right person for them?"

"Trust!"

"Your famous last words, God!"

Bill comes back to get us after taking Sally and Zoe home. Dropping me off at my apartment, Tommy gets out of the car to walk me to my door. He stands on the step below me, bringing us face to face. I can tell he wants to kiss me, but he's not sure if I want him to. So, I make the first move, kissing him, and it feels like we melt together when he pulls me in closer to him. Every time he tries to leave, we start kissing again.

"What's your phone number?" he asks.

I give it to him, and he says it a few times to himself.

"I can go inside and write it down for you," I say.

He rattles it off to me, "I'll remember," he says. "I'll call you tomorrow after work. Then he kisses me again.

"You better get going, Bill's out there waiting for you," I say.

"Oh, he can wait," Tommy says as he kisses me one more time before leaving.

I only ever really loved one person, and that was when I was fourteen. It was right before I went into Stenton. Our short time together was something out of a storybook. We lost touch with each other, and nothing ever really compared to that. While I wondered about so many other guys who came along, there is something different about Tommy. Maybe it's the way he wants to know everything about me or the way he makes me feel safe when he wraps me in his arms. I'm afraid to get too excited about it, but I can't help it, I already am.

Chapter 23 – June 1970

hen I talk to dad about my fears, he reminds me of FDR's famous line from his inaugural address, "We have nothing to fear, but fear itself." I understand what that means. What I don't understand is how to turn the feeling off or change it? The only thing I know how to do is protect myself. Right now, I'm fearing that things are moving too fast for Tommy and me. It's been barely a month since we started seeing each other, and he's already saying how much he loves me. The thing is, though, I think I love him too. Every night it gets harder to say goodbye to each other. I never met a guy who asked me how my day went, how I felt, what I wanted to do, and what he could do to make me happy. It feels kind of weird. No one has ever cared that much about me. I have been hurt too many times by guys who I thought cared about me. I need some time to get away and think. I haven't been back to visit my friend Mary Faith in Philly. That's what I'm going to do.

"Tommy, I think things are moving too fast for us. You need to go out with some other girls so you can be sure before you start talking about love," I say.

"I don't want to go out with anyone else. I know what I feel is the best feeling in the world. Why would I want to have that with someone else when I already have it with you?" Tommy asks.

"But what's going to happen when you go back to college? Maybe after being with me, you won't be so shy to ask other girls out. It's better to end it now."

"Why do you want to be with me? I have crooked teeth, I'm stupid and poor, and I have nothing to offer you but all the baggage that comes with me," I say.

"I wish you could see yourself through my eyes because I don't see that at all. You're beautiful, funny, thoughtful, and caring. I see the way you take care of your dad. How could anyone be stupid who's held her own after all you've gone through? You may not have a college degree yet, but you've gone through the school of hard knocks. It not only takes someone smart to get through that but someone strong and full of faith, someone who never gives up," he says.

"Why do you have to make this harder than it has to be, Tommy? I need some time to think, and maybe while I'm away, it will give you a chance to think things through, too," I say.

"When are you leaving?" he asks.

"Early tomorrow morning. I'm taking the Greyhound bus," I say.

"I'll pick you up and run you to the station," he says.

"You don't have to do that," I say.

"I know I don't have to. I want to take you," Tommy says.

∞ ∞ ∞

Tommy comes upstairs to get me in the morning. He kisses me as if nothing has changed. He carries my suitcase down and puts it in his parents' station wagon. Then he opens the door for me to get in. The ride is quiet. Neither one of us knows what to say.

He leans against the car when we get there and pulls me into him, laying his head on my mine. He holds me tight like he's never going to let me go. I don't know if I want him to either. I look up into those striking blue eyes of his that always have a way of melting me but quickly turn away. "I have to go, Tommy." He kisses me long and hard, with passion melting me like putty, "I have to go," I say again, only this time I break away, pick my suitcase up, and walk toward the bus. I turn to look at him before stepping onto the bus. I wave goodbye, but he dashes over before I get on the bus

"I don't want anyone else. I love you. I know you feel it, too. We both felt it the first day we meet. Think about that, too, while you're away," he says as he kisses me again.

The bus driver closes the under hatch, and says, "I hate to break this love nest up, but it's time to go."

"I'll be here to pick you up when you come back," he says and kisses me one more time.

Sitting on the bus, I look out the window. Tommy is leaning against the car again with hands in his pockets. He looks so sad, but determined, too.

"Everyone I love leaves me eventually, God. It's better this way. "

"But who's doing the leaving this time?" God says. *"Why would you walk away from the very thing you've longed for?"*

"I don't know!" I say. "I'm scared!"

"Of what?"

"Of trusting in what I can't control," I say as I wipe away my tear.

∞ ∞ ∞

When I get to Mary Faith's, we talk for a long time as I tell her all about Tommy.

"Listen to yourself," she says. "You light up when you talk about Tommy, and now you may have ruined the best thing that ever happened to you."

Hearing her say it like that makes me want to hurry back home.

"He said he'd be there to pick me when I get back. Oh, what if he isn't there?"

"You always expect the worst to happen," she says. "If Tommy's anything the way you think he is, he'll be there."

The bus depot in Philadelphia is under the train station. It's the same one that brought my family and me into Philadelphia five years ago. It's cool, dark, damp, and musty, making the smells of exhaust, cigarette smoke, and urine thick and pungent. I bring my hand over my mouth and nose to keep from gagging. A chill goes down my back as the memories of that dark early morning come flooding back. But look how far I've come since then. God has been true to His promise, and now I may have gone and thrown it all away.

"Oh, please let Tommy be at the Lancaster bus depot, God, and I'll never let him go again. I promise this time, God."

My heart begins to beat faster, and I sit up a little taller so I can see the Lancaster bus station when we go around the corner. There he is. Standing against the car in the same spot, I left him, with his hands in his pockets and a smile on his face as our eyes lock together in that special way.

I run into his arms, and he buries his face in my hair. "I love you," he whispers in my ear.

"I love you, too," I say, looking up at him.

"I know," he says as he kisses me all over my face. "You just needed to go away to figure it out," he kisses me again. "Let's not worry about me going back to school yet," he kisses me again. Let's enjoy the time we have right now." And this time, his kiss is long, tender, and full of passion. "We can figure the rest out when the time comes," he whispers again as he holds me tight.

As we hold each other, everything feels right for the first time in my life. I can feel fear's grip trying to pull me away, always snatching at the good things that come into my life. But it can't penetrate what I'm feeling. I realize for the first time that love is stronger than fear.

Chapter 24-August 1970

"Your Dad seems so different since he got out of the hospital," Tommy says.

"I know. It's nice to have my Dad back again; this is the way he was when I first came to live with him last summer."

"He's not the only one who seems better. It's nice to see you smiling more and less worried. It makes me feel a little better about leaving you to go back to school in a few weeks," he says.

"I don't know what I would have done without you this summer. You've been the only real good thing in my life. Every time I think of you going back to school, it feels as if my heart is being squeezed like silly putty," I say.

"I feel the same way," he says.

"I'm so worried about losing you," I say.

He takes my face in his hands so that he has my full attention and says, "I wish you would stop saying that. Haven't I proven to you yet how much I love you?"

"Yes, but you could meet someone at school while we're away from each other. Someone who's less complicated than me," I say.

"I don't want anyone else. I love everything about you. I wish you could see yourself the way I do," he goes on.

He kisses me with tenderness until our passion overtakes every thought, and the world disappears around us. The only thing that remains is what we become as one.

"I feel so loved and safe with you, Tommy. I think, how can love possibly be any more perfect than what we feel when we're together? But then the fear sets in, that fear of abandonment and having my life pulled out from under me. I'm afraid to let my guard down because it leaves me wide open for that unexpected rejection. I've felt it too many times in my life."

"It's like you wear all these layers of armor to protect yourself," he says.

"I never thought of it that way before, but it does explain a lot. I'm not a tough person. Life has broken me too many times, and each time I begin to put myself back together, I guess I have formed a harder shell around me. I swore I'd never let that happen again."

"That's what I'm saying. I want to help you peel those layers away. With me, I promise, you'll never feel that kind of rejection again," Tommy says.

"You've already started, and now I understand why it felt so weird to be with someone so nice to me. It meant that I had to open myself up to allow you in, and I felt...what's the word?"

"Vulnerable!" he adds.

"Yes, like being naked."

"Oh, I like naked," he says.

I hit him in the arm, "You know what I mean," I say, giggling. "Taking that armor off is like being a turtle without its shell. But then you come along and wrap yourself around me, making me feel safe and protected."

"Then why do you worry so much about losing me?" he asks.

"Because as soon as you walk out that door, I put that armor back on. I guess I can only trust what's within my grasp," I say.

"Then maybe me going back to school will help teach you how to stretch that grasp out because I'm going to prove to you that you can."

We hear the apartment door open then close, making us both jump up and scramble to put our clothes back on. We're still not used to Dad coming straight home from work since he's been sober. Tommy runs out to greet him, giving me more time to pull myself together. I dash out onto the roof, feeling a little shaky, not wanting Dad to catch me in this kind of situation. But Dad steps out onto the roof of the backroom and finds me leaning against the wall of the house where the upper roof extends. The canopy of the tree shields me, and he peeks in, asking, "Are you okay, Connie?"

"I'm fine," I say, holding my shirt together with my bra still unhooked. "It's just so cool out here under the tree is all," I go on.

"Why don't you come inside? I don't like you sitting out here. It's not safe," he says.

I pull myself together when he goes back into the apartment.

He sits us both down and talks with us about what he sees is going on.

"I know I don't have any right after all you've been through with my drinking, Connie, but I do care about what happens to you. I appreciate that you've been here for Connie too," he says to Tommy. "But you have three more years of college to get through, and Connie, you have only one more year of high school to finish. I can't pretend to stop what's already started, but you both need to be careful, you know, about getting pregnant," he goes on.

I get red in the face and can't even look at Dad.

"It's okay; I wouldn't do anything to hurt Connie. I love her, John!"

"Well, that's very admirable of you, Tom, but in the meantime, I think you should both use some protection," Dad says.

Chapter 25 - September 1970

S tartled by the sudden ringing of my little red wind up clock, I jump out of bed, grab the clock like a baseball, ready to pitch it out the window, but I don't. It's the same routine I go through every morning. Pressing the little hammer down between the bells, it stops. If it weren't for the soothing ticking that puts me to sleep at night, I'd have thrown it away a long time ago. I don't know how I can have a love/hate relationship with a thing, but I do with my little clock.

Thinking of love brings thoughts of Tommy into view. I went to the window last night to watch him as he pulled away from the curb in his parents' station wagon. He had his hand out the window waving goodbye until I couldn't see him anymore. I thought I would be all right until I noticed how quiet everything got. It was as if the electricity went out and suddenly everything becomes dark. It felt like a spark went out inside me. I burst into tears, crying hard until there is nothing left to come out.

Thinking about it now makes the tears well up again. As I lie curled up on my side, I feel them roll across my face onto my pillow. That feeling of abandonment begins to nibble away at me. I could never imagine it being more painful than when dad left all those years ago, or worse when mom gave Mary and me up. But this time, I feel like I can barely breathe. The pain in my heart feels as if it's been cracked open.

"Oh, God, I think I'll die if you don't bring him back to me."

It's 9:00 am. Tommy's probably already left by now. I was hoping he'd call me this morning. I'm not surprised though that he didn't. Tommy had a lot of last-minute packing to do since we'd been spending so much time together this past week. Feeling depressed, I don't want to get up, but it's my first day back to work since the summer break. I need the money, and maybe being around some of my friends is just what I need to get through the day.

I leave for work at 10:30 in the morning and get home at 8:00. I'm pooped. I didn't even get a break. That's how busy we were. College is back in full swing at F&M, too. We had a lot of guys going through the cafeteria dinner line. Seeing them reminded me of Tommy. I wondered if he was doing all the same things as they are, getting settled.

It was nice to see all my friends after our summer break from work. That cheered me for a little while. I wore the necklace Tommy got me today so that I could show it off. Everyone thought it was pretty and nice of him to give it to me. They all said how lucky I am to have someone who cares that much.

Then they started complaining about how much they missed their boyfriends. I thought they should be happy, at least they'll get to see them tomorrow. I don't know when I'll see Tommy next or if I ever will again. What if he meets someone else and never comes back to me? I can't let myself think like that, or I'll drive myself crazy. For now, at least I can look forward to getting his letters and to the next time he comes home.

I get the twenty-eight hours I wanted at work. I have Monday off and work after school for the rest of the week and on the weekend, 10:30-7:30. They're going to be long days like today, but at least it will keep me busy while Tommy's away. It's going be hard until he comes home, but we'll make it work. The great thing about it is that I'll be making some good money for myself to put away.

All I want to do is go to sleep. I'm so tired. I have school first thing in the morning too. I can't go to bed yet, though. I have to write to Tommy. I promised him I'd write every day, and I want to get this letter in the mail first thing in the morning. I put my pillow against the headboard and write about my day ending with a P.S. I forgot to tell you, thank you for the most beautiful summer I ever had.

Another rude awaking from my little red wind up clock. Getting up so early is the part I hate most about going back to school-how early I have to get up. It's bad enough that it's hard to get up anyway, but I feel as if I have lead in my legs. I have to drag myself to move today. I should be happy. It's the first day of my senior year. I'm at the beginning of the end of my last year of school. It seems weird. For the past four years, all I've thought about is reaching this point, but I'm not quite there yet. It almost seems like a waste of time at this point, but I have to ride the time out until it's official.

When I arrive at school, I walk across the street to join my fellow smokers. We puff away on as many cigarettes as we can before the bell rings to go in. Once school starts, there will be no more smoking until we leave to go home, unless we find a way to sneak one in somewhere else.

It's nice to see the familiar faces of my homeroom class. When Sister Arminius hands out our schedules, I'm kind of excited with mine this year. With my major being business, I'm going to get some real practice in the school office. I have a lot of free time too. I think I'll volunteer in the school library. I could even go out for volleyball, but that could conflict with my work schedule. I have POD (Problems of Democracy) this year with sister Mary Peter. I remember Tommy talking about how interesting this class is and how much he liked her as a teacher. My other classes are religion, English, typing and more office practice, home economics, and of course, gym. It looks like it's going to be an easy year.

It was nice to see my friend Cissy and catch up after the summer. We hung out a lot at the end of the last school year until she started dating Rob. She's getting married in October this year. I'm surprised she even bothered to come back this year. The rule is you can't be engaged, married, or pregnant and go to Catholic High.

"Don't you want to graduate?" I ask her.

"I'm going to take the GED test and get my diploma that way," she says.

"You can do that? I never heard of that before," I say. I'm so jealous. I wish it were Tommy and I getting married, but I'm happy for her, too.

She has her brother's Volkswagen and offers to take me home. It's pretty old and beat up, but still cool. She tells me to get in and give it a spin around the parking lot.

"I don't know how to drive a car," I tell her, but I get in and give it a try. We're laughing our heads off as I grind the gears trying to master the clutch.

"On second thought, maybe this wasn't such a good idea," she says, laughing.

On the ride home, we're both quiet. She asks me if I'm all right. I tell her I don't know what's the matter with me lately. I'm so tired all the time.

"I feel the same way since Rob went off to boot camp," she tells me.

"Maybe we both have the love bug," I tell her.

"The love bug? What's that?" she asks.

"You know, lovesickness," I say.

She pulls up to the curb in front of the apartment house. "Well, today was a nice distraction from my thoughts of Tommy," I say.

"I feel the same way," she says.

"Thanks for the ride, Cissy. I'll see you tomorrow," I say.

Walking up the steps to the apartment house, I think how glad I am that I don't have to work this evening. I wonder what's wrong with me? Opening the vestibule door, I stand in front of the mail slots, close my eyes and make a wish that by some miracle, I'll find a letter from Tommy already inside. But of course, there isn't. There hasn't been enough time for a letter to go through the mail yet.

I feel like I have to drag myself up the stairs one step at a time. The moment I get inside, I head for my room, dropping my books and purse on the floor next to the bed. Kicking my shoes off and yanking the blouse out from around my waistband, I reach for the radio, turning it on and plopping face down on the bed.

"Jim Nettleton here with you at WFIL Boss Radio. Coming up next, we have The Beach Boys singing, "Wouldn't It Be Nice." Turning on my side to listen to the words of the song, I curl my legs up close to me and hug my pillow. I've heard this song so many times before, but now the words seem as if they were written just for Tommy and me, as they express exactly how we both feel.

> Wouldn't it be nice if we were older
> Then we wouldn't have to wait so long?
> And wouldn't it be nice to live together
> In the kind of world where we belong?
>
> You know its gonna make it that much better
> When we can say goodnight and stay together
>
> Wouldn't it be nice if we could wake up
> in the morning when the day is new?
> And after having spent the day together
> Hold each other close the whole night through?
>
> Happy times together we've been spending
> I wish that every kiss was never-ending
> Wouldn't it be nice?
>
> Maybe if we think, and wish, and hope, and pray
> It might come true.
> Baby, then there wouldn't be a single thing we couldn't do
> We could be married
> And then we'd be happy
> Wouldn't it be nice?
>
> You know the more we talk about it

It only makes it worse to live without it
But let's talk about
Wouldn't it be nice?

Goodnight, oh baby
Sleep tight, of baby
Goodnight, oh baby
Sleep tight, oh baby

All cried out, drained, and exhausted; I fall asleep.

Dad wakes me up when he gets home. "You're burning up," he says, concerned. "How long have you been feeling sick?" he asks me.

"I've been getting these fevers off and on, and I don't have any other symptoms except sometimes my stomach feels sick. It started the week before Tommy left for college," I say.

"You don't think you could be pregnant, do you?" he asked me.

"Dad!" I say with shock.

"Well, after our talk last week, I wondered if it could be a possibility," he said.

"I don't know for sure. I could be, but maybe I'm just coming down with something," I say.

He tells me if I'm not any better by tomorrow he's going to make an appointment for me to see a doctor.

Washing and changing into my pajamas, I'm shivering. No matter how many covers I put on, I can't get warm. Dad gives me two aspirin to break the fever and tells me to get some sleep.

"I can't. I have to write to Tommy," I say, trying to get up.

"You can write to him tomorrow," Dad says.

"But I promised him I'd write every day," I whine.

"Not now, maybe later. Get some sleep now so you can get better," Dad says.

I wake up an hour later, drenched in sweat. I walk through the living room. The TV is on, but Dad's in the kitchen sitting at the little table with a big smile on his face talking with someone on the phone.

"Who you talking to?" I say, startling him.

He puts his hand over the receiver and says, "How are you feeling?"

"Better! I'm thirsty as heck and feel clammy all over. Do you think it's okay if I take a bath?"

"I think so, but don't stay in there too long and get the chills again," he says.

"Is that your friend Sue you're talking to?" I ask him.

"Yeah," he says with a big smile on his face.

"Tell her I said hi!"

After my bath, I change the sheets on my bed. I sit up against the backboard and start to write Tommy, telling him all about my first day back at school and how much I miss him.

∞ ∞ ∞

I walk into the vestibule as I have for the past four days, stand in front of the mail slot, close my eyes, say a prayer, stick the tiny key in the lock, lift the lid, and pull the mail out. There it is, my first letter from Tommy, sitting between the electric and phone bills. Wasting no time, I tear it open, reading it like a starving kid, wanting to gobble up every word. But it was like eating something really good too fast and not enjoying the taste of it before it's all gone. I run up the stairs, kick my shoes off, flop on my bed, lie back, and read every line again slowly, digesting the thoughts between the lines, the ones that feed my hunger. I love you. I miss you. I need you. I want you. My eyes fill up with tears of joy this time. He really does love me. I wipe them away and read it again. This time for content as he tells me what he's been doing.

September 15, 1970

Dearest Luv,

I got your letter today. It was beautiful.

Well, now you know I'm up here, okay. We got up here at 1:30 or so, but I was busy up until I left home. All we did once I got here was play cards, watch TV, and play pool. When I got back to my room, the first thing I did was pull your picture out of my suitcase, and I laid on my bed looking at your beautiful face. I miss you already so much.

On Monday, I slept until 10:00 am, got my shower, and finally unpacked my stuff. I went off to eat lunch, and afterward, I registered, getting the schedule for all my classes. Nothing else to do, so a bunch of us guys got together and played football. I got a jammed toe, sore back, arms, and legs out of the deal.

Today I went to three of my classes. For swimming, the coach said that no hair could be in the eyes, so off with the bangs. In the other two classes, I think I can survive. I went down to the dining hall for a job today, but no luck. So, I don't know where to look for work now, but I'll keep trying to find something.

Do you remember when I met your dad's friend Sandy? She's the one who picks him up for work. She mentioned that she was an alumna from Bloomsburg College. She wanted me to let her know when homecoming was so she could come up to it. She also mentioned bringing you up with her. Well, it's on Oct 17th.

I hope to be home again on the 2nd or 8th of October. We can talk to her about the details then.

Now you know everything that happened to me up here, and so you can see how boring it is without you. All I see are couples walking around together, and it reminds me of you and our summer together. Connie, without you, my life is empty. I feel a lot better when I'm doing something, but there is so much time in between things that all I do is think of you and how I can't wait for next summer or spend just a day with you.

Well, Connie, I got to go now. Sorry for the short letter, but as I told you, I'm no writer, but I will get better with all the practice I'll have this year.

By the time you read this letter, it will be three months since you said you'd be my girl. Happy anniversary, Luv. Always remember how much I love you. Be good, take care, and thank you for the wonderful summer. See you in October.

With deepest love,

Tommy (Tom)

Jumping up from my bed, I feel like someone's pulled a big heavyweight off me. Turning the stereo on, I place Tommy's "Chicago" album on the turntable. "Make Me Smile" is playing, and I sing along, "I'm so happy that you love me."

The Promise

Chapter 26 - October 1970

"Well, look who the cat drug in," I say to Dad. "I hardly see you anymore."

"You know. I met someone," Dad says.

"Oh, that's why you were asking how you looked all the time before you went to work. Is it that Sue lady you talk on the phone with all the time?"

"She only started working at the Welfare office at the end of summer. I don't know what she wants with me. She is a lot younger than I am."

"So is Sandy, but you like her, don't you?" I ask.

"Sandy's thirty-five, I'm forty-six. That's only eleven years difference. Sue's a lot younger," he says.

"How much younger?" I ask.

"She's twenty-two," he says.

"What?"

"I know. Sue's young enough to be my daughter," he says.

"Yeah, only a year older than Kathy," I say.

"I miss you, and I could use some help on some projects I have coming up in school, but it makes me happy to see you happy. You haven't been drinking, have you?" I ask.

"No, I enjoy being with Sue. She likes to do a lot of the same things I do," he says.

"Oh yeah, like what?" I ask with cursorily.

"We've been to a play at the Fulton, and out to eat. We even went to a poetry reading at the college. She's smart, sensible, and funny. I met her mom. Boy, can she cook! She made me a huge meal with all the fixings. I could hardly move when I finished. You'd like her. I met her dad too."

"How did that go? I mean, what did they think of you going out with their young daughter?" I asked.

"They like me. Amy, her mother, gave me a big hug and told me to be good to her daughter, and she'll make me some more good meals."

"So, when do I get to meet Sue?" I asked.

"Soon," he said, "I think she's a little nervous you won't like her," he says.

"Well, tell her anyone who loves you as much as I do can't be all that bad," I say.

"Ah, bless your heart," he says. "So, how's Tommy?"

"He's having a really hard time, Dad. We both are. He can hardly concentrate on the work he has to do at school, and neither can I. He's thinking of dropping out and just working at Armstrong. But we're both worried if he does that, he could get drafted. So, we thought maybe he could transfer to Millersville."

"You know it was hard for your mother and me the same way in the beginning. Once we got married, I was able to crack down and get to work on my studies. We were lucky we could live on campus after we got married. How's everything else going?" he asks.

"There isn't anything else without Tommy here for me. For the first time in my whole life, I was really happy. Every day I do the same thing: I go to school, clean the apartment, do laundry, and go to work. Oh, and I study too. I do stay up too late at night and can hardly stay awake at school, so I bought some NoDoz". I tell him.

"Don't be taking that stuff," he says to me.

"But they help me stay awake, although they do make me fill a little jittery," I say.

"What you need is to get to bed earlier," he says.

"If you need a boost in the morning, drink a cup of coffee," he says. "Now, promise me you won't take them anymore."

"Only if you promise to come home a little more, so I'm not all alone at night," I say.

"I promise," he says. But I know better than to hold my breath with his promises.

"I am enjoying home economics. We made some little loaves of bread yesterday. I brought it home if you want to try a slice. It's all good practice for when I marry Tommy. We're making a Thanksgiving meal in class, and everyone's inviting their parents to come to school that day. Do you think you could come for an hour?"

"I'll try, but transportation can be a problem for me. Let me know when it is, and I'll see what I can work out," Dad says.

"We're going to be sewing in January. I was thinking of trying to make my prom dress. If that goes well, I could make my bridesmaid gowns for when I get married," I say.

"Your mom was a great seamstress. I always said that about her. I'm glad you're enjoying it, too," he said.

He takes the change out of his pocket and puts in the big water jug Tommy brought over. "It's going to take a long time to fill this up, but when it's full, you'll have a nice saving," he says.

"Thanks for the contribution," I say. "We've been saving green stamps, too. You can get all kinds of things with them. I'm collecting those cute little glasses the jelly comes in too. Tommy and I find all kinds of ways to find things we need without spending a lot of money. That's another thing I like about him. He's smart with how to budget money," I say.

"I like Tom a lot," Dad says. "I couldn't ask for a better guy for you, Connie. I mean it. He truly cares about you and is a sensible boy. I miss him not being around here."

"He'll be home October 2," I say.

"That's only six days from now," he says

"I know. So close, yet it still feels so far away. I can't wait," I say.

"How about if I take you and Sue out to eat next week? Then you can meet her, and it will give you something else to look forward to," he says.

"That would be cool, Dad."

∞ ∞ ∞

"Home," Tommy says in his letter, "I never knew how sweet the word home could sound. That's because you are my home now, Connie."

Last night was like Christmas Eve when I was little. I'd lie awake all night, too excited to sleep, wondering what I got, wishing that Christmas morning would hurry up and get here. Now today is just as bad. Waiting till the end of the day for Tommy to get home is like having to wait until the end of Christmas day to open my gifts.

I sit at the top of the steps, waiting for Tommy to come dashing up to me. He told me all he wants to see is my smile. "That cute little smile you get when you look at me," he says, "I love it so much I could pick you up and carry you away."

The front door opens downstairs. Then I hear the familiar sound of his dash up the first flight of stairs. As soon as I see him, I jump up, standing at the top of the landing. He looks up at me and slows his stride until he stands on the step right below me. It's the same place we stood the first time we kissed. We look at each other as if we're both wondering the same thing, is this real or just another one of the dreams we've had for the past few weeks we've been apart? Our lips meet, and what starts as slow and gentle becomes long and passionate, kissing every inch of each other's face, fingers curled in each other's hair, we are like two hot candles melting into each other. It's the way we feel when we're together like there's no beginning and no end. Everything feels right and perfect.

"Home!" he whispers, holding me tight against him, and the heat of his breath gently blowing in my ear drives me crazy.

"Welcome home," I whisper back. Tommy picks me up and carries me into the apartment.

"Where's your dad?" Tommy asks.

"He's hardly home anymore since he met Sue. He asks about you all the time, says things aren't the same since you went back to college."

"As much as I want to visit with your dad, I'm glad we have the place to ourselves. You don't think he'll pop in unexpectedly as he did before, do you?" he asks.

"He likes to keep us guessing. He thinks that way; we won't fool around," we both laugh. "But, I don't think he will pop in because he's all caught up in Sue."

We spend every moment we can together. If Tommy weren't such a good son, he'd stay all night, but he doesn't want his parents to think the worst about us. I don't want them to think I'm a bad influence on him either.

"Connie, I don't want to wait to get married," he says to me.

"I don't either," I say. "Maybe you could transfer to Millersville this next semester, and we could get married in January. I could quit school and get my GED like Cissy is doing."

"I don't want you to quit school," he tells me.

"I won't be able to marry you and still go to Catholic High. It's okay. I'll still get a diploma that counts the same. This way, I could work full time while you go to college. We could live here with Dad until you finish college," I say.

"I need to find a way to talk to my parents about it," he says.

"I could go with you, and we could talk to them together. Maybe I could even get my dad to come with us so he could let them know it's all right with him," I say.

"I'll write to them when I get back to school and tell them what a hard time I'm having, how I can't concentrate on anything but you. I have to come up with the right way to tell them," he says.

"In the meantime, I'm going to talk with Father Lavelle about us and see what he thinks," I say.

"That's a great idea," he says.

"You know, Cissy has been sharing with me everything she has to do to get married in the church. You have to go to something called Pre-Cana classes. I'd have to have proof of my baptism, and she thinks you have to have all your sacraments in order. I never made my confirmation, and I don't know where my baptism took place. We have to have blood tests and a license. If we want to get married in January, we need to get moving on some of these things," I say.

"That does add pressure to the whole matter," he says. "That only gives us two months. Maybe we should try to hold off until the end of the school year. Then you could graduate with your class, and we'll have more time to plan things right."

"If only you could transfer to Millersville in January, it would make it so much easier on both of us," I say.

"To be honest, Connie, I think that might be easier said than done. I did apply there, and I didn't get accepted. I need to look into all this. I could probably transfer there easier if I wait until the next school year," he says.

"I'll talk to my dad and see if he can find anything out for you," I say.

"Do you know that Millersville college is Bloomsburg's rival? That's who we're playing football against at the homecoming game this year. Have you talked to Sandy anymore about coming up for homecoming?"

"Yes, she's excited about it and asked if you'd call her this weekend."

"Good, I found a hotel you can both stay. I'll go over the schedule with Sandy so she can figure out what she wants to do while she's there," he says.

"Aren't we lucky to know someone like her who's an alumnus? She's so excited to take me up there with her," I say.

"I can't wait to show you around the campus," he says.

"Well, I can't wait to see where you live when your away from me," I say.

∞ ∞ ∞

I talk with Fr. Lavelle today at school about Tommy and me. He asks what his last name is. When I say Rife, he knows who he is right away.

"That's a good guy you have there," he says to me.

"I know," I say. "That's why I want to marry Tommy."

"So, what can I do for you?" he asks.

I tell him how much Tommy and I love each other and that we are planning to get married. "I was wondering if I need to have all my sacraments in order before we can do that. I never made my confirmation," I say.

"It's not necessary," he says, "But it would be nice if you had it just as a Catholic. You'd have to go to the Dioceses in Harrisburg to have it done because the church would consider you to be an adult now," he says.

229

"To tell you the truth Father Lavelle, I'm not even sure if I want to make my confirmation. I mean, I became Catholic through my baptism. Isn't confirmation about choosing the faith for yourself?"

"I guess that's one way to look at it, but there's more to it than that. Confirmation is one of the three sacraments of initiation into the Catholic Church, the other two being baptism and holy communion. According to Catholic doctrine, the sacrament of confirmation enables the faithful to be sealed with the gift of the Holy Spirit, strengthening them in their Christian life. It's the sacrament by which Catholics receive a special outpouring of the Holy Spirit. Through the Holy Spirit, we're better able to practice our Catholic faith in every aspect of our lives and to witness Christ in every situation," he tells me.

"That must be the secret behind Tommy's family's faith. The Holy Spirit must be right in the middle of it. Whatever I choose to believe, I want to believe as they do. I don't ever want my kids to think I'm living one way and making them live another. I want to understand the religion I decide to follow so I can live it and be a good example to our kids. I've only ever believed in God, and I have a great relationship with Him. I don't ever want that to change," I say.

"Well, maybe you can take that relationship and let it grow through the help of the Holy Spirit through the church," he says.

"I'm going to give that a lot of thought," I said. "In the meantime, Tommy's away at college up in Bloomsburg. We're both having a heck of a time concentrating on our studies. Tommy is miserable all the time. We thought if we went ahead and got married, maybe he'd be able to settle into his studies better," I tell him.

"I don't think it's a good idea to get married before you both finish school, especially with you being here and him up there," he says.

"Tommy's thinking of transferring to Millersville. We could live with my dad until Tommy finishes college. That's what my mom and dad did when he was in college, and it worked out much better for them. My dad was able to put more into his studies then," I said.

"I want what's best for you both. You still need to finish your last year of school, and you won't be able to do that here if you get married. Tom needs to think about what he wants out of his education and what he has to do to accomplish that goal. That's what I want for the two of you to think about first," he says.

"Honestly, Father Lavelle, if I knew that Tommy's education meant that much to him, then I'd do everything I could to support him. But it doesn't seem like he wants to be in college or knows what he wants to do with that education. That's what he tells me anyway," I told him.

"I will be here for you both whatever you decide and support you in any way I can. I still think you have a lot to talk about; one should never take marriage lightly. It's a commitment you'll make for the rest of your life," he said.

Sometimes I wish I didn't talk to any adults at all because they always make you think about the things that get in the way of what you want to do. Tommy and I have a lot to talk about, but I still wish we could just run off and get married and forget about all the stuff in between we're supposed to do because that's what society tells us to do. I don't understand why I'm an adult when it comes to making my confirmation, but I'm a child when it comes to getting married.

∞ ∞ ∞

The mountains are full of Autumn colors. They are not tall and peeked like the California mountains. These are like round heads, and the trees are their hair, one head standing up against the other, all different heights and widths. They are as unique as all God's creations. I love the changing seasons of Pennsylvania. Autumn is my favorite time of year.

I look over at Sandy driving. She's singing an Elvis song. "Don't you love Elvis?" she says to me.

"He's OK," I say.

"Only OK!"

"I'm guessing it's the generational difference. When I first started liking music, it was all about the Beatles and the Beach Boys. That was when I lived in California. Then, when I moved to Philadelphia, I got into Motown music. Tommy's turned me on to the Chicago band, and our song is "Color My World." Another one is "We've Only Just Begun" by the Carpenters.

"Speaking of different generations, what do you think of your dads' new friend Sue?" Sandy asks.

"You mean girlfriend," I correct her. "She's very nice but not much older than me. I don't' know why anyone so young would want to date someone old enough to be her father. To each her own, I say. The good thing about it is that she makes him want to be a better person, and for that, I'm grateful. I don't want him to get hurt, though. That could send him right back down the drinking hole."

"You can't keep trying to save your dad from himself," she says to me. "You have your own life to live. Pretty soon, you'll be old enough to create the life you want for yourself."

"Isn't that what I've been doing for a long time now?" I ask.

"In many ways, you have, much sooner than any kid should have to. But I'm talking about getting out from under your parents' problems, making your life the way you've dreamed it could be someday," she says.

"Miss Janet, the counselor I see from family services, says that sometimes what happens in situations like mine is that the roles get reversed, where the parent becomes the child, and the child becomes the parent. I don't tell her that's the way it is at home. She's always trying to get things out of me. She's pretty good at figuring out what I need to hear, though, and I do listen. I've only ever done what I had to survive. But in truth, Sandy, all I ever wanted was for my parents to love me enough to take care of me."

Sandy doesn't say anything. She looks like she's going to cry or scream or something like she wants to say something and is trying hard to hold it in. "Are you all right, Sandy?" I ask.

"I'm fine, Connie," she says, patting my hand. "I'm so glad you have Tom in your life. You deserve some happiness. He's a good guy, and it seems like he cares a lot about you."

"I don't know what I'd do without him, especially now that Dad is with Sue. It seems as if it's meant to be. Dad and I both have someone in our lives who brings out the best in us."

"I guess that's one way to look at it," Sandy says.

"All I dream about is being with Tommy. You know he asked me to marry him. We can't stand being away from each other. Neither one of us can concentrate on our school work. We keep thinking if we could be together, we'd be able to do the things we need to do a little bit easier. Do you know what I mean?" I ask her.

"What you and Tom have is very special. Anyone can see that, but isn't his education important too?" she asks.

"But his heart isn't in it. He has no idea why he's there or what he wants to do with his education. If he were at home attending Millersville, he'd be able to think clearer. I know he doesn't want to disappoint his parents either," I say.

"As much as I hate to see him leave my alma mater, he might be better off going to Millersville State College," she says.

"We've been talking about that. I even talked to Father Lavelle at my school, and he said the same thing. I talked with Miss Janet, too, about it, and she agreed as well," I said.

"It sounds like you've both thought a lot about this, and you're talking to the right people. Has Tom talked with anyone about it?"

"He's been trying to talk with the dean at school about it but can't seem to catch him at the right time," I say.

"What does your dad think about all this?" she asks

"He understands. He said that when he and my mom started seeing each other, they had the same trouble. She was a senior in high school, too. After she graduated, they got married. They lived in one of the dorms for married couples. It was his last year of college."

"I didn't know that. Sounds pretty cool," Sandy says.

"I wish we could live on campus. Since we can't, Dad said we could live with him until Tommy finishes his next two years."

"Your dad loves you and wants the best for you. It's nice to see him finally stepping up to the plate and looking out for your best interests," she says.

"You know, Sandy, before Tommy or Sue came along, all those times you came over to play three-handed pinochle with dad and me, and the few times you had us over for dinner, I was kind of hoping you and dad would get together. I mean, you're younger than him too, but not as young as Sue. Did you ever think about my dad in that way?"

"I did, but I could never handle his drinking and always worrying about when he's going to take the next drink. He's a great guy, I enjoy working with him, he makes me laugh, but that's about it," she says.

"What do you think of Sue?" I ask.

"I guess I'm a little jealous of the attention he gives her at work all the time. We don't talk like we used to, and I miss my friend. What I don't get it why a woman as pretty and smart as Sue is would want to be with someone as old as her father," she says.

"Well, I hope it doesn't change things between you and me, Sandy. Tommy enjoys being around you, too. We can still pick up a game of pinochle between the three of us," I say.

"I'd like that," she says.

Bloomsburg State College occupies the top of an expanding hill. You can't miss it once you start driving up toward it. We find the Hotel McGee, where Tommy is waiting outside for us. It's 10:00 am, and we made it before the homecoming parade starts. After we check-in, we get something to eat, then watch a little bit of the parade. Sandy wants to rest a little before the football game starts. That gives Tommy and me a little bit of time to walk through the campus together and be alone.

"So, this is your world when you're away from me," I say. "It all seems so cool to be on your own, making your own decisions, trying to better yourself and prepare for a career. I wish I were smart enough to go to college."

"You could do anything you put your mind to," Tommy says. "But it is hard work, and not everybody here knows what they want to do with their education. I don't even know. I'd rather be with you, making our life together. I don't need some fancy degrees from college. My dad did alright; he made a good living and providing for our family working at Armstrong. I don't mind doing the same thing if it means we can be together."

"Then you need to tell your parents that," I say.

"I know, but they had such high hopes for me being the first one in the family going to college. I don't want to let them down either," he says.

We meet Sandy at Hotel McGee and head to the football stadium. Bloomsburg State College doesn't have a playing field; they share it with the local high school. Sandy and Tommy are excited because Bloomsburg is playing our local college, Millersville State College. The game starts at 2:00 pm, and it turns out to be as exciting as they anticipated, with Bloomsburg winning 23 to 17.

After we get something to eat, Tommy takes me to see his dorm room, where I meet his roommate Christopher. He wants to know what I'm doing with a goofy guy like Tom when I could have someone as cool as he is, and before I have a chance to defend Tommy, he's pushing Christopher out of their room.

"Alone, at last," Tommy says as he wraps his arms around me.

"Are you sure I'm allowed to be in here," I ask him.

"Yeah, it's open dorms every weekend," he says.

"But what if someone walks in or Christopher comes back," I ask.

"He won't," Tommy says. "He knows we want to be alone."

We meet up with Sandy back at the hotel and watch TV. Sandy falls asleep, and Tommy stays all night. Before long, we are packing up to head back home.

"It seems like you just got here," Tommy says.

"I know, I feel the same way. It's always like that when we're together, time flies by, too fast. But when we are not together, it drags.

"OK, you two, say your goodbyes. It's time for us to get on the road," Sandy says.

Chapter 27 - November 1970

call Tommy's mom to make sure it's okay if I drop by on Sunday. She invites me to supper. It's nothing fancy," she says, "just some lentil soup."

"I never had that before, but I'm sure I'll like it," I tell her.

"Oh, it's one of Russ's favorites. Nana Mary likes it, too. Why don't you come before supper so we can talk a little while before she gets here? The guys will be busy watching football," she says.

"That sounds great," I say.

As I walk over to their house, it's colder now. No one is sitting on their porches. It's quiet without Tommy and seems farther away than when we walk together.

They live in a big row home with three floors and a basement. I guess you need a big house with seven kids. There's no front yard, just a big porch. The back yard is about two clotheslines long and one clothesline wide, with gardens on both sides of the fence.

I knock at the door and see through the lace-covered window Jimmy and Bobby running to answer it. They fight over who gets to turn the doorknob first. I hear a loud voice in the background yell, "What the hell are you two nitwits doing? Open the damn door."

"It's Tommy's girlfriend," Bobby says with a big grin.

"Tommy's not here," Jimmy says.

"I know! I came to visit the two of you," I say, tickling them both in the tummy. Jimmy, Tommy's youngest brother, grins with a toothless smile. Then comes Bobby, Denny, Rusty, and Rick. Then Nancy, the oldest and only girl. She's married; Tommy is the oldest boy.

Mrs. Rife comes up behind them, drying her hands on her apron. "Let me take your coat," she says, looking for a spot to hang it on the filled coat-tree. Mr. Rife gets up out of his chair from the TV room and comes out to greet me, "Come on, give me some loving," he says, reaching his arms out to me. I hug him. Then he goes back to his chair as he hears the cheers of the football game. "What'd I miss?" he says to Denny, who couldn't care less about who came to the door. Even Mrs. Rife wanted to know what happened. They are a big sports-minded family. No wonder Tommy likes to watch the games all the time.

She invites me to sit on the couch in the living room with her. The two younger boys are already in front of the TV, with their eyes glued to the game.

"So, how's school going?" she asks me. It's an exciting year for you, being your last one. I graduated from Lancaster Catholic High, too.

"Wow, I didn't know that. School's going okay. Sometimes it's hard to concentrate on because I miss Tommy so much, but in a way, I'm doing better than I ever have," I say.

"Well, that's great!" she says. "What makes this year easier for you?" she asks.

"I wouldn't say it's easier. It's just that Tommy makes me feel like I can do anything if I put my mind to it. He encourages me always to do my best, and when someone believes in you as much as he does me, it makes a big difference."

"Only it doesn't' seem to be working for him," she says.

"He does want to do good, Mrs. Rife, but he's up there away from everyone, and at least I'm around my family the people I care about," I say. "I think, too, if he had a goal or purpose being there, he'd do better. He doesn't' know why he's there anymore or what he wants to do with his education," I say.

"But I thought he did know," she said. "I thought he wanted to be a math teacher or an accountant. He's so good with his math skills," she says.

"He told me after student teaching at Catholic High last year he knew right away that wasn't what he wanted to do. As far as being an accountant, he didn't want a job where he'd have to bring his work home with him all the time. He said that's the nice thing about working at Armstrong-he could go to work, do his job, and leave it there when he came home," I tell her.

"All we ever wanted for him was something better. Education can get that for him. Open up more opportunities," she says.

"I know from the way he talks about you both that he cares very much what you think. I think he wants to do good for you and his dad, but he's not doing it for himself. I learned when I went to an Al-Anon meeting once when my dad was drinking so bad that an alcoholic can't quit drinking just because you want them to. They have to quit for themselves first to be successful. I couldn't understand that then when I needed to. But when I look at Tommy's situation, I can see how it's the same. He has to want to do better because it's what he wants to do. Right now, the only thing that feels right in his life is when he and I are together. I feel the same way," I say.

"You really love him, don't you?"

"I don't know if God creates someone special for each one of us, but the moment Tommy and I met, we both felt a connection. Two weeks after seeing each other, I felt like things were moving too fast. He was telling me that he loved me, and I was feeling that way, too, but it scared me. As much as I wanted to be loved and treated special, it didn't feel normal to me. I couldn't trust it. Tommy was too kind and caring, and no one had ever treated me in that way. What scared me the most was that all the people in my life who were supposed to love me, left me. So, to spare myself the hurt that I believed would eventually happen, I broke it off with him. I went to visit my best friend in Philadelphia for the weekend. She knows me better than anyone and what I've experienced. She thought he sounded like the best thing that ever happened to me. I realized she was right and feared that I'd screwed it all up. But when I came back, he was at the bus station, waiting for my return. So, yes, I really do love him."

"I don't know much about what you've been through, but I can see from what you're saying how hard it must be for you to be apart from each other. Tommy wrote that the two of you want to sit down and talk with his dad and me when he gets home. I'm going to take a wild guess that it's about getting married?" she comes right out and asks.

"I don't feel right talking about this without Tommy being here, too," I say.

"Then it's true," she says.

My face gets red, and I look down at my hands, not knowing what to do or say.

"It's okay, Connie. Anyone who sees the two of you together can tell how much you love each other. I need you to know that we don't have the money to help you both out right now."

"It never occurred to Tommy and me to ask for money from you. We've already talked about the different ways we could afford to do things. Tommy has a good head on his shoulders about money and budgeting. We know what's important and what isn't. We're probably about the only two young people around who don't feel like we have to have the best. Having each other is enough for us. We're already saving green stamps and putting away every penny we can save. We don't need fancy things. Having jelly jar glasses to drink out of is good enough for us. Please don't worry about us being a drain on you. We would never think to do that, Mrs. Rife," I assure her.

"Here comes Nana Mary," she says as a little old lady with a bun on her head comes walking up the steps to the porch. "We'll talk some more in a few days when Tommy gets home," she says, patting my hand.

hen Nana Mary walks through the door, she has her pocketbook in one hand and a paper bag with a handle in the other. That must be the bag that's full of goodies that Tommy always tells me she brings. Mrs. Rife helps her off with her coat; The first thing Nana Mary does is reach her arms out to me, saying, "come over here and give me some loving," just like her son Russ does. She pulls me into her soft pudgy body, giving me a big bear hug. She smells of Jean Nate perfume and cigarettes. She hands

the bag for me to carry, puts her arm through mine, and we walk out to the kitchen together. I sit down next to her while the other Mrs. Rife stirs the lentil soup. Here I am sitting in the kitchen with two generations of Mrs. Rifes, and I realize I'm going to be the first of a third generation.

"Oh, you're wearing the ring I gave you at the Bay," she says to me.

That was a fun weekend I spent with Tommy and his family at the Chesapeake Bay. Nana Mary and I slept out on the screened-in porch of the tiny cottage. She had a little box full of beaded rings, and let me pick whatever I wanted. I remember her pulling the pins out of her bun. I was expecting to see her long hair drop to her shoulders, but the bun wasn't her hair. It was a detachable hairpiece she placed on the nightstand beside her cot. She looked at me and put her finger to her lips; it was to be our secret. That's when she told me I could call her Nana Mary, like the rest of the family, did. She snored all through the night. I wanted to ask her to turn over like I do my dad when he snores, but I didn't want to disturb her. So I put my pillow over my head to drown out the sound, eventually falling asleep. I still can't believe we all fit in that little cottage and no one minded, they just enjoyed being together.

"I have something else for you," she tells me as she pulls a box out of her paper bag. "Go ahead, open it," she says.

"Oh my gosh, you're the sales lady from Logan's. I kept thinking that you looked familiar, but I couldn't remember where I met you before. You helped me find that nice top to go with the tunic outfit I bought. Then you tried to sell me this nice green skirt. I couldn't afford it, too. I can't believe they still had it."

"I guess it was just meant for you," she says.

I reach over and give her a big hug, "Thank you, Nana Mary," I say.

I look over at Tommy's mom. She's watching the two of us with a smile on her face.

The boys and Mr. Rife come into the kitchen, "It's half-time, woman," he said to his wife. "Let's eat," he says as he starts kissing her cheek.

"Oh, for God's sake," she says, "behave yourself."

"That's why they have so many kids," Nana Mary says to me, smiling.

"Now I know where Tommy gets it from," I tell her giggling. I love this family.

Mrs. Rife puts a bowl of lentil soup in front of me. I look around to see if everyone else has the same bowl of mud that I do. Nana Mary says, "Don't worry, it tastes much better than it looks." Everyone blesses themselves. Mr. Rife says grace so fast the words run together, and all you hear is the beginning, "Bless us, oh Lord," and the end, "Amen."

Chapter 28 - December 1970

S pending the holidays with Tommy's family is like being in a Norman Rockwell picture-only; it's the real deal with everyone around the table eating together laughing, talking, and kids pinching each other. Mrs. Rife is in her glory, making all the things her family loves. As I help clear off the table, I tell her how good the gravy was. She tells me the secret is in the goodness that's left at the bottom of the pan. Nothing goes to waste in their family as Mrs. Rife scrapes what's left of the mashed potatoes into a container, getting every single layer with her spatula.

I go to mass with Tommy and his family on Christmas Day, and when we get back, I watch as the kids open their gifts in front of their Christmas tree. After everyone has opened theirs, Mrs. Rife hands me one. It's a scarf, gloves and a knit hat. Nana Mary gives me a small bottle of Ambush perfume wrapped in a pretty box. I was not expecting anything. As always, I'm grateful for their kindness.

Even at my place, Christmas was full of family as my sister Kathy and Phil came to live with us in late October. Mary was there, and Sue too. Our little apartment was festive with a pretty tree and decorations that Sue made. The only one missing was Johnny. He was still in the Navy. Mom wasn't there either. As much as I had wished to have my family all back together, I was ready to be off on my own with Tommy.

∞ ∞ ∞

Between Christmas and New Year, before Tommy goes back to school, we finally sit down with Tommy's parents to talk to them about our plans.

We go into the kitchen, where Mr. Rife is already sitting puffing on his cigarette and sipping his coffee while he reads the evening paper. Mrs. Rife asks Tommy and me if we'd like a piece of spice raisin cake.

"It's one of my favorites," Tommy says to me.

I'm too nervous to eat anything, but I don't want to be rude, so I take a piece also. Tommy gobbles his cake down. Even though it tastes delicious, all I can do is pick at mine. Before we start to talk, Tommy gets up to pour us a glass of milk to wash the cake down. I realize that even though we're about to take this big step, this is his home, and there's a sense of comfort here that seems to have a relaxing effect on him.

His dad puts the paper down, lights another cigarette, looks at Tommy, and says, "Well, spit it out, boy."

Tommy and I look at each other like two little kids facing a monster. But as long as we keep our eyes on each other, we're okay. I smile at him, and the fear melts off his face as he smiles back at me and takes my hand.

"We love each other and want to get married," he says.

"Okay," Tommy's mom says, looking at her husband. "Let's take one step at a time. You want to get married, but you need to think of first things first here."

"It's no big deal," Mr. Rife says, "So they'll get married in two years after Tommy finishes college. There's plenty of time to do the planning."

"Well, we were thinking more of this summer when I finish out this year. Then I'll transfer to Millersville," Tommy says.

"Where are you going to live? How are you going to pay the rent and pay for school, too?" Mrs. Rife says.

"We can live with my dad until Tommy graduates," I say.

"Does your dad know this?" Mrs. Rife asks.

"He's the one who said we could. He understands why it's so hard for Tommy to concentrate on his studies because he went through the same thing with my mom when he was in college," I say. "Once they got married, he was able to crack down on his studies and concentrate."

"It sounds like you both have your mind made up," Mr. Rife says.

"Russ!" Mrs. Rife looks at her husband.

"Look, woman, they've obviously thought this through and made up their minds," he says.

"When were you thinking of setting the date?" Mrs. Rife asks.

"We were thinking sometime in June," I say.

"Don't you graduate in June?" Mrs. Rife asks.

June 4th," I say. "We were thinking of the 19th."

"There's a lot to think about and plans to put together, but like I keep saying, first things first. Work on getting yourselves through this year of school. Then we can talk about each step that comes next," she says.

Tommy looks at me and I at him again. "I think we can do that," he says. "What do you think, Connie?"

"I think we just got engaged. That's a step all on its own, but with your help, Mrs. Rife, I think we can make it work," I say.

"Since you're officially engaged, I think you can do away with Mrs. Rife and call me Mom," she says.

"You'll be my first daughter-in-law. Come here and give me some loving. You can call me what you like, the big shit, pain in the ass, whatever, just so long as you don't call me Mr. Rife."

I give him a big hug, and Mom gives me a big hug, too, saying welcome to the family.

Wow, this is what it feels like to be a part of a real family. It's all I ever wanted and dreamed I could have, and it's what God promised me. All I had to do was hang in there through all those difficult years. Now, it's just a little bit longer, seven more months.

It feels so close yet so far away. I've waited this long I guess I can wait a little longer, God. But I'm still afraid of losing Tommy. I know what You're going to tell me.

Trust!"

Chapter 29 – January 1971

oday is January 27, 1971, my eighteenth birthday, and I wake up feeling nauseous. It seems like it's getting worse each day.

I go back to bed and cover-up. The conversation with Ms. Grace, my supervisor at work, plays in my head. She told me I need to see a gynecologist. It's the same kind of doctor Nurse Jones was going to take me to when I didn't get my period for nine months.

Ms. Grace, with all her years of experience behind her, puts it bluntly, "If you think your woman enough to have sex, then this is one of the things that come with it, getting pregnant."

Hearing someone else say the word pregnant out loud makes the possibility all the more real. I could actually be pregnant.

"But isn't it too soon to tell if I'm pregnant?" I ask.

"Maybe, but it would be good to get into the doctor to see what's going on anyway," she encourages me.

Maybe it's just because I've been stressing about getting up in front of my POD class to give my presentation on the death penalty. I've done a lot of research and learned a lot about how the government works. I'm afraid once I put it up for debate, I'll forget everything I want to say to defend it. I have to go to school today and do my presentation in front of my class. That's enough to make anyone sick in their stomach. Plus, I have my ob-gyn appointment right after school.

"Come on, Connie, you've done so many difficult things in your life. It's just another part of being a grown-up," I hear God's voice inside me.

Leaning my head against the window on the bus, I'm off on a new journey that's taking me into the adult world. As much as I want to grow up and take this ride, it doesn't hold the same excitement my runaway years held. I only thought of all the fun things I wanted to do and not the bad things that could happen. Part of being a grown-up means you don't run away from your problems; I have to face them head-on. It doesn't mean I'm not scared to see a gynecologist, I am. It's funny how this reminds me of when I was a little girl. I wanted to play with my doll one minute;

then I'd hide her in my closet and play with Kathy's makeup. I want to run home and pretend that nothing is wrong. I'm still the high school senior who wants to go out and party with my friends. But I want to be a mother and Tommy's wife, too.

The nurse takes me into the doctor's office and introduces me to Dr. France. He's very handsome. Having such a young, good-looking doctor examine me for the first time only makes me more nervous. He looks up and pauses for a minute as he notices I'm wearing my school uniform.

"How old are you?" he asks.

"Eighteen, as of today," I say.

"Well, Happy Birthday," he says. "It's pretty brave of you to come here all by yourself," he says.

"Oh, I've been doing things on my own for a long time," I say. "But I am a little nervous about being here."

"Well, the nurse will explain everything I need to do, and she'll be with you the whole time."

He has a calm way of making me feel a little more at ease. We go over why I'm here and what's been going on. After my full examination, he brings me back into his office and talks with me again.

"It looks like you might be pregnant. It's still a little too early to tell, but a pregnancy test will verify it for you," Dr. France says.

"Wait! Did you say you're pretty sure I'm pregnant?" I ask.

"Yes, I did."

"Holy moly!" I say.

"I'll have the receptionist set you up for your next visit, and then we'll talk about your prenatal care," he says.

I have no idea what he's talking about; it's all going in one ear and out the other.

The receptionist gives me some information on how I can pay for my monthly visits. She tells me to stop at the hospital on my way home to get the pregnancy test done.

"Is there a chance the test will say I'm not pregnant?" I ask.

"Well yes, but your body is showing all the signs that you are," she says

Before I leave, she hands me a booklet on what to expect with pregnancy.

As I'm walking from the office to St. Joseph's Hospital, my thoughts are going a mile a minute.

What are Tommy's parents going to think now? They're going to hate me for sure. What's my dad going to say? How are we going to make the doctor payments each month? What about school? Should we get married right away or wait?

Of all people, I get a nun nurse for the pregnancy test. She looks at my uniform and shakes her head.

"Call tomorrow late afternoon for the results," she says.

Tommy calls as he promised around 6:00 pm.

"Happy Birthday, Luv! Did you get my card in the mail?"

"Yes, thank you," I say.

"I'm sorry I couldn't get you anything special," he says.

"Oh, I think you may have given me the best gift ever," I say.

"What do you mean?" he asks.

"I told you I was going to the doctors today to find out what's going on with me."

"Yeah, but I thought it was just an infection or something going on that you were getting checked out. What did the doctor say?"

"He thinks I'm pregnant, Tommy." "Hello! Are you still there?"

"Did I just hear you say, he thinks you're pregnant?"

"Yes."

"But he doesn't know for sure yet?"

"I stopped at the hospital to get a pregnancy test done. I find out for sure tomorrow when I call for the results. But Tommy, the doctor's so sure I am pregnant that they are setting me up with a payment plan and prenatal care. They even sent me home with a booklet on pregnancy."

"Yikes, this changes everything," he says.

"I know, but let's not decide anything until I get the results tomorrow."

"I should figure out a way to get home this weekend. We will have to tell my parents."

"You and I need some time to think this through together before we tell anyone," I say.

"I agree," he says.

"By the way, I did my debate today in POD. I felt so much better after it was all over. I was sure that was the thing that was making me so sick to my stomach," I say.

"I'm sure it didn't help, but how did it go?"

"I was nervous, but since I was well prepared, I thought it went pretty well. I realized that I couldn't get everyone to see things the way I did, that was frustrating, but hearing all the pros and cons made me think about what I believed and made me all the more determined toward the cause I was fighting for."

"You amaze me," he says.

"Why?" I ask.

"Because everything you do, you approach with such caring passion."

"I wish I could see what you do in me because I sure don't see it."

"Well, I'm going to keep telling you for the rest of your life, until you start to believe it. I hope you don't ever get tired of me telling you how much I love you either because I'm going to remind you every day."

∞ ∞ ∞

I run up the stairs to the apartment, quickly unlocking the door. I dropped my books and purse on the bed and fumbled with the buttons on my pea coat, trying too fast to slide each one out of the hole. My hands shake a little as I pick up the receiver and start to dial the number for the hospital.

"Hello, this is Connie Miller. I'm calling to get the results of my pregnancy test. It's probably under Constance," I say.

She asks me to wait a minute while she checks her paperwork.

"Here you are," she says, "It came back positive."

I pause for a moment, "Ah, I'm sorry," I say. "What does that mean?"

"You're pregnant!" she tells me, "Congratulations!"

I hang the phone up slowly, and with my hand still on the receiver, I don't move for a few seconds. All I hear are the words bouncing around in my head; you're pregnant, you're pregnant, you're pregnant. As the words begin to sink in, my emotions start to spin around, and I'm not sure how I feel. I'm crying and laughing at the same time. I'm going to be a mother. I don't have any idea what that means or how to be one or what to do.

It's 4:00 pm, maybe I can catch Tommy before he goes to the cafeteria for dinner. I call his dorm, and he answers the phone as if he's been waiting for me to call.

"Tommy, I'm so glad I caught you before you left," I say to him.

"Are you all right? You sound like you've been crying and out of breath," he says.

"I got the results of my pregnancy test. They came back positive," I tell Tommy.

"What does that mean?" he asks.

"It means you're going to be a father," I say. "Tommy, are you there?"

"Ah, yeah. Are you sure?" Tommy asks.

"Yes, I'm sure. I asked the lady what it meant. She said positive means you're pregnant. Tommy, are you there?" I ask after a long pause.

" Yeah! I just need some time to take it all in, "he says. "I'm going to run down to the cafeteria to get something to eat. I'll call you back, hon. I love you. Bye."

"What the heck! How can he eat at a time like this?" I say out loud as I slam the phone down. I throw myself on the bed and start thinking the worst. He doesn't want me anymore, I sob. Ten minutes later, the phone rings. I pick it up, sniffing back the tears.

"Hello," I say.

"I'm sorry, Luv, I got to the cafeteria and thought, what the heck am I doing? I hardly talked to you on the most important day of our life. I guess I was in shock for a few minutes. I kind of still am," he says.

"I know I have all kinds of mixed-up feelings too. I don't know how to be a mom or take care of a baby," I say.

"I do," Tommy says. "I helped with the babies my mom had. I had to since I was one of the oldest kids. I'll show you what to do, and we'll figure the rest out together," I say.

"I was so afraid you didn't want me anymore. I started feeling all the scary feelings of my past with everyone leaving me all alone. I couldn't bear losing you, too, Tommy."

"I want you more than ever now. We're going to have a baby, and now we can be together for sure," he says.

"Are you really happy, Tommy?"

"I am, my love, more than you can imagine! Connie, I don't like it when you talk about your past. That was then, and this is now. I won't ever leave you or let you down. I won't let anyone ever hurt you again."

"I wish you were here right now so you could hold me. I always feel like everything's okay when I'm in your arms."

"I guess I'll be coming home this weekend so we can tell my parents. Did you tell your dad yet? I hope nothing changes between him and me now. Maybe you could ask him to come with us when we tell my parents?"

"I haven't told him yet. I don't even know if he'll be home tonight."

"Do you want to wait until I come home this weekend? We can tell him together?"

"I don't think I can wait that long, Tommy. I don't know what to do next. I mean, are we going to get married right away? What about school? I won't be able to stay in school if we get married. I can't wait, either. I also have to see the doctor now for regular monthly visits," I say.

"Yeah, and there will be a hospital bill to pay since we don't have any insurance," he says.

"One of us is going to have to work. It may as well be me," I say. "I'm sure I can work full time at the college," I go on.

"Ah, Connie. I don't want you to have to quit school," he says.

"I don't know what else we can do. You may as well finish out this year it's already paid for, and at least you'll have two years in," I say.

"I don't even care about that. I can get a job at Armstrong again and make good money. Plus, we'll have medical insurance," he says.

"All this stuff is making my head spin, Tommy."

"I know, that's why we have to talk with our parents," he says.

"That's true, but at this point, it's all up to us. I don't want your parents to feel like they have to figure it out for us. We're going to listen to them, then decide how we want to move forward. We have to prove to them that we are mature enough to take care of ourselves. I think we both need some time to take it all in and think things through."

"I agree," he says.

∞ ∞ ∞

It's so hard to keep this all inside, I want to talk to someone about it, but I won't until we've had a chance to speak with both our parents. Dad didn't come home last night, so I'm going to have to stop in at his work and ask if we could talk. In the meantime, I'm going in to speak with Father Lavelle. He'll be able to tell me what my options are.

"Sounds like you got yourself into quite a predicament," Father Lavelle says. "But there's no sense in crying over spilled milk. Let's figure how we can get you through the rest of the school year."

"I know, Father, but I'll be six months pregnant by then," I tell him.

"Hm! That will be a little hard to hide," he says.

"Plus, we need the money, and I want Tommy to be able to finish his second year of college," I say. "I already talked to my boss at work, and he said I could work fulltime. In the meantime, I could take the GED test and still be able to get my diploma."

"Sounds like you have it pretty well planned out," he says.

"Tommy and I don't want anyone else to feel as if they have to figure this out for us. We want to take the right steps, but we're not sure what all that is. That's why I've come to you. We haven't told Tommy's parents yet. I haven't even told my dad."

"It sounds to me like you've already thought this through and made your mind up. I think the next step then is to talk with Father Taylor, the principal," he says.

"Now that makes me nervous," I say.

"You are braver than you give yourself credit. Father Taylor isn't as scary as everyone thinks he is," Father Lavelle says.

"I know. I talked to Father Taylor when I first came to Catholic High. I'm afraid he'll be disappointed in me," I say.

"He's a good man and knows how to deal with the things that come up. Nothing surprises him. Father Taylor only wants the best for all his students," he says. "In the meantime, I'll be keeping you both in my prayers. Don't forget to come back to let me know how you make out."

"I will, and thanks for everything, Father Lavelle," I say.

As I'm walking to Father Taylor's office, I think that in all my twelve years of schooling, I never got sent to the principal's office for anything. Here I am, on what will probably be my last day of school, doing that very thing. I feel like I'm in a dream. None of this seems real to me, and everything is moving faster than my mind has a chance to catch up.

Father Taylor doesn't discipline me. All he wants to do is help me.

"Are you sure you love this boy?" he asks me.

"Oh, yes!" I say. "More than anything. He loves me too, Father Taylor. He's been there for me through some of the rough times with my dad's drinking, and we both want the same things in our life together," I tell him.

"And what is that?" he asks.

"We don't have to have all the fancy things in life. I never had much and have made do. Tommy grew up in a big family. He had what he needed, and that was enough, too. We don't ever want to be in debt. My family lost everything by doing that. Tommy has a real good head on his shoulders, and he's responsible. He comes from a good Catholic family. He goes to church every Sunday and is a good influence on me. We both want to be happy like his parents are. I want to love this baby with all my heart and give it the kind of life I never had. We both believe that we have something special and that God has brought us together. With God on our side, how can we go wrong, Father Taylor?"

"I guess I can't argue with that," he says. "I'll tell you what. Since your halfway through this school year, if you take the GED test, we'll give you your diploma from Lancaster Catholic High," he tells me.

"Wow! I never expected that. What do I have to do?" I ask him.

"I'll give you the upcoming schedule, and you can make the arrangements," he says.

"That will make my dad happy, too. He didn't want me to quit," I tell him.

"Now the hard part," he says.

"You mean coming to see you wasn't the hard part?"

"No, now you have to take this dropout notice around to each of your teachers and have them sign it.," he says.

"Oh!" I say. "Then what?"

"Then empty your locker, turn in your books, and anything else belonging to the school, as well as your signed dropout notice to the office on your way out.

"What do I do next, though?" I ask.

"Have you decided where you're going to be married?" he asks. "Usually, a couple gets married in the woman's church," he tells me.

"Hum! My parents got married at Sacred Heart, but their marriage didn't make it. Maybe that would be bad luck," I say.

"I have a feeling that you're going to be the couple that does make it work," he says. "Why don't you call over there today to get you an appointment with Father Lawrence this weekend while Tom is home from school. I'm sure he'll fit you both in, at least you can get the ball rolling," he goes on.

"Thanks, Father Taylor. You've been a big help, and I won't let you down," I tell him.

When I drop all my stuff off at the office, I ask the school secretary if she knows where I can get a bus to go into town. She pulls out a schedule and says if I hurry, I can catch the next one in ten minutes out in front of the school. As I sit looking out the bus window, I realize I not only have to tell dad I'm pregnant but that I've dropped out of school. I may as well go to his work and get it over with, just in case he doesn't come home again tonight. We have to tell Tommy's parents tomorrow when he gets home. I pull out the Bloomsburg calendar Tommy gave me and wrote down some of the things we have to do: 1-talk to dad, 2-call father Lawrence, 3-talk to Tommy's parents, 4-start working fulltime, 5-figure budget out.

I get off the bus on King Street in front of the Welfare Department and go inside. I ask the lady at the front desk if I can talk with John Miller, "He's my dad," I tell her.

She takes me back to his office, "Hi Dad, I say.

"What a nice surprise. Hey everybody, look who's come to see me," Dad says to his co-workers. It's a big open office with desks spread out. Sandy waves to me, but can't come over because she's with a client. Sue works in another section because her clients are the elderly.

"Dad, is there someplace we can talk in private?" I ask.

"Sure," he says, leading me by the arm into a private office. "What's going on?" he asks as we sit.

"I was hoping to tell you last night, but you never came home," I say.

"I'm sorry. I stayed with Sue last night," he says. "What is it? You look like you're going to cry."

"Yesterday after school, I found out that I'm pregnant," I say.

"Hum! I can't say that I'm surprised," he says. "Do you know for sure?"

"Yes. I saw a doctor on Wednesday. It was my birthday, and you didn't come home that night either," I say.

"Oh my God, I forgot, I'm so sorry, Connie," he says.

"I'm getting used to it," I say.

"Why didn't I know all this was going on?" he says, as if angry.

"Because you're never home anymore for me to talk to," I say. "You may as well know, too, that I already talked with Father Taylor about everything, and I dropped out of school today."

"Why'd you do that without talking to me first?"

"For the same reason—because you're never around anymore, and this isn't your problem now. It's Tommy's and mine. Don't be mad at me. Ever since you started seeing Sue, you haven't had time for me. It doesn't matter anyway. All I want is to be with Tommy. I won't be a burden to you anymore."

"A burden! You've never been a burden to me. Don't ever think that," he says.

"I'm sorry, Dad. I'm just so emotional right now and a little scared," I say.

"Of course, you are. Come here," Dad says, hugging me.

"The good news is that I'm still going to get my diploma from Catholic High as long as I pass the GED test before the end of this year," I tell him.

"Okay, that is good news," he says.

We hear a light tap on the door, and Sue peeks in her head. "I heard you were both in here. Is everything all right?" she asks.

Dad looks at me and asks, "Is it okay if we tell her?"

I shake my head, yes.

"This is a call for a celebration," Dad says. "How about if I take us all out to eat and we can talk some more about this? What are you hungry for?" he asks me.

"Ba-ghettie," I say like I did when I was a little girl.

"Spaghetti it is," he says, smiling. He reaches out and hugs me again. "It's going to be all right," he says.

"I know it is. It just feels as if everything is moving too fast," I say.

"Well, it has my head spinning, that's for sure," Dad says.

∞ ∞ ∞

Tommy's sitting on the front porch steps when Sue pulls her car up in front of the apartment house. He stands when he sees my dad and asks if he can talk to him for a minute. They walk to the corner and both light a cigarette I wish I could be a fly on one of their shoulders so I could hear what they are saying. They shake hands, and then dad hugs Tommy.

"What was that about?" I ask Tommy.

"I wanted to ask properly for your hand in marriage and assure him that I'd always love and cherish you for the rest of our life," he says as he holds me.

"Oh, Tommy, every time you hold me, I feel like I'm going to melt away."

"No, not away. We melt into each other, becoming stronger, whole, and complete," Tommy says.

"When did you become so sentimental?" I ask.

"The moment I met you," he says. "Have I told you how much I love you today?"

"I could never get tired of hearing you say that," I tell him.

"Good because I'm going to tell you every day for the rest of our life."

"Hey, how'd you get here so quickly anyway?" I ask.

"I hitched a ride with someone from school," he says. "When I called my parents last night and told them that we needed to talk with them, they said to come over tonight after mom's done work."

"Isn't that going to be late?" I ask.

"She kept asking me what it was about, and I told her I'd rather wait to tell her in person. She said there was no sense in putting it off. We should be there when she and dad get home at 9:30 tonight."

"By the way, your dad said he wanted to come with us tonight when we talk with my parents."

Sue drops Dad, Tommy, and me off a little after 9:00 pm. As we walk into Tommy's house, one light in the TV room casts a dim dreary appearance. It does not look like the active, cheerful home I've experienced all the other times that I've been here. It's so quiet you can hear the refrigerator humming in the kitchen.

"Where is everyone?" I ask Tommy.

"The younger boys would be in bed by now, and the older ones are either out or upstairs."

As soon as we get our coats off and sit around the table, Tommy's parents come through the front door. His mom looks a little agitated but smiles when she's introduced to my dad.

"Oh, boy, this looks serious," she says as she goes to sit down, then jumps back up. "Can I get anyone anything? She puts a pot of coffee on."

"Sit down, Dot," Russ says to his wife. "Let's see what all the suspense is. Well, boy," he says, lighting a cigarette, "spit it out."

"Connie and I are going to have a baby," he says.

Mrs. Rife jumps up from her chair, "Oh, for God's sake, not another one," she says as she starts pacing. "I don't get it, Russ, where are we going wrong with our kids? We try to give them something better, then they go out and get pregnant." Before she can say another word, Mr. Rife says, "Oh, for God's sake, woman, calm down."

I'm sitting there with my head down, wanting to cry because I love them already and don't want them to hate me. Dad, reaching under the table, pats my hand, and I squeeze it back. Tommy is holding my other hand, and I can feel the sweat on his palm.

"So, where do we go from here?" Mrs. Rife looks at both of us.

"We plan to get married as soon as we can," Tommy says.

"What about school?" she asks.

"I'm going to finish out this year and go back to Armstrong to work as Dad does," he says.

She shakes her head with sadness. "We wanted better for you, Tommy," she says.

"What could be better than following in your own dad's footsteps and building a life the way you both did?" Tommy said proudly.

They look at each other and smile. Then Mrs. Rife asked us, "What can we do to help?"

We went on to tell them the steps we've already taken, my dropping out of school, working full time at the college, and how we were going to meet with Father Lawrence Saturday afternoon.

"We don't want this to be a burden on anyone else," Tommy says. "But we sure could use your advice along the way."

"Whatever you need, Tom," his dad says.

"And the same goes for me," his mom added. "As soon as you have a date, we'll sit down and talk over the details."

"I told Tom and Connie that they could live with me in the apartment until they can get on their own two feet," Dad says.

"As far as our wedding goes, it won't be anything fancy," I say. "It will be as simple and inexpensive as we can make it. That's the way we want it anyway."

"I guess it's official then," Mrs. Rife says. "Welcome to the family!" She reaches her arms out to give me a big hug.

∞ ∞ ∞

Tommy and I walk up the steps to the Sacred Heart rectory and ring the doorbell. A handsome young priest answers the door.

"You must be Tom and Connie," he reaches his hand out to Tommy first, then me. "I'm Father Lawrence. Come in." He stands aside, and with his hand raised toward the office to the left, he directs us to go in.

As he closes the door, he says that he was telling Father Taylor this morning about a young couple he was going to meet today.

"He asked your names, and when I said who you were, he filled me in a little about your situation," Father Lawrence says. He doesn't sit behind the desk but joins us in another chair where we talk as if we're in a sitting room instead of an office.

"So, do you want to get married, or do you feel you have to get married?" he asks us.

"We want to get married!" we both say at the same time.

"More than anything," Tommy says, looking at me.

"Tell me a little bit about yourselves," he says.

Neither one of us is too quick to say anything. We can talk up a storm with those we know and feel comfortable with, but we both tend to be shy around people we don't know. I hate the uncomfortable quite feeling it creates, so I'm often the first to say anything to break the ice.

"I don't know where to start. I have a long history of dysfunction in my family. All I ever wanted was to make my life the way I wished it could have been for me," I say. "That was the promise that kept me going every time life got unbearable."

"Wait a minute, what promise?" Father Lawrence asks.

"God made me a promise a long time ago when I was a little girl. I felt like I wanted to die because things were so awful at home. It was like being in a dream, where He showed me how things were going to get worse in the years to come. I remember being angry with Him, telling Him that it wasn't fair because I was just a kid. Why would He give me two parents who had so many problems that they couldn't take care of my siblings and me? I didn't remember what He showed me; all I remembered is the promise. When times got bad, and I was tempted to give up, God always found a way to help me hold on," I told Father Lawrence.

"That's a special kind of faith to have at your age. Did you learn all about that from the church?" he asked.

"No. We hardly ever attended mass. God was kind of like my friend. He was the only one who never left me. No matter how angry I got with Him, He loved me anyway."

"That's called unconditional love. If you can take that same kind of love into your marriage, you'll have a solid foundation to build upon," he said.

"How about you, Tom, what's your life been like growing up?" he asked him.

"I don't know. I never thought of my life as being anything other than ordinary, but being with Connie, I've realized how lucky I've been all these years. My dad works hard to provide for us, and my mom works hard taking care of us. I think everything they do has been to give us a good life. We're not an affectionate family, being all boys except my sister Nancy. I know that I've disappointed my parents by not taking my schooling more seriously. I do understand that they just wanted the best for me. But even when I let them down, they turned around and loved me anyway-with that same kind of unconditional love you are talking about, Father."

"You are both very young, with dreams that are not flighty like most young people your age. Your dreams are not the ones of a fairy tale happy ending, but a happy ending that comes with hard work, sacrifice, and most of all, love. I'd normally be wary of marrying a couple as young as the two of you. I feel confident that your marriage will only grow stronger in the years to come," he tells us.

Tommy and I look at each other, smiling, yet with a bit of surprise on our faces, too. We never expected anyone in the adult world to see things our way, let alone believe in us.

"Thank you, Father. It means a lot to know that you understand us so well," I say.

"Well, it means a lot to know that the couple I join in the holy sacrament of marriage love each other as much as you both do." He goes around to the desk and pulls out his calendar. "You want to get married as soon as you can, correct?" he asks us.

"Yes," we both say.

"We need time to announce the banns of marriage. That requires three weeks before the wedding," Father Lawrence says.

"I never quite understood what the purpose of that was except to announce a couple's engagement," Tommy says. "Why is it required before you can get married?"

"The purpose of banns of marriage is not only an announcement of a couple's engagement. It also allows the community to raise any doubt as to why a couple should not get married in the eyes of God and the state, things like a pre-existing marriage that have not been annulled by the church yet," he explains to us. "If I start the banns of marriage next Sunday, we could have the wedding on February 27, he says, looking at us.

We look at each other, making sure we both agree. We don't need any words between us; our smiles say it all. We look at Father Lawrence and speak at the same time, "Yes!"

"Okay, that's' settled. Now there are a lot of things you'll need to do before then. I'll jot them down for you as we go over them. I'll need proof of your baptism. You can get a certificate from the church you were baptized in," he says.

"I have no idea what church that was. I was born and baptized in California," I say.

"Your dad would know," Tommy says.

"You could write the church and have them send it to you. I suggest you do that right away," he says.

"Then you'll have to go down to the courthouse and fill out the papers for a marriage license. You'll need a blood test done for that as well," Father Lawrence says.

"Why do we need a blood test to get married?" I ask.

"The state requires premarital blood tests to check for venereal disease or rubella," he says.

"I always thought it was to make sure you had compatible blood for having children," I say.

"Yes, that's another reason," he says.

"Oh, we don't' have to worry about that. We already know we don't have the same blood type," Tommy says.

"Good," Father Lawrence says. "The next thing we have to do is meet for Pre-Cana," he says.

"What's that?" I ask him.

"It's required by the church that all couples have pre-nuptial preparation sessions with the priest. It's a chance to talk about marriage and the commitment that you're making," he says.

"Do we both have to be present to do this together?" Tommy asks.

"Ideally, that's the way we like to do it, but since you'll be up in Bloomsburg, we'll have to have you meet with a priest up there. Tom, what parish do you attend up at college? I'll call the priest there and fill him in. You'll have to set your own time to meet with him."

"I can do that, and I guess I'll have to have my blood test done there, too," Tommy says.

"I'm going to give you a book to look through together about the commitment of marriage. It also has lots of explanations for the ceremony. It's called "Together for Life." I've already marked a few pages I especially want you to read. During the ceremony, you'll each say a prayer. If you'd like to make up your own, that's fine, or you can read the one in the book."

He hands me the book and a list of the things we need to get done before the ceremony. My first meeting with him for Pre-Cana is February 9.

Chapter 30 - February 1971

"Oh, Tommy, you should have seen me when your mom opened that door. I was oblivious as to what was about to happen. I barely stepped inside the doorway when I heard everyone shout, "SURPRISE!" There were all these women looking at me, and the only ones I knew were your mom, Nancy, and Nana Mary. I thought we were going to a knit-in. That's what your mom called it. I thought I was going to learn how to knit. Did you know she was doing this?" I asked Tommy.

"I had no idea. Mom must have gotten my aunts together and planned it. That's the way my family is. Everyone takes care of each other. Now you'll be a part of the knit-in group," he says.

"I don't have any idea how to be like them," I say. "But I guess I'll learn as I go."

"And who better to learn from than my mom?" Tommy says.

"They were all so nice to me. I was worried that your family would hate me because I got pregnant, but they don't seem to be judgmental at all. I never knew people like this existed, except maybe on TV," I say.

"What kind of things did you get?" he asks.

"You mean, did we get. Everything is for us. I'm telling you, Tommy, I never opened so many gifts at one time. We got cake, cookie, and cupcake pans, two Teflon frying pans, Corning ware casserole dishes, some other glass baking pans, and a teapot. Then there's sheets, pillowcases, blankets, towels, table cloth, hot pads, a toaster cover, dish towels, and an apron. Oh, and even a set of Mr. & Mrs. hand towels. Just think, Tommy, this is only our shower. I can't imagine what we'll get for our wedding, can you?"

"Your mom was funny. She whispered in my ear to remember to send thank you notes. That she'd help me if I wanted. I was glad she told me about doing that because I never remember getting anything from anyone that required a thank you note."

"That's my mom looking out for you, as if your one of her own already," he says.

"She is such a good example for me in a way that my mom never was, and I appreciate it. I think I'm going to learn a lot of helpful things from her. I love the way she takes care of all of you. I know it's hard work, but she makes it look like it's second nature to her. She seems to love being a mom and wife," I say.

"I'm glad you like her. That means more to me than you know," Tommy says.

"There were all kinds of goodies to eat, like cake, chips and pretzels, peanuts, and colorful candy mints and punch to drink in a big glass bowl with little matching cups.

"I'm so glad you had a good time at the shower. You see, Connie, everyone likes you. My Mom thinks a lot of you because you are making me very happy. That's one of the most important things that she wants, to see her children happy," he says.

"Thank you, hon, you always make me feel so special," I say.

"That's because you are special," he says.

"So, tell me how the wedding plans are coming along?" Tommy asks.

"Well, I'm still seeing Father Lawrence for Pre-Cana tomorrow. I think this will be the last one for me. I've enjoyed talking to him. He makes me think about my faith, and even though I have a great relationship with God, I think I'd still like to know what the church has to teach me. I never practiced the Catholic faith the way you have. I didn't even know if I wanted to be Catholic. But then I thought, how will I ever know if I don't give it a chance. Plus, I do like going with you and your family to church," I say.

"That makes me happier than you know," he says.

"My dad and Sue took me out to get my dress. I couldn't find one I could afford, so they told me not to worry that they wanted to pay for it. It looks like a gown; only it goes below my knees. The sales lady said it's one of the new styles today. I got a beautiful mantilla that goes past my shoulders and a pair of white heels. Guess what else dad bought me, a sewing machine that sits in an oak case. He also got us two engraved champagne glasses, one with my name and one with yours. Both have the date of our wedding on them, too. Sue got us a cool wedding book also for people to sign as they come into the church. We can write all our memories about our special day and put pictures in it, too. Sue also asked if she could buy my flowers? And I gave her a big hug and a thank you.

"Did you get your baptismal certificate yet?" he asks.

"Yes, thank goodness," I say.

"I was getting worried that maybe we wouldn't be able to get married without it," he says.

"All we need yet is the license, and that's sure to get here any day now," I say. "Other than that, all we need is for you to come home, and everything will be in place. The only thing left will be to get married."

"I'll be able to come home for sure on Thursday. I talked with all my professors, and they were supportive and said they would work with me so I could come home a day early," he says.

"Oh, honey, I get so excited at the thought of waking up next to you every morning and watching you lie there asleep because you look so cute when you're asleep. Then I want to get up every morning and fix you breakfast and surprise you, giving it to you in bed. I'm going to learn how to cook all the things you like and keep you good and healthy. I'll also make you all kinds of goodies to help you put back on that weight you lost. Oh, Tommy, I sure hope you'll always love me as you do now because if you do, we're going to have a happy, fun life together," I say.

"In your letter, you talked about how you hoped I would never regret marrying you that you were going to do everything in your power to make me happy. Connie, the only thing you have to do to make me happy is to be yourself. You don't have to go out of your way for me or change in any way. I'm marrying you for who you are. I love you just the way you are," he says.

"Father Lawrence says. We'll have to learn about each other. Sometimes we might not like some things about each other. I can't imagine what that would be with you, but I guess we know ourselves best and how ugly we can sometimes be," I say.

"We are all human and make mistakes, but we can worry about those things when and if they happen," he says.

"Let's promise that we'll always be honest with each other, no matter what," I say.

"I promise," he says, "and when and if we ever get mad at each other, let's promise never to go to bed before making up," he says.

"We will stay up all night if we have too, I promise," I say.

"With all the trials and tribulations, we'll have through the years, I believe there will be more good in our life to build upon than bad because what we have is special," he says.

"With God at the center of our life, Tommy, how could we ever go wrong?" I say.

"We are two minds that think alike in so many ways. I miss our talks like this while I'm away from you. You help me see life so much clearing," he says.

"And you make me feel so safe and secure in a way I never was before," I say.

"We could talk all night like this, but we can't afford this phone bill to be any higher than it's already going to be. I love you so much, but I better get going," he says.

"Only a few more days and you'll be home. It seems so close yet so far away. It will be here before we know it and then we'll be Mr. & Mrs. Rife.

∞ ∞ ∞

"It's soon 7:00 pm," Dad says to Tommy, Sue, and me. "Time to head over to the church for the rehearsal."

"Where's your maid of honor?" Sue asks.

"I just got off the phone with Mary Faith. She couldn't make it here on time for the practice, but she promised she'd be here in the morning for the wedding."

We meet Bill, Tommy's best man, outside the front entrance of the church. He's already swaying all over the place, slurring his words, and laughing out loud.

"Boy, do we have plans for you tonight, Scuzz," he says, slapping Tommy on the back.

"Bill, I told you not to call him that," I say.

He puts his finger up to lips, saying, "I'm sorry. I forgot."

"Oh, great, Tommy, I don't have my maid of honor here, and now your best man is drunk," I say.

"Don't worry, I'll take care of him," Tommy says.

I watch them as I wait to walk down the aisle with my dad. Bill is trying to hold it together, but the harder he tries, the worse he acts. The shiny cobblestone aisle makes me feel dizzy as I follow it with my eyes all the up to the altar. I feel nervous and shaky all over. What makes it worse is that I can't make it go away. The harder I try, the worse I feel. Dad can feel me shaking and pats my hand. Tears well up in my eyes, and he hugs me for a moment as I let out a little cry.

"I don't know why I feel this way," I say. "I should be feeling happy."

"It's normal to feel a little nervous. That's all it is," Dad says. "Sometimes, our feelings get all jumbled, especially before a big step like this. Those aren't sad tears, Connie, they're happy tears."

"I guess that makes sense. I hate when I get so anxious and can't make it go away," I say.

"The harder you fight anxiety, the worse it feels. Just take a few deep breaths and let it pass through you," Dad says to me.

"Oh, Dad, how'd you get so wise?" I asked, hugging him again.

"From lots of experience," he says. "By the way, I thought your mother was going to be here today too. Where is she?" he asks.

"She's not coming," I say. "I got a letter yesterday. That's all I want to say about it, Dad."

"No wonder you're so upset," he says.

"I shouldn't have expected anything else," I say. I can't tell Dad how bad the letter was or the terrible names she called me. I was glad my friend Cissy came by. She took me out for something to eat, and I was able to talk with her about it. She's about the only friend I have who understands the pain our parents can inflict on us emotionally.

Dad and I practice our descent down the aisle toward the altar. When we come before Father Lawrence, he proceeds to go over the entire wedding ceremony in short form, what we will say and when to say things. Standing next to Tommy, holding his arm, I'm so excited. I can't wait to marry him tomorrow, even if I have to walk up this wobbly aisle to do it. I'd walk across a bed of coals if I had to so that I could spend the rest of my life with him.

"Bill's determined to get me drunk tonight. I'll have a few beers with him, but that's it," Tommy says.

"I know. I'm beat and want to go to bed, but all my friends are back at the apartment waiting for me. At least you can go home and go to bed. They'll be there all night with me. I probably won't be able to go to sleep anyway. I'm too excited.

"One more day and it will just be you and me," he says.

"I know, but I guess it's nice to know how happy everyone is for us. I think our family and friends want to be a part of it. They've all helped out so much. It's cool, don't you think?" I say.

"Okay, you two," Bill says. "It's time to go. You're not supposed to see each other now before the wedding."

Tommy gives me a long kiss, but Bill pulls on his arm.

"Come on, Romeo. You'll have the rest of your life to kiss as much as you want after tomorrow. It's time for this bachelor to say goodbye to the single life," Bill says, laughing.

Tommy gets in Bill's car, and before they pull away, I say, "Don't get him drunk, Bill. He might not get up on time tomorrow," I say.

Bill puts his foot on the gas and screeches off.

"Don't worry," Dad says, "There's no way that boy's going to miss tomorrow."

Dad leaves with Sue for the night after he drops me off at the apartment.

By the time morning comes around, I'm dead tired. I was too excited to sleep. I sit in the middle of my bed, the same one dad and I carried from around the corner, and up the steps the summer of '69. The same bed, Dad's old girlfriend, threw down the steps because she didn't want me here. I look at Dad's bed on the other side of the room. I remember how he sat on the edge of it, drunk as a skunk when I asked him if he had any money left to pay the rent. He cried like a baby, saying how sorry he was that he'd try to do better. The vase I hide his money in still sits on the nightstand beside it. It's empty now but came in handy back then as the weeks passed by and the bills needed paying. A shiver goes down my back, and I wonder why I'm thinking of all the bad things that happened in this room. It's supposed to be the best time of my life. I'm marrying Tommy today, the sweetest, kindest, and most loving person I've ever met, and this is going to be our room now. Dad will sleep in the backroom in my bed after today, that is when he's home.

I've spent two summers, two Christmases, and two birthdays here. It seems so much longer, yet it's only been a little over a year and a half that I've been here. Each part of my life has been like its separate chapter with unbelievable experiences. But today, February 27, 1971, is the end of that story and the beginning of a new chapter in my new life, the one that God promised me. How that story will begin and end will be up to Tommy and me to build together.

Chapter 31 - February 27, 1971

I want everything to be perfect today. My friends are all around me fussing like fairy godmothers, wanting to make me and my simple wedding into something magical. But no one seems to know what to do with me, and all I want is to be alone so I can fuss over myself.

I make a clean getaway by telling them I need to use the bathroom. As I sit on the edge of the tub, looking around, I wonder how this ugly bathroom ever became the little oasis it has been for me.

Standing in front of the mirror, I push my hair back so I can get a good look at my face. Pausing for a moment, I meet my own eyes in the mirror. *God, I know You're somewhere inside there. You've always been with me, and if I hadn't felt you there all these years, I would have never been able to hang onto your promise. Here we are. Today's the day I marry the man of my dreams. I know I have a lot of hard roads ahead of me, but at least I'll have Tommy walking beside me, and You will always be at the center of our love like the glue that binds us together. How can I go wrong with two strong forces in my life like You, God, and Tommy?*

"Hurry up, Con," my sister Mary says, interrupting my thoughts." I have to get ready, too."

"I'll be out in a few minutes." I quickly tease my hair at the crown on my head, smoothing it back into a nice bump, then swoop the rest of my hair back into a French twist, pinning it in place, pulling a few curls to dangle in front of my ears.

I then apply my makeup and step back to observe and smile. I've accomplished what I set out to do, looking refreshed and as happy as I feel. When I come out, my sister, Mary, pushes past me, and my friends are waiting. They like what I did with my hair, but still, have to touch tuck, and spray, so every piece of hair is in place. Another friend holds my unzipped dress so I can step into it. My maid of honor, Mary Faith, puts the mantilla on top of my hair, pinning it in place. I look at the friend who's been there for me through the worst of times. It's been five years. She never judged, was always honest, upfront, and sincerely cared, but most of all, she never gave up on me. If it hadn't been for her telling me that Tommy was the best thing that ever happened to me, I wouldn't be standing here in front of her right now. I think she knows from here on out I'm in good hands. Maybe she's relieved in a way that she won't have to pick up the pieces of my life for me anymore.

"It's getting late," she says to me, "it's time to go." She's not a touchy-feely kind of person, so when she smiles at me, and I smile back at her, we know the fondness we feel in our hearts for each other. No matter where life takes us, the memories of these teenage years, we share will always be with us.

I hear the key in the apartment door. It's Dad. He and Sue have come to take me to the Church. "You look beautiful, sweetheart," he says as his eyes begin to well up. "I have one more thing to add, your garter," he says, holding it for me to see.

"Oh, yes! Tommy's friends will be disappointed if not allowed to tackle each other for it," I say.

"Well, don't be surprised if they don't. Your friends are young. Not everyone's as eager to get married as you and Tom are," he says as he slips it on my leg. He bows and says, "Your chariot awaits" and points the way.

"We have about ten minutes to get there," Dad says, looking at his watch.

"Thank goodness it's only around the corner," I say to Mary Faith as we dash toward the car.

"Connie," I hear Sue's voice in the back of us. "Look here."

I turn, wondering what she's doing in the back of us when her car is up ahead. I smile when I see her snapping a picture. I feel like the rabbit in Alice in Wonderland, turning to say, "I'm late, I'm late, for a very important date.

Sue hands me my bouquet; I had no idea that it would be so beautiful. I left it up to Dad and Sue to pick it out. They did ask me what kind of flowers I liked. All I could think of was how much I loved the sweet, spicy cinnamon smell of carnations, and I knew red roses stood for Love. It had eight red roses in the center surrounded by red and white bright ruffled carnations and greens. Mary Faith's bouquets are the same, except the center has red carnations. The flowers on the altar are the same red and white carnations in my bouquet, and the boutonnieres are white carnations.

I can see through the open doors how many people there are. It's much more than I thought, and most of them are sitting on Tommy's side of the Church.

"This is your big day," Father Lawrence says as he comes up behind me. "Are you ready? "Ready as 'I'll ever be but nervous," I say.

"That's normal," he says. He places his hand on my head, blessing me before the ceremony.

Three altar boys line up, one at the point of the procession carries the crucifix upon a tall ornate pole. The two remaining boys stand behind him side by side, each holding a tall, lit candle. As the entrance hymn begins to play, they slowly walk up the aisle. Father Lawrence follows a few feet behind them. Mary Faith now steps inside the doorway, ready to walk down the aisle next. She wears a sleeveless powder blue lace dress that comes right above her knees with a matching shoulder-length Mantilla over her long dark hair. White elbow-length gloves cover her hands and arms. She looks for the signal from Father, and as he nods his head, she begins her lonely descent down the cobblestone aisle. At least I have dad's arm to hold onto, but she doesn't seem nervous at all.

I stand now in the doorway with my dad. My heart is beating fast, and my palms feel hot and sweaty.

"I'm so nervous, Dad," I say. "My legs feel like those two candles we had in the apartment that fell over from the heat.

He pats the hand that grips his arm tightly.

"You'll be fine. I won't let you melt away," Dad says. "Take a deep breath and keep your eyes on, Tommy. He's why you're here."

I catch Tommy smiling at me. I take a few more breaths as the organist stops to pause before she begins to play "Here Comes the Bride." Everyone turns the moment she pounds on the keys, da-da ta-da. Dad is leading me down the aisle, and I feel like it takes a few moments for the rest of me to catch up. As I search for Tommy's face to focus on, all I see are people's eyes locking onto mine and bouncing like a tennis ball back and forth from one person to the other. I smile the way I always have in difficult situations to hide what I'm feeling inside. Dad places my hand in Tommy's, and he kisses my cheek before stepping aside.

Tommy and I look at each other, trying to get past our nervousness-remembering why we are here and how much our love means to each other. I don't want anything to take away from this special moment in time. I know deep down inside, neither does Tommy.

Father Lawrence stands before us with one hand raised in blessing as he reads the Rite of Marriage according to the Church.

"Tom and Connie, you have come together in this Church so that the Lord may seal and strengthen your love. Just as Christ abundantly blessed you through the consecration of baptism, He enriches and enhances your love through the sacrament of marriage. And so, in the presence of the Church, I ask you to state your intentions.

Tom and Connie, have you come here freely and without reservation to give yourselves to each other in marriage?"

"Yes, we have," we say, looking at each other.

"Will you love and honor each other as husband and wife for the rest of your lives?"

"We will."

"Will you accept children lovingly from God and bring them up according to the law of Christ and his Church?"

"Yes!" We say again together.

"You may be seated for the reading of Liturgy of the Word," he says. We sit beside each other at the edge of the altar rail, still holding hands.

I hear bits and pieces of the old testament from the book of Genesis 2:18-24,

"The Lord God said, "It is not good that the man should be alone. I will make him a helpmate."

The next reading is from the New Testament Romans 8:31-35, 37-39, but once again, I only hear what resonates with me.

"With God on our side who can be against us?" and the end where it says, "For I am certain of this: neither death nor life, no angel, no prince, nothing that exists, nothing still to come, not any power, or height or depth, nor any created thing, can ever come between us and the love of God."

As Father Lawrence stands for the gospel, so do we and the rest of the congregation. A reading from the Gospel of John 15:9-12.

"Jesus said to his disciples:

"As the Father has loved me, so I also have loved you. Remain in my love.

If you keep my commandments, you will remain in my love, just as I have kept my Father's commandments and remain in his love. I have told you this so that my joy might be in you, and your joy might be complete. This is my commandment: love one another as I love you.

"The word of Lord,"

"Thanks be to God."

Father Lawrence pauses for a moment as we sit for his sermon.

"All these readings are about Love. Of course, it is appropriate to talk about as we join these two in holy matrimony. But I have to say in the short time 'I've had a chance to get to know Tom and Connie. There is an understanding of love between them that goes beyond their years. What struck me the most in our conversations was their understanding of unconditional love. There is a pureness to the word where one loves with their whole heart, their whole soul, and their whole mind. There is no condition for how I feel about you; there is nothing you need to do to make me love you. I love you for who you are. I give it freely. But when two people come together in holy matrimony, they become one. Entering into a bond of commitment that comes with the promise of expectant love. Now we are no longer looking from our point of view, but from the view of the one, we love. Will you love me in sickness as well as health, and through the years of growth and change, even when I am old and gray. These are the conditions of marriage, and yet in your commitment, you still offer to love each other no matter what. It is as simple and yet complicated as following the Way, the Truth, and the Light. There is no expectancy in love because all we can do in love is give and receive. So, those who go into a marriage with the idea that 'it's a 50-50 proposition will only find themselves fighting over who did what the last time of equal value. If you must put a number on it, then give 80% by doing the best you can and let the 20% fall where it may. True Love gives without condition because that's what it's designed to do. The only condition that God asks of us is to love one another as he has loved each one of us. To do onto your brother as you would want to have done onto you. I know it sounds so simple. In truth, it is until we let our pride get in the way. Marriage is not about your way or my way. It's about finding common ground that brings two people together as one. It's only the beginning of your love story, Tom and Connie. There will be many ups and downs yet to come; it's all a part of growing into a deeper love for one another. I pray that you always see the blessing of God's promise that has brought you here today and that you will create many happy memories of lasting love in the years to come."

Tommy and I look at each, smiling because Father Lawrence found a way to fit the promise God made to me into his words today. He did it in the form of showing us that that promise will carry through into our new life together now. It all feels so unreal to me. Too good to be true. The kind of thing I would dream about to escape from the bad that was happening in my life. I don't want anyone to pinch me for fear I'll wake up and find out that none of this is real.

Standing before us, Father Lawrence says, "Since you intend to enter into marriage, join your right hands and declare your consent before God and one another."

Tommy and I turn toward each other. We join our right hands and then our left as well. I look up at him, and he smiles down at me. Everything around us disappears, including Father Lawrence. We hear his words but only see each other standing face to face surrounded by light. "Thomas Richard Rife, do you take Constance Fay Miller to be your wife? Do you promise to be true to her in good times and in bad, in sickness and in health? To love her and honor her all the days of your life?"

"I do," Tommy says, smiling at me.

"Constance Fay Miller, do you take Thomas Richard Rife to be your husband? Do you promise to be true to him in good times and in bad, in sickness and in health, to love him and honor him all the days of your life?"

"I do," I say, smiling up at him.

"You have declared your consent before God. May the Lord in his goodness, strengthen your consent and fill you both with his blessing.

What God has joined together, let no one divide. Amen."

"Lord, bless and consecrate Tom and Connie in their Love for each other. Tom and Connie, let these rings be a symbol of your love for one another. For just as they are a circle with no beginning and no end, so will your love be from this day forward. Amen."

"Connie, take this ring as a sign of my love and fidelity. In the name of the Father and the Son and the Holy Spirit."

"Tommy, take this ring as a sign of my love and fidelity. In the name of the Father, Son, and Holy Spirit."

"Tom and Connie, by the power vested to me by our Lord Jesus Christ, I now pronounce you husband and wife. You may kiss the bride," Father Lawrence says with a smile.

"This concludes the marriage ceremony. I now present to you, Mr. and Mrs. Thomas Rife," he says.

Tommy kisses me again, and we turn toward the congregation as they clap for us. We hold hands, and I look up at him and he at me. I pull at his hand, and he bends down so I can whisper in his ear, "Did you see the light around us when we said our vows?"

"Yeah!" he smiles. "I was hoping you saw it, too."

"I love you so much, Tommy." He leans down and kisses me while Father Lawrence and his altar boys wait to walk down the aisle behind us."

So, many smiling faces are looking back at us. They are happy for us when we thought the whole world was against us. I have never been this happy myself or smiled as much. We head out of the church, and everyone throws rice. We climb into the backseat of Bill's parents' car. It's white, and Bill has written- "Just Married" on it with black shoe polish. Tommy leans over to me and whispers, "Did I tell you how beautiful you are yet today?"

"All I know, Tommy, is that you've made me the happiest girl in the world. Thank you for loving me the way you do."

Epilogue

orty-eight years, four children, nine grandchildren, and one great-grandchild later, we are still together. Ginny was our love child, as we often refer to her. Two years later, we had our son, Tommy, and that's when my sweetheart Tommy became Tom. Two years after that, Shannon was born, our bicentennial baby, and twenty-one months later, at the age of twenty-five, we had our last child, the baby of the family, Teri. We loved being young parents and having the energy to keep up with them. Tom worked seven days a week, three different shifts, in these earlier years, making enough money for us to live comfortably. Tom was good at budgeting our money, and we both had that shared value of making sensible choices with the things we bought. While Tom was busy providing for us financially, I tended to our family's needs at home. I became resourceful with the things we had by making them stretch out as long as they could. I mended our clothes, even made some of the kid's outfits. I learned how to make the most out of the food we had. We grew vegetables and canned as well as froze many things. It was hard work, but we never felt deprived of anything. We felt lucky to have what we did and proud of our accomplishments, and the many things we learned along the way.

During those earlier years, my mom had settled in Lancaster, as well. She became an intricate part of my life as we now shared the commonality of motherhood. It created a bond between us. I was better able to appreciate how difficult it had been for her as a mother, especially when my dad left us. She was always over, helping me in one way or another with the kids. She loved being with our little family so much that she wanted to live with us. Even though I had come to love her, there would be periods of unexpected irrational behavior from her that often left me with the hurtful memories of my childhood. Of course, it was part of her mental illness, but it still hurt. It was ironic that she gave Mary and me up when we needed her the most, but now she wanted me to take care of her. I could tolerate being around her when she'd visit, but there was no way I was going to let her move in with us, nor would Tom.

By the time I turned thirty, our sweet little life had begun to change. Once the kids were all in school, it felt as if it was finally my time to discover myself. While I still had plenty to do at home, I found that being alone gave me too much time to think. I'd find myself crying all the time and not knowing why. I became angry with my dad for what I wouldn't allow myself to see growing up. It felt as if my past was caving in on me, and that's when my anxiety attacks began to set in. I thought maybe it was time for me to stretch my wings and get out in the world. After all, I had gone right from high school to being a wife and a mother and never had the chance to discover what I wanted to do or what I was capable of doing. I was always impressed with Tom's aunt, who had made a career working in banking. After talking with her, I decided it was something I wanted to do. I got myself dressed up and went for my first job interview at a fancy bank in town and got the job. I was excited and felt alive in a way I'd never experienced before. As long as I didn't have to think about my past, I was okay. But as exciting as my new job was, something was missing at home. It was the attentive mother I had been, and I found it challenging to do both jobs at the same time. The anxiety attacks returned; only now, I would get them at work. Tom and I realized that whatever was going on with me was more serious than either of us could fix. It was time for me to find a therapist with whom I could talk things through.

The person I found was so fascinating with my story that he asked if he could videotape our sessions. He introduced me to the book "*Adult Children of Alcoholics*" by Janet Woititz. For the first time, I understood why I felt and reacted to things the way I did. I no longer felt alone, and eventually, we formed a group that got together and shared. But that was only the beginning of many more years of therapy, as I would later learn that the trauma of my childhood had created PTSD, Post-traumatic Stress Disorder in me. I couldn't understand why I was so depressed all the time when I had such a good life. But my episodes of depression could be easily triggered by merely looking at my kids and seeing myself in them at that age — another form of therapy healing the inner child. Eventually, I learned how to recognize the signs and symptoms of my disorder, and with the proper tools, I was able to control it before it got too bad. The real healing came about through the writing of my story. Each time I'd rewrite it, the deeper the healing would go, and the better I'd feel about the person I'd become. It is my fourteen-year-old self who tells the story. She wouldn't leave me alone until our story came to an end. Usually, when I'd get a writer's block, she'd tell me to get out of her way. She was telling it from her point of view, not from my grownup point of view. It was as if she needed validation for the part she played in getting us through the worst of times. Once my story was finished, that inner child was willing to let me embrace her and show her what we had become because of the sacrifices she endured. We made it to the age where the Promise could become our reality. I was not only being a parent to my children but also tending to the various ages of my inner child. I worked hard to recognize and validate each part of my inner child that had suffered, and now the pain of their wounds is gone and healed.

The Promise didn't end with my marriage and the beginning of my new life. It has carried through every lesson, stage, and decision along the way, and still does to this day. The Promise encompassed all that I wanted my life to be, but it wasn't a magic fix. It was a gift that came without any instructions. To keep this gift alive, I had to learn how to hold onto it, bringing about many lessons along the way. I was at a prayer meeting once and asked prayer for patience as a mother. A wise woman told me that when you pray for something, God gives you lots of opportunities to practice it. That realization became the understanding behind every lesson that came along, and I would have to practice, practice, practice everything because the things I asked for came with an even bigger responsibility to maintain.

I often wonder what my life would have been like without Tom. When he came into my life that first summer, he seemed too good to be true. Later I'd tell him he was my angel sent from God. Just as Father Lawrence said to us on our wedding day, True Love gives without condition because that's what it's designed to do. Tom has lived that every day since we've been together. As much as I loved him, I could never truly love anyone until I learned to love myself. He believed in me when I didn't believe in myself. He was always telling me that he wished I could see myself through his eyes. Through my healing, I was eventually able to begin to see my own goodness.

Our grown children often tell Tom and me that we are a hard act to follow. Even people we don't know see how happy we are and ask us what our secret is. It's sometimes hard to give others the answer to what seems so easy for us. But marriage takes two people, both working together for the same common purpose. Just because we become one as a couple, doesn't mean we stop being the individuals God created us to be. That's where the real work comes into play: two people finding a way to be happy as one. How do we do that? Through God. As I said to Tom many times before we got married, "With God on our side, how can we go wrong?" "The Promise" was nothing more than a way to connect me to God. Now, that same God sits at the center of our marriage and has become the connecting factor for us. That is our secret ingredient and, while we are as human and selfish as anyone else at times, having God as part of the mix has a way of reminding us of the better part of ourselves.

I have come full circle in my faith walk. I walked the path as a young girl with God at my side and somehow lost him along the way as I went looking for him outside myself. We became the perfect Catholic family filling three-quarters of a pew with our family of six. We lived our faith, the same as Tom's family had done. They were our models. Yet it was never enough for me. I was continually learning about my religion, taking part in everything they had to offer. We started Bible studies, taught religion classes, took part in Marriage Encounter, did Pre Cana sessions for couples, became Extraordinary ministers, took communion to the sick, led prayer meetings, and women's groups. It went on and on, and for me, it never seemed to be enough. As I was doing my daily Bible readings, looking deeply into what God was trying to tell me, the word "simplify" started jumping off the pages at me. It kept happening until I finally saw what God was genuinely trying to say to me. "*Your making things much more complicated than they are meant to be.*" Ah! I hadn't heard that voice from within in a long time. I started to ease off and go more inside myself, trying to reconnect with that inner spirit I once knew. But I had to deal with the fear that I'd developed about heaven, hell, and purgatory. What if I was wrong?

I was in my forties at this time when I started spending a lot of quality time with my dad. We always did share a similar belief, not in religion, as much as a loving God. It was at this time that he began to share a few more books with me, one of which was called "*Many Wonderful things,*" by Robert W. Huffman. Dad said he was waiting until he thought I was ready to read it. Then there was "*In Tune with the Infinite*" by Ralph Waldo Trine and the inspiring books by Emmet Fox. These were all books that spoke of the God I'd known as a child. Dad helped me to find my way to the God that was within me all along. I finally got back the dad I enjoyed spending time with, and together we shared some of the best conversations. He told me again how he could never forgive himself for leaving us behind. I told him that I forgave him, and if I could forgive him, then he should forgive himself. Even with all the positive changes he made in his life, Dad said he would take the shame he felt with him to his grave. He finally told me how proud he was of me," the mother I'd become, and the faithful wife — the person I'd made of myself.

It was when the people I cared about started to die that my faith walk took its most significant turnaround. The way people would come out of the woodwork, worrying about my loved one's salvation. I would think to myself, if these people knew who this person was, they would have seen the same God inside them that I had. It was when Tom's mom was dying, and she questioned her salvation, wondering if she'd have to go to purgatory before going to heaven or possibly hell, that I could see how powerful the church had incorporated fear into each faithful participant. I'd come to love her more than my mother. She was the most unselfishly giving person I'd ever known and devoted to her faith and family. If she wasn't going heaven, then there wasn't much hope for the rest of us.

It wasn't long after she passed away that I left the church. I don't condemn the Catholic religion or any other ones. It was a path I believe I was meant to walk, and I was like the prodigal son on a journey, only to find my way back home with so many lessons that made my faith even stronger. God isn't out there for us to find. He's the same God I saw on the day of my wedding when I looked in my own eyes and saw Him within me. He has always been there,...and learning to *trust* in that knowledge has been the lesson of *"the promise"* all along.

Made in the USA
Middletown, DE
20 January 2020